Planning for Serfdom

Planning for Serfdom

Legal Economic Discourse and Downtown Development

Robin Paul Malloy

UNIVERSITY OF PENNSYLVANIA PRESS   *Philadelphia*

Library of Congress Cataloging-in-Publication Data

Malloy, Robin Paul, 1956-
    Planning for serfdom : legal economic discourse and downtown development /
Robin Paul Malloy.
        p.   cm.
    Includes bibliographical references and index.
    ISBN 0-8122-3055-8
    1. City planning and redevelopment law—United States. 2. Real estate
development—Law and legislation—United States. 3. City planning—Economic
aspects—United States. 4. Real estate development—Economic aspects—United
States. 5. City planning—Political aspects—United States. 6. Real estate
development—Political aspects—United States. I. Title.
KF5692.M35   1991
346.7304'5—dc20
[347.30645]   90-29188
                                                                              CIP

For Celia, Margaret, and Gina: The three most important individuals in my life

Contents

Preface   ix

1. Prologue   1

Part I: The General Framework

2. Renaissance and Counter-Renaissance in Urban Life   9
3. The Classical Liberal Prespective   16
4. The System of Checks and Balances   30
5. The Political Means Versus the Economic Means   38
6. A New Commons—A New Tragedy   45
7. Classical Liberals and Individual Liberty   49
8. Government Regulation by General Rules   53
9. Comparative Ideology   61
   Conservative Theory   66
   Liberal and Left Communitarian Approaches   70
   Libertarians   76
   Classical Liberalism Compared   79
10. First Principles and the Concept of Faith   84

Part II: The Urban Development Context

11. Planning and Serfdom: The Police Power   89
12. Planning and Serfdom: The Purse Power   98

13. Indianapolis: Example of Renaissance and Counter-
Renaissance in Urban Life   103

14. The Politics and Economics of Urban Development   113

15. The Philosophical Constraints on Urban Development   123

16. Recommendations for Proper Urban Development   129

17. Conclusion   140

Notes   143
Index   181

Preface

This book is the culmination of a prolonged study of ideology in law and economics and of the relationships that govern human interaction in the urban development context. In defense of liberty, human dignity, and freedom I have tried to set forth a theory of law, economics, and the state that will be of interest to the general reader, as well as to those engaged in the study of law, economics, and politics. My views and theory in this area have been generally influenced by the writings of Adam Smith, Friedrich Hayek, and Milton Friedman. While building on some of their general ideas, I have, nonetheless, tried to develop a theory or perspective independent of these earlier works. I do not purport to offer a theory that is merely a guess as to what each of these earlier scholars might think about the problems I address.

Much of this book consists of completely new material although there are portions that rely heavily on earlier publications and these sections have been updated and revised to fit in with the scheme of the book. In many places I have limited the note citation information related to these earlier publications. For readers interested in more detailed references, I suggest that they turn to the extensive footnote materials that correspond to my earlier articles.

The portions of the book that rely in substantial part on earlier publications are as follows: Chapter 3: Malloy, *Invisible Hand or Sleight of Hand? Adam Smith, Richard Posner, and the Philosophy of Law and Economics*, 36 KANSAS LAW REVIEW 209 (1988); Chapter 5 (in part): Malloy, *The Political Economy of Co-Financing America's Urban Renaissance*, 40 VANDERBILT LAW REVIEW 67 (1987); Chapter 8 (that portion dealing specifically with rent control): Malloy, *The Economics of Rent Control—A Texas Perspective*, 17 TEXAS TECH LAW REVIEW 797 (1986), and Hoeflich and Malloy, *The Shattered Dream of American Housing Policy— The Need for Reform*, 26 BOSTON COLLEGE LAW REVIEW 655 (1985); Chapter 9 (the later portion of "Classical Liberalism Compared"):

Malloy, *Invisible Hand or Sleight of Hand? Adam Smith, Richard Posner, and the Philosophy of Law and Economics*, 36 KANSAS LAW REVIEW 209 (1988); Chapter 11 (the part dealing with "takings"): Malloy, *The Political Economy of Co-Financing America's Urban Renaissance*, 40 VANDERBILT LAW REVIEW 67 (1987); Chapters 12 to 16: Malloy, *The Political Economy of Co-Financing America's Urban Renaissance*, 40 VANDERBILT LAW REVIEW 67 (1987). I thank all of these journals and reviews for authorizing the use of their copyrighted materials.

The reader will note that Chapter 3 is referenced with substantial detail. I intentionally did this because of the value of detailed citations of the many works of Adam Smith. All too often books and articles make numerous textual references to the works of Adam Smith without giving adequate note citations. A distinct value of Chapter 3 is, therefore, to provide the reader with specific references in order to make the true complexity of Smith's many works accessible to a broader readership.

In the preparation of this book I benefited greatly from the willingness of my wife, Margaret, to listen to, discuss, and comment upon my ideas. I also benefited from comments by and discussions with a number of friends including Professors Paul Cox and Joe Tucker at Indiana University and Dean Michael Hoeflich (my friend and mentor) at Syracuse University. Some of my ideas were further sharpened by my preparation of papers and participation in programs sponsored by the International Association For Philosophy of Law and Social Philosophy at Pace University (New York), at Edinburgh University (Scotland), and at the University of Utah; by the Center for Semiotic Research in Law, Government, and Economics at Pennsylvania State University; by Tulane University's Mellon Lecture Series; two exchanges with Judge Richard Posner including a live debate at Valparaiso University; a presentation to the American Culture Association concerning Law and American Culture; being the 1990 Distinguished Lecturer for the Ben Rogge Memorial Lecture Series at Wabash College (Indiana); and, by presentation of faculty seminars titled "Law, Morality, and the Marketplace" at Oklahoma State University and at The University of Tulsa. My work on the metaphorical and symbolic function of economics was particularly aided by my association with Roberta Kevelson and her willingness to share her insight on Law and Semiotics. She generously approved my appointment as a Special Research Fellow of the Center for Semiotic Research in Law, Government, and Economics at Pennsylvania State University for 1989–90, and I benefited from discussion with her on a variety of topics.

Finally, I benefited from a small group of faculty members who were especially influential in my own education: these include Professors G. R. Huekel, Phil Burstein, and Michael Pustay while I was a student at Purdue University's Krannert School of Management; and Professors Robert C. L. Moffat and Winston P. Nagan while I was a student at the University of Florida, College of Law. This small group of faculty, more than any other, inspired me to ask new questions, to stretch my imagination, and to see the world in a new light. Although none of the people or organizations I have mentioned necessarily shares my views on the subject addressed in this book, each has played an important role in encouraging me to develop my thesis.

In addition I would like to thank Stephanie Payne for her research assistance in revising the original manuscript for this book, and everyone in the Tulane Law School Word Processing Department (especially Ms. Sherry Bachus and Ms. Stephanie Mitchell) who helped put this material together in its initial book form. I also wish to thank all of the people at the University of Pennsylvania Press who helped to bring this project to a successful completion. In particular I wish to express special thanks to Arthur Evans and Jo Mugnolo, for their strong support of my work throughout the long effort of bringing this book to print, and to Ruth Veleta, who oversaw the editing process.

Robin Paul Malloy
Professor of Law and Economics
Associate Dean for Research
College of Law
Syracuse, New York

Chapter 1
Prologue

As a society, late twentieth-century America seems trapped in a preoccupation with the public rather than the private; with planning rather than spontaneity; with material objectives rather than spiritual triumphs; and consequently, American society has drifted increasingly into the allure of statist ideology. An infatuation with planning and with appeal to the exercise of the political over the economic means has led us to the doorstep of a new age of serfdom; a serfdom where, once again, personal status rather than individual talent and human dignity becomes the measure of one's worth.

In this book I will offer an explanation for this rising acceptance of statist ideology in American society.[1] At the same time I will provide a theoretical framework for considering the delicate balance required for the maintenance of a free society despite the rising tide of American statism. The theory expounded in this book does not assume a conspiracy against the individual, nor is it a theory which accepts as inevitable the class struggle; rather it is a theory of counterbalancing forces striving for equilibrium. Throughout this book a theory of law, economics, and the state will be posited as a means for understanding our current situation. At the same time a conception of free society will be offered as a basis not only for criticizing current social, political, and economic arrangements, but also for delineating the path to a better and more humane future founded upon a belief in freedom, individual liberty, and human dignity.

In seeking to make the theoretical both easily understandable and practical, I will allude to various examples from everyday life throughout the book. Reference will specifically be made to the way in which various theoretical principles are manifested in a particular context. This book deals with the legal, political, and economic considerations of modern urban development and revitalization strategies. My focus on real estate development and revitalization is useful for several reasons. First, a theory is most practical when understood within the bounds of a particular discussion, even though that theory has broad implications for the greater society. All of the virtues and vices that make up American society can be found in the give and take, the politics, and the economics of real estate development.

Second, it is the urban environment with its dense population, its diversified and specialized enterprises, its ability to generate excess capital, and its influence on surrounding regions that first reveals the emergence, stagnation, or death of a great society.[2] Consequently, it is by looking at the forces and dynamics of urban life that we can learn something about the individual communities and the society in which we live.

Third, the process of urban development and revitalization is important because of its significance in defining the observable dimensions of an urban culture's legal, political, and economic aspirations. The types of real estate projects, the design of spaces inside and outside urban structures, and the legal, political, and economic arrangements employed for their completion are all important indicators of the way a society views itself. Through the study of these activities and arrangements a great deal can be learned about the normative boundaries that govern the relationship between various individuals, groups, and the state, with the hope that they will create a sufficient backdrop for the explanation and understanding of our current drift toward serfdom. In addition, it is the purpose of this book to offer a theory of law, economics, and the state that rejects current statist trends in favor of a commitment to individual liberty and human dignity within the confines of limited government.

This book will focus on the general practices of urban planning and development. The discussion, however, is not meant to be a detailed or exhaustive treatment of the underlying real estate and constitutional law issues addressed. Rather, the context of urban development serves as a point of reference for conducting a dialogue on the proper relationship between law, legal institutions, and economics. One should keep in mind that I am concerned primarily with an analysis of legal arrangements to see what they tell us about the ideological composition of a given community. I seek to examine the types of legal economic discourse validated by a given community for purposes of achieving certain "desirable" ends, and ask what these validating norms can tell us about the values and ideological beliefs of the community. As such, I will examine approaches to urban development to see what types of values and norms are being validated by particular forms of legal economic discourse.[3] In this sense economics is treated as a creative process of discourse and the focus is on its symbolic and metaphorical use in law, rather than on the empirical dimensions of economics as "science."[4]

By reference to the symbolic and metaphorical use of economics I mean several things. First, I want to clearly distinguish my efforts from those that have used mathematics and econometric models to analyze empircal data about urban development. While such economic analysis has its usefulness, my primary concerns are elsewhere. Second, I intend to liken my inquiry to that followed in law and semiotics.[5] This means that I consider economics as a process. Economics is a creative process of discovery and it is a structured process of discourse concerning the appropriate relationship between individuals, the community, and the state. In economics, market theory establishes certain ideological boundaries for discussion. Central to the establishment of these abstract boundary lines of legal economic discourse are a set of ideological norms and values. Key among these are: (1) the central role and referential function of the individual; (2) the rationality and appropriateness of individual empowerment and decision making; (3) the importance of counterbalancing power sources that stimulate an everchanging creative process; (4) the recognition that self-interest is incompatible with selfishness; (5) the understanding that economics, as a form of classical liberal discourse, is concerned primarily with the promotion of individual liberty and freedom as an *end*, rather than with "scientific" efficiency or wealth maximization; thus, capitalism or free market economics is a *means* to the ends of individual liberty and freedom and not an end in itself; (6) the acknowledgment that classical economic theory includes the recognition of a natural rights discourse and consequently of "welfare" claims related to a conception of human dignity; (7) the recognition that prior distributions of power and resources may not have been fair and are thus subject to constant reconsideration; (8) the understanding that general rules are preferred to outcome-specific rules; and (9) an understanding that the universe around us is never fully knowable; thus, no experts or planners can adequately control, in a manner consistent with individual liberty, the creative and spontaneous energies of countless individual decision makers.

By examining these constructs from the standpoint of their semiotic function in legal economic discourse we can begin to map the contours of our legal and economic culture. One can understand Adam Smith's classical theory of economics as a process of reconstructing the way in which we talk about the proper relationship between the individual, the community, and the state based on the subjective historical and economic context of a given society. Likewise, we can begin to see our own system of constitutional checks and balances as a legal construct intended to mirror the competitive market metaphor of economics. Furthermore, we can compare alternative ideological forms of legal economic discourse to this baseline. This allows us to uncover the conversational shift in boundary line values at work in alternative approaches to law and legal institutions.

This new way of considering the relationship between law and economics is not without its critics and may be misunderstood by those seeking to apply a different or more traditional perspective. The approach I take relies on a large number of sources, some of which may be unfamiliar to the traditional scholar of urban development, zoning, and takings law, but it is by sifting through unusual sources that one sometimes gains the greatest insights. With this in mind I undertake, in Part I of the book, to reconstruct traditional discussions of Adam Smith, urban life, constitutional checks and balances, political versus economic decision making, externalities, transaction costs, government regulation, and alternative legal theories.

Likewise, my view of economics, as a symbolic and metaphorical construct concerning social, political, and economic relationships, informs the essence of the critique of urban development that follows in Part II. From this perspective, it should become clear that law and economics are concerned with much more than the production of buildings or the generation of localized wealth. Urban development is not, after all, a collection of capital goods. Nor should urban life be merely the pursuit of efficient capital accumulation. The values at stake are much more important and fundamental than these. Democracy, for example, is said to be hopelessly inefficient; constitutional guidelines for criminal procedure, such as the exclusionary rule, are said to make law enforcement by police less efficient. But in such cases alleged inefficiencies are tolerated because the underlying values are normatively important. Similarly, a symbolic and metaphorical understanding of law and economics provides a valuable method of analysis to understand the sometimes hidden ideological messages contained in particular forms of legal economic discourse or social interaction. Such an analytical process is useful in allowing one to consider in a new light the particular context of urban development.

To explore a contextual application of the general theory of law, economics, and the state, it will be helpful to focus attention on a study of a model city. The city of Indianapolis, Indiana will be considered. The reason for its selection is fourfold. First, books on urban life all too often limit their conception of "city" to several extremely large urban environments, such as New York, Chicago, London, Tokyo, or Paris. While such cities play significant roles in worldwide human interaction, it is a shortcoming to focus on them to the exclusion of smaller cities that make up the majority of America's and the world's urban environments. Second, Indianapolis has followed the current trends in financing urban development and revitalization to a great degree. While larger cities such as New York and Chicago have also witnessed new approaches to government-sponsored financial innovation, the impact in Indianapolis has been far greater. The spending, for instance, of $1 billion has more impact in Indianapolis than in a larger and more diversified city such as New York. Third, the political and economic ideology of the Indianapolis community is, at least at the rhetorical level, much more defined and cohesive than the more pluralistic and factional politics of larger urban environments such as Chicago. This makes it easier to identify the elements underlying the city's changing approaches to urban development. Fourth, Indianapolis has received national as well as local press coverage concerning its urban revitalization efforts. As a model city, Indianapolis has been reported on by the Reagan administration[6] and by such distinguished journals as *National Geographic*,[7] *The Smithsonian*,[8] *Urban Land*,[9] and *Newsweek*.[10]

It is hoped that the discussion of urban development will serve as a useful example of the reconstruction of classical liberal theory presented in Part I. This book focuses on the manner in which the ideological perspective that one brings to law and economics affects not only the structure of legal economic discourse but also its content. The theory espoused in this book and the critique of urban development presented are designed to offer a new interpretation and use of the classical free market economic metaphor. At times the theory of this book may seem at odds with "scientific" approaches to economic efficiency or public choice, but this should not be troubling since it is my objective to reconsider the goals and values of traditional interpretations of classical and neoclassical economic theory.

This book presents a theory of law, economics, and the state by looking specifically at urban planning and development. The theory developed here has emerged from the observation of the changing legal arrangements in urban development, but it has significance beyond city life. The lessons of urban development and revitalization are the lessons of changing attitudes and changing times in America. This book seeks to identify the importance of these changes while offering a theory to explain their emergence. Finally, it offers a conception of law, economics, and the state that emphasizes the individual rather than the state, spontaneity rather than planning, and spiritual triumphs rather than material objectives.

Part I
The General Framework

Chapter 2
Renaissance and Counter-Renaissance in Urban Life

America is experiencing an urban renaissance and revitalization that is transforming downtown areas into entirely new urban environments. The visible products of this renaissance are new office buildings, shopping centers, hotels, historic preservation districts, and luxury housing. Promoting a unique blend of public and private cooperation, today's planners and politicians are hailing a new era of urban affluence, forged from the creative talents of lawyers, accountants, financiers, and urban planners, among others. Working within the political process, these creative planners for America's future have concentrated their efforts on project-oriented objectives. Deciding first on what projects need to be built and where and when to build them, they then use and devise the most creative methods for completing their goals. As a result, American cities of all sizes and in all parts of the country have seen real estate projects undertaken and completed that just a few years ago would never have gotten off the drawing board.

The products of our urban renaissance mark the skylines of America's urban landscapes. Their visibility, in fact, is partly what makes such projects politically viable; they are immediate and durable monuments to the people and political processes that made them possible. Not so visible and seldom, if ever, discussed is a counter-renaissance in ideas that underlies the philosophical structure of current urban revitalization efforts. This counter-renaissance involves an implicit rejection of important normative values concerning freedom, liberty, individualism, private enterprise, and democracy. In place of these progressive ideals of the Enlightenment stand the everincreasing trends toward central planning, communitarianism, and statism.

Public entrepreneurism, the phrase used by some to describe the current era of public/private cooperation, is a contradiction or counterproposition to itself and thus a fitting label for the current course of urban life.[1] *Entrepreneur* is a term common to American rhetoric and is used to invoke images of private enterprise, individual risk taking and the sink-or-swim success or failure stories of the American marketplace. To be public, on the other hand, runs counter to the individual or to private initiative. Thus, in the marriage of these two words is the symbolic fusing of the private into the public and the elimination of the individual as the key point of reference in favor of the community.

To change or initiate new legal relationships often takes new philosophical conceptions of the politically and economically good and just society. Urban development and revitalization are no exceptions. Unfortunately, lawyers are seldom trained to think about the political, economic, and philosophical consequences of their actions; rather, to "think like a lawyer" is to be creative in reaching an objective—to find new ways to win the case or to finance and structure a downtown real estate project. It is just this type of myopic task-oriented thinking that underpins much of the current counter-renaissance in urban life. While lawyers and others seek new ways to implement political objectives at the local level, they seldom put themselves in the position of evaluating their objectives from the perspective of how they might infringe upon underlying and accepted norms.

As an example of this problem, consider the consequences of public entrepreneurism in the city of Indianapolis, Indiana. As a city of about one million people, Indianapolis prides itself on recent revitalization efforts that have been reported on by the Reagan administration and by *National Geographic, The Smithsonian, Urban Land,* and *Newsweek.*[2] From each of these quarters comes an unquestioning endorsement for the can-do spirit of public and private cooperation that has led to numerous new structures in the Indianapolis downtown area. Local residents are pleased with the impressive changes to their skyline that they believe give evidence of Indianapolis as an important metropolitan area, rather than a sleepy crossroads that only a few years ago was referred to by many locals as "India-no-place."[3] In achieving this impressive new construction, despite an unimpressive midwestern economy, Indianapolis seems admirable to some people; the epitome of good and effective government.

But Indianapolis's success story is subject to at least two interpretations. In contrast to the visible monuments of political power in Indianapolis, there is an invisible restructuring of cultural values and norms. This restructuring builds on a simplistic and egotistical conception of community, while reconfiguring urban life into something almost completely inconsistent with local political rhetoric. First, Indianapolis and cities with similar aspirations foster a local conception of community, anchoring it in a zero-sum game vision of the world. The community, or the public, meaning the immediate residents of the city, are considered better off when diverse state and federal revenue and tax subsidies are used to build projects in Indianapolis rather than in other communities. But if community were understood as something greater than the city itself—at least as broad as the state and national levels from which revenue and subsidies are generated *for* Indianapolis—then it could be seen that the community is hurt in terms of overall job creation, productivity, and prosperity. Resources that would, by economic forces, find themselves employed more effectively elsewhere are instead transferred to the use of Indianapolis politicians. Such a zero-sum game vision of community is harmful to the long-run growth of the greater community and the national and global economy in which we now operate.

Interestingly enough, a different and greater view of community seldom escapes local politicians when they speak rhetorically of *world* peace, of *transboundary* air and water pollution, or of the need for their constituents to have new avenues of *international* trade opened. But the zero-sum view and the narrow definition of community prevail when special interests and continued political survival require these same politicians to favor such things as "free trade" legislation designed, in fact, to reduce or eliminate competitive pressure on local labor and business. Another example is the need felt by politicians to get their "fair share" of the construction and employment benefits of economic growth. This means, in fact, that they want more than their fair share so that they can provide local special interest groups with more than they deserve. This is usually accomplished by displacing market-oriented investment decisions with legislative fiat and politically coerced wealth transfers from one region of the country to another.

This view of community and the political means by which these developments occur will be explored more fully later, but it is important, at this point, to see the backdrop against which urban life is being reconfigured by structural changes in our official and socially validated forms of dialogue. Structural changes in legal economic discourse reveal inconsistencies between surviving forms of free market rhetoric and dramatic ideological shifts in foundational social norms. Such inconsistencies can lead to confusion concerning a community's self-image. Again, consider Indianapolis, located in the "heart of the heartland," a community where most of the people take pride in traditional, conservative, republican values. They value hard work, capitalism, the free market, and individualism. In dramatic contrast to the rhetoric of these "down-home" values, however, Hoosiers in the state's capital city live under a rather different set of political, legal, and economic norms. In its quest for urban revitalization the city has worked hard to promote creative new financing and legal arrangements that have helped change the city skyline, and, some would say, improve the quality of life. But the underlying philosophical change in community norms has gone essentially unnoticed and consequently unevaluated.

Although most Indianapolis lawyers, politicians, and business people have focused their attention on "how to get the job done," no one has reflected on the issue of how certain methods of getting the job done may affect community norms. Thus, in a city where private property, free enterprise, and the individual entrepreneur stand as rhetorically supreme, the reality is that most of the commercial real estate activity in the downtown area is heavily subsidized, administered by central planning boards, and owned in some significant way by the "state." The realities of this "state capitalism" or "urban socialism" stand in dramatic contrast to the rhetoric and self-image of most residents of the Hoosier state.

The inconsistency between rhetoric and reality is seldom acknowledged publicly in a city like Indianapolis where local politicians and business leaders busily orchestrate a vast cheerleading network. The troubling element in this process is that legitimate and critical evaluation of government activity is being foreclosed. Even the local *Indianapolis Star* newspaper tends to side with the cheerleading interests, while presenting contrary views in minimal detail and frequently only after key decisions have already been made.[4] The people of Indianapolis and elsewhere need to be given the opportunity to evaluate the consequences of local approaches to urban revitalization. Through exposure of the inconsistency between rhetoric and reality, critical evaluation might lead the community to a restructuring of their communal order. They may decide to relinquish outdated norms in order to recognize those newly emerging from current legal arrangements, or instead, they may decide to reject the encroachment of new norms upon existing and highly valued norms.

These questions are of great importance, because they are being confronted in a variety of contexts and in a number of localities. Indianapolis is not the only city engaged in urban revitalization activities that are detrimental to important social norms and values, although Indianapolis is an excellent example of the problems associated with the transformation of our legal and economic discourse. Other cities engaging in public/private ventures similar to Indianapolis include Boston, Louisville, Pittsburgh, and St. Louis.

In Boston, for instance, there was over six billion dollars of real estate construction between 1975 and 1985.[5] There are many factors at work in the complex economic environment of Boston that have accounted for recent economic growth and decline. But, in recent years, Boston, like Indianapolis, has been actively engaged in an urban development process that has mixed public and private resources and blurred distinctions between public and private interests. The city has made arrangements to suspend property taxes and instead take payments for such projects as the Prudential Center. In addition, the city provided tax breaks, land, and over $12 million in public funds in order to assist the private development of Faneuil Hall Marketplace.[6] Lastly, in order to complete Copley Place almost $20 million in public funds were mixed with loan and tax breaks to private parties, while the city provided other planning and assembly assistance. The Copley Place project, like similar ventures, establishes long-term agreements and working relationships between the public and private parties engaged in the enterprise.

Louisville, Kentucky, is another city that has gained publicity for its willingness to engage in extensive public/private partnerships. Between 1970 and the mid-1980s, Louisville expended $1 billion in downtown development.[7] Notable projects included the Riverfront Project, the Fourth Avenue Mall, the Commonwealth Convention Center/Hyatt Regency Louisville, the Galleria, the Seelbach Hotel, the Kentucky Center for the Arts, and the Broadway Renaissance project.[8] Typical of the public/private cooperation in these ventures is the Riverfront Project, for which the city contributed a thirty-acre site and $13.5 million in financing. The city accessed $11.5 million from federal sources for the development as well. By linking the resources and efforts of public entities and private parties, the city initiated the redevelopment of a central business district (CBD), a wharf area with open space, a hotel, offices, and an underground parking garage. The city and the private investors are bound together in a long-term business relationship as they manage and operate this project.

Like Louisville, Pittsburgh is a river city, although it is much larger and is home to fifteen Fortune 500 companies.[9] Many costly projects have been undertaken as public/private ventures in Pittsburgh, and Point State Park Gateway Center is typical of the Pittsburgh approach.[10] It is a twenty-three-acre, mixed-use site located in the heart of downtown and developed in conjunction with the thirty-six-acre Point State Park.[11] The power of eminent domain was used to acquire

the land for the private developers' mixed-use development project.[12] This use of eminent domain was one of the first to transfer
substantial amounts of private property to another private party by
way of a public taking. The use of eminent domain powers and the
contribution of additional public funds allowed this project to become a new commercial center in the city. The Allegheny Center
project was another major development undertaking in Pittsburgh.[13]
This seventy-nine-acre mixed-use project was billed as "a $60 million
city within a city." It consumed over $24 million in public funds and
benefited from tax and other incentives. That led to the subsidized
construction of, among other things, badly needed parking space.[14]
Public and private entities worked together in bringing these projects
into existence and that partnership will continue in the future.

St. Louis is a final example of the significant use of a public/private
partnership for urban development and revitalization. Using
constant 1985 dollars, it is estimated that public financial assistance
to redevelopment projects between 1960 and 1979 amounted to
$1.1 billion ($55.5 million per year) and $2.1 billion between 1980
and 1986 ($301.5 million per year).[15] An example of the projects un-
dertaken in St. Louis is St. Louis Union Station. The former train
station first opened in 1894 and included seventeen acres of property.[16] Today St. Louis Union Station is a marketplace shopping center with parking facilities and a 550-room Omni International Hotel.
Public subsidies for this private commercial venture included a 25
percent federal tax credit for historic preservation.[17] This allowed the
private developer to get back one of every four dollars invested. The
project also received $11 million in public funds and a significant
property tax abatement. Furthermore, the project owners/operators
were given the power of eminent domain under Missouri law and
control of more than fifty acres of land in and around the project.[18]

The common theme that runs through each of these public/private
partnership arrangements rejects traditional and classical liberal notions of the importance of maintaining a distinction and a balance
between public and private interests. Indianapolis, Boston, Louisville,
Pittsburgh, St. Louis, and other cities all share this transformation in
legal and economic discourse and in underlying values and norms.
All of these cities have moved toward a new set of legal, political, and
economic arrangements that blur the distinction between the public
and private sphere of property ownership and between counterbalancing power sources. The consequences of this transformation are
significant. Although Indianapolis serves as the primary illustrative
city for this book, it is important to keep in mind that many other
cities are experiencing similar transformations. It is also important to

note that, as a society, we seem to be praising and validating the methods undertaken by these cities without engaging in a clear and thoughtful dialogue concerning the implication that public/private partnerships have on the basic norms and values of our society.

Unfortunately, what is occurring in the area of urban real estate development in Indianapolis and elsewhere is a microcosm of our society, and it can provide a meaningful basis for discussion regarding the broader concepts of freedom, individual liberty, and human dignity. Urban planning and revitalization are also important because they are examples of areas where lawyers too frequently approach problems with a myopic task-oriented perspective rather than with the broader political, economic, and philosophical vision necessary for a moral or ideological evaluation of certain activities.

Chapter 3
The Classical Liberal Perspective

Since this critique of current trends in urban planning and revitalization follows in the philosophical perspective of classical liberalism, it is important to provide a description of classical liberal philosophy. Classical liberalism as used in this book refers to a political and economic philosophy characterized by a strong belief in individual liberty. In general, the philosophy embraces a free market approach to law and social policy as the best method of insuring the greatest possible personal liberty for the individual. Classical liberalism is not, however, a philosophy that requires the completely unfettered operation of a *laissez faire* economy. On the contrary, it is a philosophy founded upon high standards of moral conduct and human dignity that transcend purely utilitarian cost and benefit calculations and simplistic notions equating morality with wealth maximization and market efficiency.

Generally speaking, categorizing classical liberals as either "liberals" or "conservatives," as those terms typically are understood in the United States, would be inappropriate.[1] The term "classical liberal" derives from the British liberal tradition of Adam Smith and David Hume and is espoused by such notable contemporaries as Friedrich Hayek and Milton Friedman. A classical liberal is one who advocates freedom of the individual and reduction of governmental power and control. Over the course of American history, however, the promoters of active government acquired the label "liberal."[2] This role reversal has been the most pronounced since the 1930s, when the term "liberalism" came to be associated with a readiness to rely on state intervention and paternalism rather than on private voluntary arrangements to achieve certain social objectives.[3]

Classical liberals are not, properly speaking, liberals. But neither are they conservatives. Conservatives do not quarrel with liberals over how governmental power should be limited to protect personal liberty. Rather they concern themselves with who should wield government power. In this sense modern conservatives and liberals are merely opposite sides of the same coin. Both philosophical views endorse the use of government power, disagreeing only on the appropriate political agenda. Classical liberals, in contrast, seek to reduce and limit the exercise of government power as a means of protecting individual liberty. Friedrich Hayek, for instance, has described his break with conservatism on the basis that

it neither understands those spontaneous forces on which a policy of freedom relies nor possesses a basis for formulating principles of policy. Order appears to the conservatives as the result of the continuous attention of authority, which for this purpose, must be allowed to do what is required by the particular circumstances and not tied to rigid rule. A commitment to principles presupposes an understanding of the general forces by which the efforts of society are co-ordinated, but it is such a theory of society and especially of the economic mechanism that conservatism conspicuously lacks.[4]

In order to understand more fully modern classical liberalism and the theory of law, economics, and the state one must understand the work of Adam Smith, since it stands as the foundation for the contemporary works of Hayek, Friedman, and others.[5] It is a general misunderstanding of Smith's work that confuses both supporters and detractors of the classical liberal tradition.[6] A brief but comprehensive reconstruction of Smith's work is, therefore, in order.

Adam Smith's theories of law, economics, and society are inevitably linked to his vision of social order. He has been called a reformer, a libertarian,[7] a conjectural historian, and a sociological evolutionist,[8] but whatever term is used to describe Smith, he was undeniably a leading figure in the Scottish Enlightenment.[9] He had a vision of an unequivocable link between economic and social organizations,[10] and viewed society from a historical perspective.[11] He believed that people were subject to uniform principles of self love, a natural desire for action and improvement of their material condition.[12] On the basis of the identification of these natural and uniform human propensities, Smith and other scholars of the Scottish Enlightenment endeavored to discover the interrelationship between the historical changes in civil society and the constant principles of human nature.[13] They visualized social order as the outcome of innumerable self-directed actions and reactions taking place within an everchanging socioeconomic environment.

Adam Smith believed that all people had certain inherent natural rights.[14] These natural rights were part of the endowment of human beings and, for Smith, those endowments were equally distributed among all people, except where the state or the powerful had inter-fered with perfect liberty.[15] Regulations to restrict employment and the free mobility of labor and resources, for example, would violate Smith's theory of natural liberty.[16] On the other hand, Smith was never an advocate of a completely *laissez faire* society. He expressly condoned limited restraints on natural liberty when the restraints served a significant social purpose and were general in their applica-tion.[17] He also postulated certain affirmative duties for government such as providing the poor with adequate public education.[18]

Smith's balancing of the protection of natural liberty and the deter-mination of higher and more significant social purposes was not a utilitarian one.[19] He gave paramount value to the protection of the indi-vidual's natural liberty and sought to balance the greatest possible protection of this liberty against the imposition of restraints for a greater social good. Thus, for Smith, the balance was not simply one of cost and benefit efficiency. Rather, he sought justice in the protec-tion of individuals within the confines of a society governed by gen-eral rules and legal principles.[20] Furthermore, in acting within the confines of these general rules and principles, the state was obligated to treat all people equally; to do otherwise contravened Smith's no-tions of justice.[21]

In at least one sense, Smith's theory of individual liberty seems to be multifaceted and, one might think, contradictory. On the one hand, Smith viewed individual liberty as a natural right. As such, it would seem that individual liberty would be a nonrelative concept. On the other hand, Smith justified restrictions on individual liberty when necessary to serve significant social purposes. Smith also as-serted that human necessaries went beyond what was indispensable for subsistence to include those additional comforts of life that have become part of the customs of society.[22] In this respect, Smith seemed to postulate individual liberty as a relative concept. His two ap-proaches are not, however, contradictory.

Smith was concerned with restraining the power of the state and protecting individuals from the coercive power of both the state and powerful private citizens or special interest groups.[23] Smith's require-ments that there be an independent judiciary and that action occur within the confines of general rules and legal principles demonstrate that he was concerned with process and fairness.[24] Individual liberty in its nonrelative sense refers to placing paramount value on the ideas of individual freedom and respect for the human dignity of each and every person. For Smith, people, because they are human and because they possess natural liberty, are entitled to a process that protects this liberty and dignity to the fullest extent possible within the boundaries of communal society.

Smith's notion of the relative dimension of individual liberty must be viewed against this backdrop. His acknowledgment that individual liberty must sometimes be restrained for more significant social purposes is merely a recognition that in society there must be limitations on one's freedom to preserve for everyone the greatest possible personal autonomy.[25] Any limitation on individual liberty would be subject to procedural guidelines and would be measured against principles of fairness and justice rather than notions of social utility.

Additionally, Smith is not being contradictory when he discusses a relative conception of human necessaries. For the fulfillment of individual liberty and for the respect of personal dignity, it is appropriate that material well-being be measured by the custom and standards of a society rather than by biological criteria for human subsistence. In other words, the degree to which society respects the individual liberty of all its members can be measured, in part, by the degree to which even its poorest members enjoy material well-being.

Smith, therefore, is not contradicting himself when he discusses individual liberty as a natural right. The natural rights of liberty, freedom, and human dignity are steadfast and protected by a commitment to equality, justice, and fairness. At the same time, the measure of a society's success in protecting individual liberty is, by necessity, linked to that society's history and the socioeconomic conditions of its time.[26]

Given this perspective on the nature of individual liberty, Smith presents a historical explanation of the evolution and advancement of freedom and liberty.[27] Smith identifies three separate and distinct stages of development: the age of hunters, the age of shepherds, and the age of commerce.[28] Each of these stages involves its own peculiar social, political, economic, and moral arrangements.[29] Furthermore, each stage represents an increasingly higher societal order involving greater realization of the individual's natural right to liberty. Progression from the lowest stage, the age of hunters, to the highest stage, the age of commerce, is made possible by the division of labor and each individual's natural desire to advance his or her own interests and material well-being.[30]

An important consequence of progressing through the three stages is that the source and nature of power within the community shifts.[31] In the age of hunters, power and authority were earned with bravery, strength, and skill. There was little on which to spend one's resources and there was little ability to preserve or store up capital in the form of beads, crude tools, and short-term supplies of food. As society progressed to the age of shepherds, basic conceptions of property law emerged. A more advanced form of government was required to protect emerging notions of property and to secure the benefits of ownership.[32] Thus, in the age of shepherds, the ability to acquire and store large amounts of wealth in the form of animals, land, and crops gave rise to a base of power in the community that was not dependent upon one's physical strength, cunning, or bravery. With the transferability of wealth from one generation to another, the age of shepherds also allowed for families, rather than individuals, to exercise power over one or multiple generations. Finally, in the age of commerce, creativity and mobility of capital became the source of power. Of Smith's three stages, the age of commerce, by dispersing wealth and power, allowed the greatest realization of individual liberty.[33]

An important reason for the enhancement of individual liberty during the age of commerce was the increased availability of alternative ways for the rich to spend their wealth.[34] In the early stages of social progress, those who acquired wealth by power, force, or authority had few ways to spend their money. Consequently, most wealth was tied up in the ownership of land and its produce. Because a person can consume only a small amount of such goods, much wealth was used to support servants, agricultural workers, and serfs.[35] In this social arrangement, one or a few wealthy lords might support everyone in a town or village.

As the division of labor increased and more manufactured goods became available, the wealthy spent their assets on conspicuous consumption, no longer spending their excess capital to support others.[36] Instead, the rich used their money to obtain goods and services from independent merchants and sellers. Because these merchants and sellers served many buyers instead of one overlord, they developed a sense of independence. Thus, through the enhancement of voluntary market exchanges, the ownership of land became less central to social organization and the rich lords lost much of their power.[37] Power follows capital. The opportunities for spreading and sharing wealth are increased because the capitalist society rewards an individual's product rather than his or her status. In this manner, capitalism assures greater individual participation and less bondage to powerful overlords than in any other stage of development.

The other important reason that a capitalist society results in greater individual liberty is that it creates a power base for individuals to challenge and constrain the state.[38] The state protects the individual while providing necessary services for the protection of human dignity. It often, however, can become the tool of special interest groups bent on using the state's power to further their own selfish interests.[39] Yet capitalist society, by having multiple sources of capital outside the direct control of the state, empowers individuals.[40] This dispersion of capital helps to prevent the state from becoming a mere bureaucratic substitute for the coercive domination of an overlord.

A basic understanding of each of Smith's three stages of social development is important because, according to Smith, law and government also evolve within these stages.[41] In the age of commerce for instance, the rule of law and the role of government are linked to the interest of capitalism. And, for Smith, capitalism is linked to the greatest fulfillment of individual liberty.

Furthermore, individual liberty for Smith is linked to spontaneous social order which can emerge in a society where individuals are allowed to pursue their own self-interest. Such order emerges, not as the result of omnipotent design or central government planning, but as a result of what Smith terms an "invisible hand."[42]

Interestingly enough, Smith's characterization of an "invisible hand" gained its notoriety from a single mention in his famous book, *The Wealth of Nations*,[43] even though he had more fully explained the concept in an earlier work, *The Theory of Moral Sentiments*.[44] Consequently, Smith's "invisible hand" concept often is not fully appreciated because readers are frequently unfamiliar with its construction in the earlier work. In *The Wealth of Nations*, Smith described the nature and benefits of an exchange economy. He depicted the quality of self-interest as the pursuit of one's own material gain. The result of this self-interested pursuit was beneficial not only to the pursuer but to everyone in the society, because of the generation of positive externalities through the market system of incentives and disincentives. The pursuit of self-interest, therefore, benefited both the individual pursuer and society without the need for central planning. With a market framework that allows self-interested individuals to exchange information, individuals themselves can coordinate numerous opportunities for human interaction. Thus,

It is not from the benevolence of the butcher, the brewer, or the baker, that we expect our dinner, but from their regard to their own interest. We address ourselves, not to their humanity but to their self-love, and never talk to them of our own necessities but of their advantages.[45]

Viewed only in the context of *The Wealth of Nations*, the "invisible hand" characterization could easily be misjudged as a purely utilitarian appeal for, or justification of, the pursuit of materialism. Such a judgment, however, would be a mistake. Smith's conception of self-interest is far different from selfishness and is even antagonistic to the pursuit of materialism as a means to human happiness.[46] A fuller appreciation of the "invisible hand" concept can be gleaned only by reading its more comprehensive treatment in *The Theory of Moral Sentiments*.

In *The Theory of Moral Sentiments*, Smith asserted that true human happiness cannot be attained by wealth.[47] He admitted that for many people the pursuit of wealth and riches is a preoccupation that drives and motivates their self-interest and, consequently, their productivity.[48] But they do not necessarily seek a specific material outcome. Rather they feel that by possessing a certain object or certain riches they will have more and better means for attaining human happiness.[49] Smith argued, for instance, that wealth and riches are not pursued by people for their own sake,[50] but because people perceive a beauty and harmony in the wealthy, who have at their disposal greater means for the attainment of happiness.[51]

In describing the almost pathetic quest for wealth that some people exhibit in their unrelenting labors, Smith concluded that, in the end, even the most ambitious of people

find that wealth and greatness are mere trinkets of frivolous utility, no more adopted for procuring ease of body or tranquility of mind, than the tweezer-cases of the lover of toys; and like them, too, more troublesome to the person who carries them about with him than all the advantages they can afford him.[52]

They discover that the real values are happiness and liberty, which cannot be attained by the mere accumulation of material wealth.[53]

In *The Theory of Moral Sentiments*, it is evident that Smith's characterization of spontaneous social order through an invisible hand is much more complex than would appear from a mere review of his passage in *The Wealth of Nations*. It is also clear that Smith's conception of the "invisible hand" is one that embodies complex moral considerations that go far beyond simple notions of utility, efficiency, or wealth maximization.

For Adam Smith, individual liberty is the essential ingredient of a good life; it is the one ingredient that satisfies people and makes them equal.[54] Individual liberty, however, is a concept that, like self-interest and the "invisible hand," takes on meaning only in a social context. All members of human society stand in need of each other.[55] Consistent with this recognition of human beings as social animals, Smith denounces selfishness and distinguishes it from self-interest, which embodies a concern for living with others.[56] To understand the harmonizing of individual liberty with social cooperation, Smith offers his theory of moral sentiments.

His theory is basically a subjective model of human conduct. In the first part he postulates that people judge the conduct of others only from their own perspective.[57] To the extent that one agrees with or identifies with the conduct of other people, one sympathizes with them,[58] and shares an almost altruistic compassion and understanding for what they are experiencing. In the second part of his theory, Smith postulates that people judge their own conduct only as they imagine that others are judging them.[59] In this the individual is guided by a hypothetical and impartial spectator that represents a subjective view of how one imagines others will sympathize with one's conduct.[60] Therefore, one must live in society with others to judge oneself and to understand the basis upon which to judge others.[61]

In Smith's model, a community of individuals subjectively views others and itself on the basis of how it thinks others view it from the perspective of the impartial spectator. Individuals seek praise and try to avoid blame.[62] They voluntarily adjust to and accept societal norms for behavior and cooperation.[63]

At a superficial level, Smith's theory of individuals seeking praise and avoiding blame can be viewed as a moralistic formulation of economic cost-benefit analysis. Yet, on a more complex level, Smith offers a conception of individual conduct that is governed by a process that reflects concern for others and for the community, a process where gain is measured in a societal context. Smith, in fact, specifically rejected the notion of selfish gain in the marketplace.[64] He allowed for an individual to use his or her best efforts in the pursuit of personal fulfillment, but such efforts must be constrained by values of fair play and justice.[65] Thus, Smith did not postulate a selfish survival of the fittest with individuals acting to maximize their own wealth and success. Rather, Smith saw a society comprised of individuals who act within the guidelines of social norms to achieve praise and success.[66] In this manner, one's individual merit is contingent and dependent upon the happiness and merit of others.

From this theory of moral sentiments Smith derived the basis upon which morals are founded. He wrote that the general rules of morality

are ultimately founded upon experience of what, in particular instances, our moral faculty, our natural sense of merit and propriety, approve or disapprove of. We do not originally approve or condemn particular actions, because, upon examination, they appear to be agreeable or inconsistent with a certain general rule. The general rule, on the contrary, is formed by finding from experience that all actions of a certain kind, or circumstanced in a certain manner, are approved or disapproved of.[67]

For Smith, general rules of morality are not divinely ordained, but emerge from the self-conscious introspection of individuals living and pursuing their self-interest in the society of others. Consequently, individuals do not always act to their own advantage. Rather they are constrained in the pursuit of their own self-interest by their moral sentiments.[68]

To appreciate Adam Smith's understanding of the relationship between law and economics, it is necessary to review his conception of the rule of law and of government's proper and limited role. Smith believed in the need for general rules of law as the building blocks for the stages of society.[69] Smith's conception of the many ends to which government can be directed must be viewed from a backdrop of social organization governed by general legal rules and principles. Against this backdrop there are probably few activities that government could not engage in if the people desired it, especially if that activity served a significant public purpose and could not be achieved by private means.[70]

General rules are important to a Smithian conception of the rule of law.[71] Regulations governing economic activity, for instance, would be acceptable to Smith because they subject all participants to the same constraints.[72] And, assuming no restrictions on price in a competitive market, the consumers of regulated commercial activities receive valuable information about their cost relative to other alternatives. This function, which occurs through the operation of the marketplace, is important for the realization of Smith's spontaneous social order.[73] The marketplace allows numerous individuals to coordinate their goals without central planning. General rules facilitate both this process and the optimal use of scarce human and economic resources by providing non-outcome specific guidelines for individuals to consider as they decide to buy, sell, enter, or exit the marketplace.

General rules in a democratic society can be understood as those underlying principles on which a majority would agree.[74] True agreement among a majority will, in a given society, rarely extend beyond some set of general principles that can be maintained only to the extent that they are known by most of society's members.[75] For instance, the legislative process that brings forth new law as the result of compiling special interest legislation, does not necessarily meet the test of generality.[76] Only to the extent that a majority believes in the general principle does legislation meet this test. Legislation passed as the result of a combined series of special interest proposals does not meet the test of generality if all the special interests make up a majority, but the legislation itself represents no principle upon which they agree. It is through this requirement of generality that a Smithian conceives a restraint on the ability of the people to change the rules to favor their own interest.[77] Similarly, it is this restraint on changing the rules for the benefit of a particular person or group that protects individual liberty and spontaneous social order from encroachment by the coercive power of the state or others.

Given Smith's conception of the role of general rules, it is now possible to consider the proper and limited functions of government that are compatible with his notion of a free society. For Smith, the first and paramount purpose of civil government is to protect individuals from the coercion of others.[78] In a society that has no civil government, power is exercised by those who control the resources and command the personal respect appropriate to the given stage of social development. Unless there are multiple sources of nongovernmental power, there will be no basis for checking the unlimited coercive conduct of people possessing private power.[79] Government, therefore, is formed to protect individual liberty and human dignity by protecting the weaker or less powerful members of society from the coercion of those stronger and more powerful.

Although governments are formed to protect individual liberty and allow for beneficial social cooperation, governments themselves are composed of members of the very societies they govern. Democratic process seeks to assure a continuous feedback of information between individuals in the society and the people and apparatus that emerge as the manifestation of representative government in the form of the state. But democratic process alone is not sufficient to protect individual liberty if government, in the form of the state, is able to act in the same coercive fashion as the power elite or as special interests would in the absence of government. Preventing government from becoming a mere substitute for coercive individuals or private entities involves a proper regard for constraining governmental power.[80]

In his works *The Wealth of Nations, The Theory of Moral Sentiments,* and *Lectures on Jurisprudence,* Smith observed that the power of government is frequently used to benefit the rich and powerful at the expense of other members of society.[81] The conception of the law of property and the power of government to enforce that law is, according to Smith, an example of the means by which people with property seek to affect the rules that identify and protect that property from others.[82] Smith, however, was careful to acknowledge the value of human productivity and material well-being resulting from the evolution of general rules of property.[83] Because productivity and material well-being are secondary to Smith's concern for individual liberty, he is cautious about the exercise of state power to mold and enforce property rules.[84]

Dealing with this continuous tension between the benefits and costs of government activities requires a concern for process. Just as Smith was concerned with the process by which individuals were treated, he also seems to have envisioned a process of checks and balances between individuals and their government. Reading all of Smith's publicly available literature, one senses that Smith was aware of the need to maintain extensive sources of capital in private hands. Not only does the accumulation of private capital spur on the division of labor, thus greatly benefiting the individual and society's material well-being, but it also preserves sources of power that are beyond the reach of the state. Those privately owned resources ensure that there is some source of real power that can be used to keep the state in check. This source of private power, when combined with the notion of general rules and other principles of limited government, gives real meaning to the notion of limitations on state power.[85]

When viewed in a positive sense, the proper restraint on civil government can be embodied in the principles that government should act only to protect individual human dignity and only to provide services or goods that are of a type private enterprise would not provide.[86] Smith, consistent with this view of limited government, tempers his call for governmental restraint by outlining the basis for proper government action.

According to Smith, government has an important role to play in the protection of individual liberty.[87] For the most part, Smith's definition of that role centers around the traditional activities of providing for roads and other basic services important to the advancement of social cooperation and material well-being, but which usually are not fully profitable for private individuals.[88] Smith also accepted government as the administrator of justice and the provider of police and military services.[89] But he went beyond this limited conception of the role of government when he addressed, in *The Wealth of Nations*, the need for government to provide public education.[90]

The Wealth of Nations is primarily dedicated to the celebration of the division of labor and the benefits resulting from capitalism. Smith, however, was very much aware of a detrimental consequence of the division of labor—the alienation of workers.[91] Despite increased productivity, wealth, and material well-being, the division of labor alienates workers by continually reducing their identification with the product of their labor.[92] In addition, by continually having his or her attention focused on smaller and simpler tasks, the worker becomes dehumanized in the sense that there is no longer much opportunity, and therefore very little reason, to think about the job.[93] This dehumanization even extends beyond the job, for the experiences of the workplace consume a considerable amount of time and importance for the worker.[94] As a result, the numbness of the mind caused by the division of labor carries over into everyday life.[95] The worker, in the process of the division of labor, becomes increasingly unable to contemplate the nature of self, society, and government, and consequently becomes increasingly unable to enjoy the fruits of individual liberty.

To counteract the negative consequences of the division of labor without sacrificing its many benefits, Smith requires that government provide everyone with a public education.[96] He argues that the necessity for public education is especially great in the case of the poor because they are unable to afford private schooling.[97] Most important, Smith imposed this affirmative duty on government even if the state could gain no advantage from the education it provided for its citizens.[98] He argues that although education can benefit society by preparing citizens to better understand liberty, its primary purpose is to benefit the individual.[99] Smith's position on this point is in harmony with his concern for individual liberty and morality as expressed in his earlier work *The Theory of Moral Sentiments*. He believes that individual liberty is a value worthy of the highest protection and admiration and that education is one way to preserve that liberty and to protect human dignity.

Smith's position on education has important implications. The overriding theme in his discussion of public education is concern for the respect of the individual as a human being. This concern for human dignity and individual liberty is made a duty of government precisely because it is one of the fundamental reasons *for* government. The marketplace will not provide adequate educational opportunities because it responds not to the desires or needs of individuals but to their ability to purchase goods and services.[100] For Smith, the poor are as worthy, if not more worthy, of education than the rich.[101] Thus, the obligation to provide education to members of society is based not on an ability to purchase education but rather on a recognition of education's importance in protecting individual liberty, making the ends of government and social cooperation in the age of commerce worthy of attainment.

Smith's position on education should be considered together with his views on the relative aspects of individual liberty.[102] Earlier it was concluded that Smith judged a society's protection of individual liberty relative to its wealth and stage of development. It follows, then, that a modern day Smithian or classical liberal would use Smith's analytical approach in addressing issues that go beyond Smith's original concerns for matters such as public education. As a consequence,

Smith's approach requires a continuing evaluation of difficult social policy issues such as minimum guaranteed income, low-income housing, job training programs, and minimum health care protection. These important social policy issues cannot be dismissed by our simply saying that the inability to purchase these goods and services in the private marketplace is the determining factor in one's inability to receive them. On the contrary, the Smithian approach would require that one consider the requirements of fulfilling individual liberty in a society that has a certain level of wealth and standard of material well-being. In this respect therefore, the Smithian approach to pressing social problems centers on a critical libertarian analysis of what is right and proper for the fulfillment of individual liberty, rather than on the pursuit of simplistic notions of utilitarianism or wealth maximization.

It is useful, finally, to consider Smith's comments on the social contract theory of government. In *Lectures on Jurisprudence*, Smith expressly rejects the social contract theory as unsupportable.[103] The state never asks for the individual's consent and, to Smith, it stretches the imagination to assert that the individual consents, in a contractual sense, to the government.[104] Interestingly, one of his objections to the social contract theory is that it ignores the situation of the poor. There is, for many members of society and especially for the poor, an inability to move one's person and posssessions freely.[105] As a result, the notion that one can freely emigrate and withdraw consent to the alleged social contract is a myth. The consequence of accepting such a construct is surely to assure de facto consent to all but the most outrageous of state actions. Therefore, Smith rejected the social contract theory and offered an alternative theory based on notions of authority and utility.[106]

Smith believes that the organization of society and the advancement of social cooperation depends upon some degree of authority.[107] This authority must abide in social organization and, presumably, would be subject to the procedural requirements of law sufficient to preserve individual liberty. As for the concept of utility, Smith perceived that there was social utility in having government and authority. From a review of his historical analysis of the stages of social development, one can conclude that he viewed notions of authority and utility based on social, political, and economic changes over time as evolving with society.[108] As a result, Smith's work is primarily concerned with analyzing the nature of society and the means for effecting and protecting individual liberty while advancing the material well-being of society. Authority and utility combine in the sense that the rule of law and the role of government provide for authoritative dispute resolution, thus creating social utility by allowing progress and cooperation not possible in a state of anarchy. At the same time, this use of authority and the measure of its social utility is limited by the degree to which individual liberty and material well-being are protected.

An important implication emerges from Smith's rejection of the social contract theory. Because there is no contract between the individual and the government, the relevant basis for evaluating the government's performance is not an alleged contract, but the appropriate norms, moral sentiments, and morality upon which human interaction and individual liberty are based.[109] Such an approach allows one to evaluate law and society with a concern for values that otherwise might not be fully explored. This is possible because Smith is not constrained by the current status quo of society's politically expedient legal arrangements. Consequently, Smith's rejection of the social contract theory allows the individual greater freedom to evaluate government continually and critically, not on terms offered by the government, but on terms which place paramount value on the protection of individual liberty and human dignity while simultaneously advancing society's material well-being.[110]

Thus, Adam Smith had a much more complex view of the relationship between law and economics than most people realize. Smith was a moral philosopher and a philosopher of political economy, and his vision of human interaction and society never lost touch with the interdisciplinary dimensions of his own background. Smith saw both the advantages and the disadvantages of government and of economic development. Democratic government and capitalist economics were seen as means for achieving higher purposes, not as merely ends in themselves. Ultimately for Smith, the value of the division of labor, of capitalism, of material well-being, of law, and of government is always measured by the degree to which it successfully harmonizes with his concern for individual liberty and the morality of our moral sentiments.

In an effort to recapture the original meaning of "liberalism" as stressing individual liberty and human dignity, the terms "classical liberal" and "classical liberalism" are used in this book. They refer to a liberalism with roots in the tradition of Adam Smith as distinguished from the current ideology of both conservatives and liberals. The term "individual liberty" is meant here to incorporate the duality of Smith's relative and nonrelative conceptions of human dignity and, in this regard, promotes what might be called humane libertarianism.

Chapter 4
The System of Checks and Balances

In this chapter I will make an effort to explain a classical liberal vision of government, to establish a framework for a discussion of the proper relationship between the individual, the community, and the state. In classical liberal theory, that relationship is based on the establishment of a process capable of stimulating and maintaining a creative and everchanging spontaneous social order. It is a social arrangement that is dynamic and fluid rather than static and arrested, and it requires multiple and competing sources of power and authority. In many respects such a social system must metaphorically resemble the economic marketplace—as a dynamic environment where an impersonal process assures the greatest degree of individual autonomy. This chapter, therefore, incorporates some traditional discussion of the system of checks and balances, but posits them in a new light by considering them as part of a delicate and dynamic process—a process that cannot operate effectively in a noncapitalist environment and that is subject to abuse by special interests capable of capturing the power of the state for their own benefit.

The classical liberal perspective on the role of the state is, therefore, skeptical of the ability of democratic processes to restrain fully the pervasive exercise of state power.[1] Classical liberals are skeptical of statist claims that the state can be restrained by the electoral process and by an internally orchestrated system of governmental checks and balances. Although most Americans seem to accept them implicitly, each of these claims can be criticized. The power of the vote retains some validity at the local level, but is in fact quite mythical in such things as a presidential election.[2] At the local level, if the group is small enough, the members of the group will know each other personally and each of their votes will have consequence by virtue of the small size of the total votes cast. There is direct accountability and immediate feedback between voter and politician because of the small town nature involved. Examples of this process are the legendary New England small town meeting or the law school faculty meeting where only twenty-five to thirty members may make up the voting faculty. To extrapolate from these settings to the national level can be symbolically and rhetorically powerful imagery but remains more myth than reality.

In the United States much is made of the presidential sweepstakes that occur every four years and are currently operated like any other sporting event.[3] The candidates, sensitive to voter sentiment, prepare positions on topics. They then state vague and grand ideas about the resolution of complex problems. They seldom take a firm stand on any issue and, if they do, feel free to change those views later. In fact, the public has come to expect that campaign promises are unlikely to be fulfilled. Furthermore, the notion that a president, even if committed, can accomplish much is removed from reality. There are the Congress, the states, and the judiciary to deal with, as well as a large number of entrenched civil servants who can hinder or help the efforts of an administration as they choose. In such a setting it should be no surprise that we tend to pick our presidents on the basis of their good looks, quality of voice, quick wit, or attractiveness of spouse and family. Neither is it surprising that so many Americans fail to vote; unless one is allied with an interest that seeks power, one has little or nothing to gain regardless of who is elected.

Concerning the system of checks and balances, one finds almost uniformly that the discussion of such a process lacks its most important elements. Our civic lessons typically focus on the checks and balances between the three branches of government—the executive, the legislative, and the judiciary. A more sophisticated model accounts for counterbalancing forces such as federal versus state and state versus local governmental authorities. But this is only half of what is required for a government committed to individual freedom, human dignity, and self-realization.[4]

Although government is needed in a free society to protect individuals from the coercive interference of powerful individuals or groups, there must also be an effective means for checking the power of government. Sources of wealth and power must exist outside of the control of government in order to prevent government from becoming an institutionalized coercive bully.[5] If we are to advance beyond a simple and primitive society of "might makes right," we need to recognize the role of government in protecting and nurturing the rights of those less powerful members of the community while also recognizing that, if left unchecked, the power of government could become the most coercive and all-encompassing threat to individual liberty.[6] What holds true in other markets also holds true for government or state power. Just as monopolies can be bad for consumers of gasoline or cameras, so too can they be bad for individuals when a coercive power is a person (a parent over a child for instance),[7] a group (the mafia or a collusion of chemical companies), or the state itself. A capitalist system of private ownership is, therefore, an essential element of a free society, because it is the only context in which the necessary balance between public and private can be maintained.

Competing sources of power are essential for the preservation of an environment favorable to creativity, freedom, and spontaneous social order. This has been the lesson of traditional economics since the time of Adam Smith. It is, however, impractical to establish *competing* governments within a country. First, it would be administratively unmanageable to have multiple governmental structures of *equivalent* status operating within the same geographical boundaries; there is difficulty when no institutionalized hierarchy is established. Thus, the sharing of power in the United States between the fifty states and the federal government is possible only because the federal government has supremacy. The sharing of power between the three co-equal branches of the federal government is workable because the Supreme Court, leading the most undemocratic branch, has the power to interpret the constitutional authority of the other two branches. Second, the notion of competitive co-equal governments would be unworkable for state propaganda, because it could not unify the mass population behind a single identity. Propaganda need not be viewed in a negative sense, but can be seen as the basis upon which a common cultural identity is communicated to an otherwise diverse population.

In the absence of competitive governments, a system of checks and balances can be implemented. To be effective such a system must be comprised of both internal and external checks and balances. The system must also be founded upon an effective source of power. The internal governmental restraints on the power of the state include a system of checks and balances that divide the federal government into three assertedly co-equal branches—executive, legislative, and judicial. A system of checks and balances is also constructed between the federal, state, and local governments in the United States. In each instance the power base upon which governmental entities operate is the power of coercion manifested in such sources as the police power, the military power, and the power to tax and spend (the purse power). The power to tax is coercive not only because it appropriates private resources for public purposes but also because it is a vehicle for social planning; it can present benefits and detriments to various identifiable interests that the state wishes either to encourage or to discourage.

If the state is to function in a limited way to protect individual liberty, it must be subject to outside or external restraints, as well as to a system of internal checks and balances. Internal checks and balances can serve a long-term function of carving up the market for state power but cannot serve as a means of protecting the individual from unwarranted state intervention and coercion. Internal checks and balances must be considered in a context of external restraints on the state itself. Meaningful external checks and balances can come only from the existence of a capitalist free market economy.[8] For only in the capitalist system do individuals have ownership of substantial wealth sufficient to present a challenge to encroachment by the state. Great Britain is a good example of the difficulties in maintaining a free society in the midst of extensive state ownership. Consider the British Broadcasting Corporation: run by the state, it has a commitment to the free exchange of ideas but ultimately is beholden to the power of the state and has, therefore, been successful in banning such anti-establishment songs as Paul McCartney's "Give Ireland Back to the Irish" and the Sex Pistols' "God Save the Queen and Her Fascist Regime."[9] Both songs were played on American radio. One reason for the greater freedom of expression in the United States is that private ownership increases the likelihood that diverse messages will be transmitted, because various suppliers of information will compete for the chance to air materials. One must also think of the multitude of foundations and institutes on both the left and the right of the political spectrum in the United States that support the creation and distribution of diverse and sometimes controversial ideas. For the most part this is possible because capitalism has provided private individuals with the ability to spend their resources on such institutes and foundations.

The private sphere of individuals, like that of the state, is subject to internal restraints. These restraints can be summarized as follows: (1) group dynamics—we live with others and thus fall into patterns of behavior that tend toward acceptance rather than ostracism; (2) custom—in addition to any formalistic law we also succumb to various customs that regulate our behavior; and (3) norms—certain community norms about acceptable behavior also tend to govern and limit the extent to which our actions will be approved or disapproved by others.[10] The private sphere must also have a source of power in order to exercise a counterbalancing force upon the coercive power of the state. The source of power for individuals exists in two primary capacities. First, power emerges from the ability to control wealth and resources that are outside the direct control or ownership of the state. Second, the power to bear arms limits how much state police power may be exercised in an authoritarian fashion. Anyone who doubts this proposition need only consider the potential difference that a fully armed Solidarity Union might have had in the dynamics of Poland's political struggles of the early 1980s or of the Chinese student revolt of 1989. Although individual autonomy and power help to check or counterbalance the power of the state, the existence of the state serves as a counterbalance to the coercion of some individuals by others.

The chart below illustrates the necessary system of checks and balances for a free society.

INDIVIDUAL / PRIVATE	STATE / PUBLIC

1. Internal restraints
    (a) group dynamics
    (b) customs
    (c) norms
	1. Internal restraints
	    (a) co-equal divisions of
	        government: executive,
	        legislative, judicial
	    (b) subordinate divisions of
	        government—federal
	        vs. state and state
	        vs. local

2. Source of power
    (a) private wealth
        and capital
    (b) private weapons
	2. Source of power
	    (a) police and military
	        powers
	    (b) taxing and spending
	        powers

It is possible to compare this conception of government in a free society with that of other instances of market competition. Namely, competition serves to protect the interests of consumers. When the product is government, competition means protecting the individual from the tyranny of the state while providing an institutional means, via government, for protecting the individual from private coercion. But as a competitive construct this model tells us something more. It says that there will be constant conflict between the competitive roles or boundaries of the private versus public domain. Concepts such as public/private partnerships tend to break down and destroy these boundaries. The breakdown of such boundaries is detrimental because tension can produce positive externalities. As in the commercial marketplace, however, losing the will or means to compete can leave one increasingly at the mercy of other, more powerful players. In the

United States we have witnessed a loss of both will and means in the private sphere. Normative values have changed or are being changed as Americans look ever increasingly to the use of the political means and the expansion of the state as a way of avoiding the effort and potential failure of competition.

Such a result is compatible with the distinction between an impersonal marketplace and a personal state. Just as most of us believe that we will be the lawyer who gets rich and famous, the soldier who will not be killed in battle, the person who will not be victimized by crime, or the person who will not be subjected to AIDS, we believe that a properly functioning state would give greater recognition to *our* goals and aspirations than would be possible in the marketplace. We also believe that the "right" people in office can make a difference and that a system of status will give us personal recognition whereas the impersonal market may respond negatively to *our* goals and aspirations. It is easier to accept failure or rejection as a result of the ignorance or the lack of understanding of a person than it is to be left with the impersonal rejection of the marketplace. It is also easier to mobilize a special interest group to exert influence on the political process than it is to attempt to change the outcome of the marketplace in which, by definition, individuals and small groups have a minimal impact.

This vision of a free society emerging from the competitive forces of checks and balances between individuals and the state contains the basis for understanding the inevitable progression toward statism currently confronting us. The continued progression toward statism is the result of two primary factors. First, the interaction between incentives for exercising the political means and the phenomenon of overgrazing (to be discussed later) and, second, individuals' continuing loss of will to compete in the private sector.

The forces at work promoting the use of the political means are strong. Politicians and government bureaucrats are rewarded with the indicia of power and respect more frequently when they exercise political power on behalf of special interests rather than when they refrain from action. This creates a natural incentive to seek the use of such power. It also gives politicians an opportunity for self-actualization by invoking legislation or decision-making power that promotes their perceived wisdom, insight, and programmatic changes over those of others. The peculiar dynamics of the political means are discussed more fully in the next chapter, and the resulting tragedy of treating state power as a "free good" is explored in the subsequent chapter. Simply stated, however, the individual or group that can successfully harness the coercive power of the state for the achievement of its own ends stands at an advantage vis-à-vis its competition. Similarly, since the operatives of the state are seldom reluctant to expand the "good works" of the state, there is a tendency for every individual to conclude that they too should do something to invoke the power of the state on their behalf. The end result is an overreliance on state power (overgrazing) and the continuing progression toward statism.

The changes in social values, norms, and dynamics are complex yet understandable contributors to statist tendencies. For one reason, we live in a society which believes fundamentally in the miracles of science rather than of God, creativity, or uncontrolable forces of nature. This means we have become believers in the ability of people to solve many if not all of our problems. We believe that the right people in the right positions with the right resources can solve all of our difficulties. We no longer seem able to accept the natural dynamics of winning and losing in a competitive marketplace. We love to win and when we lose, we try to overcome the disappointment by working for the right kind of changes; those that will correct such problems in the future, if not totally redeem us in the present.

This false scientific mentality is part of what is behind the so-called litigation explosion. Americans no longer want to believe in acts of God, fate, individual and shared responsibility, or the inability of people to control their environment. Rather, they want to believe in scientific explanations. Today everything is thought to be foreseeable and preventable. Therefore, if only the right people were in the right places, bad consequences, whatever they were, might have been prevented. Thus, every plane crash seemingly must result in airline liability or aircraft manufacturer liability and, just as surely, every playground injury must be the result of some faulty design or improper supervision. Someone is always liable and something or someone else can always correct the problem. Consistent with other formulations of this "scientific" approach to statism, Americans seem to have turned their liability law into a call for better planning and management. Behind this approach is a mind-set that is ripe for the growth of statism and the death of liberty, for it is an attitude underpinned by a belief in humans' ability to control and manage vast and complex social, political, economic, and environmental factors and to control them in a way that leads to an objectively better future based on planning rather than spontaneity. Such is the ideological framework for forms of legal economic discourse that reject the marketplace and its focus on the individual as the key referential sign or value.

Interestingly enough, science itself, especially in the areas of biology and evolution, shows us that such an attitude can be very unscientific and that spontaneous, counterbalancing power struggles are as vital to human evolution as those forces at work in political and economic struggles are to our social evolution.[11] Nonetheless, it is this erroneous scientific mentality that helps to explain public disenchantment with people who seek to limit or restrain government intervention in the private marketplace. People who seek to limit or restrain government within a moral and principled framework are simply labeled as unscientific. Consequently, classical liberals and libertarians are not convincing to most liberals and conservatives because classical liberals and libertarians *reject* the underlying notions that (1) the right people in the right places with the right resources can solve all our problems; and (2) even if they could, the sterile world of technocratic planning could not substitute for the creative advances of counterbalancing social dynamics. Yet the myth of planning seems easier to accept given the alternative of an impersonal, spontaneous, and for some, incomprehensibly anarchic marketplace. The myth, however, is statist in origin and leads to the decline of individualism and individual liberty while promoting elitism in state planning.

Without a commitment to a strong private sector as a counterbalance to the public sector, the power of the state is unlikely to be adequately restrained. Thus, the impersonal and spontaneous social order of the marketplace will give way to the pervasive intrusion of state planning and increasing reliance on the political rather than the economic means for the allocation of rights and resources in our society. Such a process of setting the political means over the economic means results in the elevation of personal status over impersonal market outcomes and leads to a new age of serfdom in which *individual* rights are subservient to the group, institutional, and organizational claims of the state.

Chapter 5
The Political Means Versus the Economic Means

In order to understand the legal and economic implications of the classical liberal view of the individual, the community, and the state, one must understand the two principal ways in which scarce social resources are allocated. According to classical liberal theory, the allocation of scarce resources in a society can occur either by economic or by political means.[1] In either case, the primary objective is to allocate limited supplies of resources to competing users. This chapter addresses the two methods of resource allocation, and the purpose of the discussion is not to reiterate prior debates concerning public choice theory,[2] but to make some distinct observations about the ideological significance of choosing one form of resource allocation over the other. Although a society is unlikely to be absolute in its form of resource allocation, it is significant when one form predominates over the other, or when an evolutionary process that seems to be transforming the relative positions of the two alternative approaches is at work. American society today is undergoing an important transition from the use of the economic to the political means; a transition that shifts the framework of legal and economic thinking from a focus on individualist values to a focus on communitarian values.[3] For these reasons it is important to describe and explore the meaning and consequences of both approaches to resource allocation.

The economic means for accomplishing the allocation of scarce social resources are based on the operation of a marketplace of exchange. Although the marketplace of exchange can be a barter system, it typically is understood as a market in which price and currency act as the medium of exchange in order to facilitate transactions between numerous strangers. At the same time it offers a wide variety of goods and services in exchange for an equally wide variety of return goods and services. Thus, people are continually interacting as both buyers and sellers; each buyer is at some point a seller and each seller is at some point a buyer. The price mechanism provides participants in the market with a ready source of information on the cost of certain actions relative to possible alternatives. In allocating the use of resources in the system, the market allows the buyer or buyers willing and able to pay the highest price to obtain the resources. Thus, resources are put to their most valued use.[4]

The political means, on the other hand, are typically a method of allocation employed when market allocation is thought to be undesirable. Exercise of political means occurs through the power of government.[5] Having been entrusted with a monopoly on coercive power, government can direct resources to politically desired uses and away from market allocations.[6] The government can do this by virtue of its purse power (taxing and spending), police power, and the other powers that give it the ability to enforce redistribution of resources in a way not possible in the competitive marketplace. In this way, the political means can allocate resources according to the most influential participants in the political process and not according to the highest bidder in the marketplace.

The distinction between the economic and the political means can also be understood as a form of discourse related to our earlier discussion of checks and balances. The economic means represent the process of private choice and individual empowerment. The analysis of private choice in law and economics discourse employs the methods of economics and, most frequently, a view of that science known as neoclassical economics. In contrast to the economic means, the political means correspond to the public or state sphere of the checks and balances system. The analysis of the exercise of political means is sometimes referred to, in law and economics discourse, as the study of public choice.[7] The theory of public choice, in this context, is primarily concerned with the relationship between political science and economics and undertakes the study of majority-rule decision making by political bodies.[8] Thus, the economic means concern the private choice system of allocating scarce resources while the political means concern the public choice system of allocating scarce resources.

In classical liberal theory it is important to recognize the distinction between the allocation of scarce social resources by the economic means in contrast to the political means. One also needs to keep in mind that classical liberal theory provides a normative critique of both methods of resource allocation. For instance, although classical liberal theory relies to a great extent on neoclassical economics, it is not concerned with the achievement of efficiency as the ultimate end. Rather, it seeks freedom and individual liberty as the ultimate social end and thus rejects certain forms of social organization, such as slavery, even if they can be shown to be the most efficient methods of organization.[9] Similarly, classical liberal theory finds little comfort in a discourse of public choice theory that predicts the actions of cities like Indianapolis. Economic perspectives on public choice theory inform us, for example, that urban development programs will elevate the discrete and identifiable short-term interests of a few over the broader long-term interests of the many. But though such a theory might help one better understand the problems of invoking the political means, it fails to respond to the classical liberal critique of such a view. That critique, offered in this book, rejects such end-state rationalizations as those provided by the discourse of economic efficiency and public choice theory. Classical liberal theory, although sympathetic to these various forms of legal economic discourse, rejects their end-state objectives and predictions as inappropriate forms of social discourse. Classical liberal theory seeks to promote other, more fundamental end-state norms and values, such as individual liberty, human dignity, and freedom as creative and spontaneous processes of individual social evolution. This means that classical liberal discourse cannot end with the alleged determination of an efficient or predictable outcome. Instead, the classical liberal must engage in an ongoing dialogue of persuasion based on context, experience, and reason.

This book asks us to reconsider the current direction of our social evolution. It asks us to reconsider important classical liberal norms and values and ultimately to readjust our preferences in order that the current drift toward serfdom and the increasing exercise of the political means can abate. In an effort to clarify this position a more detailed discussion of political process and political means will be provided.

Political process in a democracy is a process of coordinating the desires and objectives of special interest groups within the society.[10] The focus of political process becomes the group, institution, or organization while the individual is relegated to a peripheral position. The legislative process rewards legislators who use political means to favor highly motivated special interest groups at the expense of fragmented, diverse and possibly unknown interests.[11] For example, legislated rent controls provide immediate and identifiable benefits to a known constituency. Current tenants have an intense, unifying interest in obtaining favorable rent controls, and once those controls are passed into law the tenants become obvious recipients of any alleged control benefits. The full benefits of a rent control program go to only a small percentage of the population, whereas the costs of such a program are spread out at minimal levels to numerous people.[12] These costs are not only spread around to a much larger group of people than those who receive the benefits, but many of the costs may be hidden to the casual observer. For instance, what legislative impact can potential tenants have when they are deprived of rental housing because landlords find it an undesirable investment under rent control?[13] In the legislative process the future tenants affected by market divestment and a resulting shortage of housing are no match for the well-defined and motivated special interest group.

The rent-controlled housing situation is no different from the effects of special interest legislation protecting a particular industry or labor union. One can consider, for example, protective tariff legislation designed to protect the steel industry by reducing foreign imports.[14] This legislation is said to be necessary to prevent "unfair competition," which is another way of saying it is needed to reduce competition and competitive pressure on American steel companies. In this situation, the steel workers and the steel companies have a strong and somewhat unified interest in protecting their industry, which translates into protecting their jobs and their income. A protective tariff for the steel industry, however, means that United States steel purchasers will have to pay more for the steel they use, and all products using the higher priced steel will cost the consumer more. To the extent that less of the cheaper, foreign steel is imported, the steel importing business will lose jobs.

From the perspective of the legislative process, the special interest group has a strong motive for invoking government intervention, while consumers, who may pay only pennies more for small consumer products using steel, will have little reason to be aroused. In the language of the now familiar Coase Theorem, the consumer, by opposing the special interest legislation, will have transaction costs that far exceed his or her own benefits.[15] In addition, the legislative process cannot even identify workers who would have gotten jobs in an expanding steel importing business. In this manner, the legislative process provides a mechanism for using government power to benefit special interests at the expense of the general welfare.

Unfortunately the twentieth century, especially since the 1920s, has been marked by an ever increasing appeal to political means. An important reason for the increasing dominance of the political means for the allocation of society's scarce resources, in addition to those already suggested, is that the political means represent power personified while the economic means are relatively impersonal and even impossible to control. By this distinction I refer to the impersonal nature of the marketplace that is played out by the price mechanism. The market simply brings many unknown parties together in the exchange of goods and services based on price; corresponding notions of quality and service are reflected in the market price. In this system of exchange the involvement of any particular racial, ethnic, or religious person or group in the production of a product is not important. What is important is the product and the price. Similarly, in an impersonal marketplace with many buyers and many sellers, it is difficult, if not impossible, for any one party to have a significant impact on the market.

In a perfectly competitive market individual sellers must take their price and terms from the market. This means that unless one's product is clearly distinguishable or production costs are much lower than others in the market, one will have to offer his or her goods at the market rate or buyers will go elsewhere. This fact often leads to controversy among observers of the marketplace. Some erroneously argue that when all manufacturers or sellers offer similar prices or similar terms, this is evidence of a conspiracy in restraint of trade. This observation on its own cannot, however, support such a conclusion. Evidence of only a few suppliers and of high market entry costs would be necessary to demonstrate the claim of conspiracy.

In contrast to the impersonal functioning of the marketplace and economic means, the political means are distinctly personal. Exercising the political means involves the cooperative effort of politicians and, in this regard, requires an ability to influence people in a position of power. The notion of influence should not be understood merely as the process of buying votes or contributing to campaign funds, although such methods of influence appear to be a common fact of political life. Influencing the sources of political power can be done in other ways and can include long-time and personal friends of an influential politician. Although the friendly relationship may raise no legal or ethical questions, it is true that a friend's ideas are more likely to reach the politician and to be of some persuasive value. Regardless of the method or motive of such influence, it is clear that the political process works on a personal level.

The distinction between the personal and impersonal nature of each means of resource allocation is of great importance. At a practical level it affects individuals or groups with an intense interest at stake. The marketplace, for example, is so impersonal that even the fabulously rich Hunt brothers of Texas were unable to control their fortunes and were thrown into bankruptcy as a result of billion dollar ventures into the silver and oil markets. On the other hand, the personal nature of the political means can allow influential individuals or groups to get special legislative protection or financial assistance to help their business or cause. Thus, political means are valuable if one already has wealth or position and is seeking to maintain or enlarge upon one's current status. Similarly, political means are important when one organizes a group of people with a strong and narrowly defined special interest. As an organized group one need only persuade a handful of politicians of one's cause to have a chance of winning something that would otherwise never materialize out of a massive and impersonal marketplace.

From the politician's perspective the use of political means is also advantageous, since the ability to deliver or block legislation expands one's power and importance within the system. All politicians benefit in this regard as the political sphere expands, especially if it expands while the private sphere contracts, or at least while the private sphere becomes more heavily regulated and thereby less private.

Finally, the political means are self-perpetuating for those special people and interests that can capture the power of the state for their own benefit. Once special interest legislation is enacted, such as rent control or protective tariffs, a group of bureaucrats, technocrats, consultants, and writers emerge in both the public and the private spheres to deal with the new regulations. This process further develops vested interests for additional untold people who, by virtue of their training, expertise, personal and financial investments, have become linked to the special interests that obtained the original intrusive action of the state. Consequently, the saying that "success breeds success" is especially relevant in the personalized world of political action and the exercise of the political means.

The dynamics of this process are significant for our prospects of freedom versus serfdom. One of the great attributes of the modern capitalist age has been the departure from a world of status to an impersonal world of contract and markets. Capitalism has made a more egalitarian society possible precisely because one's abilities rather than one's status is the key to success in the marketplace. On the other hand, the expanding use of the political means threatens the egalitarian principle of equal opportunity by returning us to an age of title, status, and connection as the means to power or success.

In the dawn of this new age of serfdom, not only do we find incentives for people to invoke political means, we find that those who fail to invoke political means may be hindered in the attainment of their goals. Thus, there becomes a market for state power and a tendency to overgraze in this market. A conspiracy is not needed in order to allege an alignment of special interests that works against the fulfillment of others' aspirations. To the contrary, the market for state power is much like other markets. Individuals and groups see costs and benefits associated with the use of the good and they can independently determine that it is often more profitable to invoke the political means than not. From the viewpoint of a person committed to individual liberty and classical liberal ideals, there is an overgrazing of political means because we have allowed the concept of limited government to be defined by the state itself. This places the power to define state power in the hands of the people entrusted with the exercise of that power and thereby produces an incentive to generate an ever-expanding definition for its legitimate exercise.

Classical liberals and libertarians share a similar apprehension about the expanding role and acceptance of political means, though others on the philosophical and political spectrum seldom share this apprehension concerning the exercise of state power. In part this lower threshold of concern can be explained by realizing that many people, whether conservatives or liberals, share a distinct interest in promoting statism and the exercise of political means. The primary difference in American politics between liberals and conservatives is which special interest groups are likely to be most influential and successful in harnessing state power on their own behalf. Thus, the Reagan administration proved itself little different from the Carter administration in terms of the exercise of state power. Although each administration may have had different special interest groups or constituents to please, neither administration retreated from the pervasive exercise of state power in pursuit of its own political agenda.[16] In contrast to these right or left orientations, classical liberals are concerned with controlling the exercise of state power so that a premium can be put on the exercise of impersonal and individual choice rather than fighting about which special interest groups will be the benefactors of governmental largesse in the next era.

In either case, be it from the left or the right, the general trend seems to be toward a greater exercise of the political means. Understanding the ever-increasing appeal of the political means to people across the political spectrum is essential to understanding the continuing drift of American society toward a new age of serfdom. This drift, it seems, is fueled by the emergence of state power as a "free good" subject to overexploitation that is the result not of a conspiracy, but of traditional economic dynamics. The explanation of this concept is considered next in the context of a new tragedy occurring on a new commons.

Chapter 6
A New Commons—A New Tragedy

In order to understand how American society continues to drift down a statist road toward serfdom, one must first understand the concept of the tragedy of the commons and its resurgence as a new tragedy on a new commons in today's urban environments.[1] To understand the tragedy that is being played out on the "political commons" of representative government, it is best to review the concept from its earlier formulations.

The local commons was visualized as a common pasture or greenspace where residents of the village could bring their cattle for grazing. As conceived in basic economics the commons, limited in size and capacity, could not sustain an infinite number of livestock. Given limited ability to generate edible grasses, the commons could be studied in much the same way that one might study a firm in the economic marketplace. With use by only a few cattle the commons could not be used efficiently and could have an overabundance of grass and weeds. On the other hand, if too many cattle were brought to graze on the commons they would soon devour all of the edible grasses and overgraze the acreage, destroying root systems and leaving patches of space unable to sustain even the smallest amount of livestock. Somewhere in between these two extremes lies an optimal level of grazing that properly maintains the grasses while feeding the most animals. This fanciful quest for equilibrium has employed countless economists throughout the ages but its exact calculation need not concern us here.

The tragedy on this quaint but historic commons of a by-gone era results from an inability to internalize the cost of one's conduct when setting an animal to graze. The commons is an example of a free good and thus, while one's grazing of cattle might impose a cost on the common good in question (the pasture), this cost bears little direct relationship to the total social cost of the activity itself.

Consequently, the owner of the cow has an incentive to graze as many cattle as possible. If we assume unlimited access at no charge to use a hypothetical commons, we can illustrate its resulting tragedy.

Assume that if only five cows graze on the commons each day they will produce fifteen quarts of milk valued at one dollar per quart. The total value of their production would be seventy-five dollars. Assume further that the more cows that graze on the commons the less grass is available for each cow and the more competitive and aggressive the cows must be in order to get their share of the food supply. Milk production for each cow will diminish as more cows are set to graze on the commons. Thus, if ten cows graze each day they will produce ten quarts of milk each and at one dollar per quart the total value of their production is one hundred dollars. If fifteen cows graze each day, they will produce only four quarts of milk each, and at one dollar per quart the total value of their production would be only sixty dollars. On this simple commons the optimal level of grazing would be ten cows each day for a total output of $100 per day. Since the commons is a free good, however, there will be no incentive to limit grazing to ten cows. Individual cow owners will want to graze as many cows as will be profitable to them even if a lesser number might lead to a more profitable *total output* from the pasture. Thus, one could expect overgrazing on the commons; fifteen or more cows might be set to grazing each day as long as each of the several cow owners received a positive cash flow.

The tragedy of the commons has been played out many times. The problems of air pollution and water pollution have, in part, been linked to their nature as a free good.[2] Water and air have been treated as a "commons" where polluters could freely discharge wastes with no established mechanism for internalizing the social cost of such activities, thus leading to overgrazing. Similarly, studies of traffic congestion reveal that if a limited number of cars are on an urban highway at any given time, more cars can travel the distance in a given period than if unlimited access leads to bumper to bumper traffic that backs up and results in many cars moving slowly and fewer cars passing over the measured distance.[3] The Kennedy Expressway in Chicago is an example of a highway that uses computers to monitor traffic flow, and by use of lights on entrance ramps seeks to limit access resulting in more cars traveling through within a given period.

The above situations are all examples of the tragedy of the commons. They are examples of individuals who have no incentive not to overuse the free good—if they do not use it someone else will—and this attitude results in overgrazing that is not only inefficient but can lead to the ultimate depletion or destruction of the resource in question such as clean air or clean water.

Allocating private property rights in the free good is one way to avoid the tragedy of the commons. By assigning property rights to the pasture area or to water in a stream, a market in those rights will emerge and they will ultimately be bought, sold, traded, and priced in a manner similar to any other goods in the marketplace.[4] One could as easily buy the right to discharge X units of pollution as one could graze X cattle each day or buy one quart of milk at the grocery store for one dollar. The problem for some people is that they feel that some resources are not like other goods in the marketplace; clean air or water should not be packaged and sold like toothpaste or beer. For them the way to internalize costs to the consumer or prevent overgrazing is by government regulation.

When looking at governmental regulation in the area of real estate development and finance, one can see the emergence of a new commons and consequently a new tragedy not unlike the examples discussed above. But this can only be appreciated by realizing that government has now become a major commodity sought after by many consumers. As such, government or, more appropriately, the powers available to the government acting as the state, have become goods subject to overgrazing. When one is politically connected, the power of the state allows the political means to be exercised in a way that frees one from the rigors, competition, and discipline of the marketplace. Government becomes a free good like the water or the air in the sense that the special interest groups that successfully capture the power of the state are not responsible for the true social cost of their activities. They see only the cost of *their* exploitation of the resource and do not have the social costs of such conduct internalized. Consequently, there is overgrazing of the political process and of the power of the state.

When a group or organization is able to direct the power of the state on its behalf, it not only gets results not attainable in the marketplace, but also gets institutional legitimacy by working with government. In the sense that government opens itself up like a public commons to address infinite social, political, economic, and environmental issues, it can be no surprise that groups and organizations with special interests will press their agendas on the commons of government until the commons becomes completely inundated and depleted of its original vitality, vision, and legitimacy. The internal dynamics of government seem to invite overgrazing. Maybe this is because politicians are also consumers of state power; *their* prestige, power, ideas, and place in history are furthered not hindered by the expansion of state power and by the tendencies toward overgrazing and statism. Eventually, the depletion and continued pollution of principled and restrained government, however, results in the demise of any moral claims upon which that government originally rested. This in turn may lead government to shore up its weakened moral authority by appeal to the gamesmanship of a more direct and coercive demonstration of its will.[5] The ultimate tragedy on this commons is the loss of an environment conducive to the social evolution of individual liberty and human dignity.

In Part II, the tragedy of the political commons will be explored further by an examination of urban development. The increasing appeal to and the use of political means will be in evidence, and challenge us to rethink the current direction of American society. Part II also offers an innovative critique of "the-business-as-usual" approach of urban planners and lawyers. While multiple interpretations might be placed on some data, the observations made in Part II will illustrate the way in which modern urban development embraces an ideological shift in values and norms that can be uncovered by a careful critique of emerging trends in new forms of legal, economic, and political relationships.

Chapter 7
Classical Liberals and Individual Liberty

It is appropriate at this point to expand upon the concept of statism and the classical liberal concern for individual liberty and human dignity by defining them and putting the classical liberal vision into perspective with other lines of legal and economic thought.

Statist ideology involves a philosophy that is dominated by a preoccupation with the state or public side of a free society. Much scholarship is dedicated to discussions of checks and balances limited to the internal restraints on the state. Lawyers often preoccupy themselves with the struggles for power between the three co-equal branches of government and the subservient divisions of federal versus state and state versus local government. But to maintain this focus to the substantial exclusion of private property as the major external check on the state is to be constrained by a vision devoid of the importance of limited government and of the very real benefits of competitive forces at work.

Unlike proponents of other schools of thought, classical liberals and libertarians are concerned with the grander conception of competitive tensions between the individual and the state. Scholarship in this area sometimes focuses on descriptive legal arguments about what the United States Constitution provides, such as debates about original intentions versus a living constitution.[1] At other times such scholarship can take a more normative tone, such as focusing on the nature of the requirements for a free society rather than limiting discussion to the structures of the constitution, whatever they might be.

For classical liberals the beauty and necessity of a competitive social framework is the potential it provides for spontaneous social order, creativity, and the enhancement of individual liberty. Capitalism and the operation of a free market are not necessarily ends in themselves, but are seen as necessary prerequisites to freedom. In this sense, the classical liberal position is in accord with the observations of Milton Friedman that capitalism is a necessary, although not sufficient, requirement for freedom.[2] But, more specifically, what do we mean by the grandiose words of freedom, individual liberty, and human dignity?

Individual liberty and freedom are delicate concepts whose meaning requires a discussion of human dignity. Together these constructs provide ideological structure to the classical liberal discourse of law and economics and have a substantive impact on the evolution of social values. The starting point for understanding is the presumption that, by virtue of being human, one is entitled to certain fundamental rights—rights not in a technical sense, but in the sense that the essence of being human is somehow tied to a certain level of dignity, respect, and reverence from others who make up the community in which we live and interact.[3] Some people disdain the idea of natural, fundamental, or inalienable rights because they believe that such conceptions stem from theological underpinnings that must obviously be rejected by educated members of the scientific age. This need not be the case, however. Although it is true that some people find theological support for the sacredness of human rights and dignity, it is unnecessary to require such a foundation for the egalitarian principle that individuals are not doormats and that there is a personal autonomy beyond which no outsider or state should be allowed to penetrate coercively.[4] Individual life, if it has any purpose, has a purpose of being; to achieve that which is possible by the individual unimpeded by the coercive influence of others. Of course, individual liberty cannot be limitless, because it must embody the notion that we live in community with others and must accommodate the rights of others. Thus, certain restrictions on personal autonomy, such as prohibition on murder and rape, can be justified and, in fact, may be required in order to protect the social harmony necessary for the continued viability of civilization as we know it.[5]

Such a discourse also embraces natural and inalienable rights as structural guideposts for asserting an ideological presumption in favor of limited state power. It is a form of conversation that posits the existence of certain human rights as predating the state or being superior to the claims of others acting through the power of the state. Natural and inalienable rights need not be thought of as a list of eternal and absolute rights, but as fundamental referential roadblocks to particular forms of legal economic conversation. In this way the structure and content of legal economic dialogue is affected and such natural and inalienable rights become part of our subjective cultural experience which Adam Smith identified as forming a foundation for individual and social morality.

Individual liberty, in this context, should not be viewed in the narrow tradition of some radical libertarian philosophers. It should not be defined by going back to a hypothetical state of nature and simply protecting the product of successful individuals under a regime of inviolate property rights. On the contrary, individual liberty requires an ongoing debate concerning the fundamental nature of being human in our society. This is a difficult issue, but debate should, nonetheless, focus on it. All too often we find lawyers and others debating such crucial issues as abortion and the right to death with dignity in the removed and detached language of privacy and constitutional law that, while interesting, is a distraction from the gut-wrenching moral and philosophical issue of what it means to be human.[6] To direct the legal, economic, and political dialogue to this question is essential, regardless of the ultimate position one may take on a subject. The classical liberal attempt to persuade by reference to context, experience, and reason requires a continuing legal economic dialogue on competing values.

In a conception of free society as fundamentally being tied to an environment of creative competition, the meaning of individual liberty must include the ability for meaningful participation in the marketplace. This participation is two-pronged. First, one must have a viable basis for participation in the public sphere—democratic institutions and the right to equality of vote. Second, in the private sphere, one must have a viable and equal opportunity for participation in the free marketplace with at least minimal assurance that continued viability will be maintained even for those people down on their luck. It is just as important to assure women and minorities of a right to vote as it is to assure that certain racial, ethnic, or gender groups are not systematically excluded from participation in the economic, educational, and social areas of the private sphere.

When searching for the definition of individual liberty it is important to reject the libertarian's state of nature justification of our original and current distribution of political power and scarce resources. It seems inappropriate to justify a current social order by asking what things were like in an original state of nature, especially when history reveals relationships based on exploitation and dominance. In the private sphere this means that we cannot find guidance on such issues as minority or women's rights by looking at or accepting the institutional frameworks of the past, since such frameworks are from the start biased against women and minorities. In the public sphere history seems replete with examples of the suppression of freedom and the use of state power to aid and benefit special interest groups that have effectively harnessed the power of the state. Although in feudal times the lords used the power of the state to exploit the peasantry, and in mercantilist times merchants used the power of the state to exalt their interests over those of others, now in the capitalist age, the rich have repeatedly tried to use the power of the state to retain their advantage over those of lesser means and over other members of the community.[7]

As Adam Smith revealed centuries earlier, individual liberty has both relative and nonrelative dimensions. In its nonrelative aspects it embodies fair treatment, equality, and process, which is to say that all individuals deserve the same respect for their person. In its relative aspects individual liberty must be viewed in the context of the society under discussion. Although concepts of life and human dignity in a primitive tribe may make living without permanent shelter or many clothes acceptable, the contrary should hold true in an advanced and materially rich society such as that of the United States. Thus, the measure of well-being and the guide to actual participation in the society is measured by the degree to which the wealth and prosperity of the society improves the experience of its most humble members. If government is not instituted for the purposes of fending off private coercion and protecting individual fulfillment and aspiration, why should we accept a government? Government will never be legitimate and will never complement the conceptual harmony needed to enhance and inspire the human experience if it is the instrument of oppression by the few against the many and vice versa. A government that does not meet these objectives should be corrected or replaced.

The classical liberal, inspired by the work of Adam Smith, seeks first and foremost to keep the idea of natural rights, freedom, individual liberty, and human dignity as part of a legal and economic dialogue. These concepts may be hard to define, difficult to describe, and incredibly complex to integrate and recognize in our present discourse on law, economics, and the state, but ideologically, their presence or absence provides valuable insight into community culture. The deletion of those terms from the vocabulary of social discourse is significant because the validated discourse of society reveals important aspects about the values and norms of that community. In Part II, I will attempt to uncover the ideological implications of the legal means by which urban development currently proceeds. Ultimately, this critique will reveal a transition in community values and call into question the soundness of current government policy.

Chapter 8
Government Regulation by General Rules

In respecting individual liberty and protecting individuals, we must be prepared to restrict some personal actions in order to protect the liberty of others and promote social harmony.[1] Individual liberty in the classical liberal sense is *not* equivalent to unfettered *laissez faire*. Rather, the protection of individual liberty can be accomplished in the midst of varied and extensive government regulation though such regulation requires general, rather than special, rules or legislation.[2]

The classical liberal conception of the goals of government can only be understood against a backdrop of social organization governed by general legal rules and principles. There are probably few activities that government could not engage in if people desired it, and if such activity served a significant public purpose, especially when it could not be achieved by private means.[3]

General rules are important to a classical liberal conception of the rule of law. General rules or regulations governing economic activity, for instance, would be acceptable because they subject all participants to the same constraints. And, assuming no restrictions on price in a competitive market, the consumers of regulated commercial activities receive valuable information about the cost of these activities relative to other alternatives. This information function, which occurs through the operation of the marketplace, is important for freedom.[4] The marketplace allows numerous individuals to coordinate their societal goals without the need for central planning. General rules facilitate this process and the use of scarce human and economic resources by providing non-outcome-specific guidelines for individuals to consider when they decide to buy, sell, enter, or exit the marketplace.

General rules promote an impersonal process of counterbalancing power sources that allow for a continuous evolution of creative activity while permitting individuals a preeminent role in the structuring of their daily activities. Economic efficiency is not the determining criterion or the measure of the proper relationship between law and economics. Rather the power of economics, as a creative process for social organization, becomes paramount for achieving individually directed outcomes (individual liberty). Such process-oriented outcomes, it would seem, can be completely independent of any concern for calculatable economic efficiency.

In a democratic society, general rules can be understood as those underlying principles that a majority would agree on.[5] True agreement among a majority will rarely extend beyond some set of general principles that can be maintained only to the extent that they are known to most of its members.[6] The legislative process that brings forth new law as the result of special interest legislation does not necessarily meet the test of generality, for instance. Only to the extent that a majority believes in the general principle does legislation meet this test. Legislation passed as the result of combining special interest proposals does not meet the test of generality if the combined special interests make up the majority while the legislation itself represents no majority. It is through this requirement of generality that a classical liberal conceives a restraint on the ability of the people to change the rules in favor of their own interest. Similarly, the restraint on the ability to change the rules for the benefit of a particular person or group protects individual liberty and spontaneous social order from encroachment by the coercive power of others or the state.

It is useful at this point to consider one brief example of the difference between approaches governed by the concept of general rules and those governed by specific outcome-oriented rules. A city seeking to revitalize its downtown area may be used as an example.[7] A number of actions could be taken by a local government for urban revitalization that would be consistent with classical liberal views on the rule of law. For instance, the city could spend public resources to upgrade educational and job training facilities, streets, utilities, and police protection. Or the city could conduct studies, promote itself, and revise zoning codes and other regulations to create a better business climate attractive to entrepreneurs willing and able to make the best use of the resources of the city. Through these efforts the city would be able to upgrade its economic environment. The improvement in its business climate would hopefully cause individuals to react positively by entering and choosing to remain in the newly enhanced urban marketplace. The ultimate decision to buy, sell, enter, or exit the marketplace, however, would still be left to individuals. Governmental power is thus used to improve the economic environment for everyone rather than to benefit unfairly a few special interest groups.

The approach using specific rules is quite different from the general rules approach. The specific rules approach to urban revitalization would encompass such practices as predetermined site-specific zoning, tax incentives, and subsidies for specific projects and developers. Examples of these activities include the so-called cofinancing projects recently undertaken by many cities. With cofinancing, city departments for economic development select specific projects, such as downtown malls or hotels, for specific locations. Public subsidies are then used to encourage the completion of the projects. Consequently, subsidies are given out and projects are constructed, not in accordance with general principles, but at the direction of government officials acting in response to special interests. As a result, power is shifted to those politically connected with outcome-specific decision makers. The coercive power of the state becomes available to those pursuing a special interest rather than a general one. Such a result is contrary to classical liberal conceptions of spontaneous social order and natural liberty. While the issue of urban revitalization will be more fully explained later, its brief mention here helps in understanding the significance of general rules in the classical liberal theory of the rule of law and the role of government.

The key to understanding classical liberalism is, therefore, to view it not as a philosophy of unfettered *laissez faire* but as a philosophy that seeks to delineate the boundaries within which government should act. The classical liberal approach to law and economics seeks to establish a process for creative discovery by structuring an urban development environment compatible with the metaphorical and symbolic functions of economics; that is, to foster a legal and political environment of spontaneous and creative evolution related to economic analysis as a metaphorical and symbolic form of discourse rather than as a mathematical science. From this perspective the classical liberal argues not that government should be prevented from acting, but rather that government should act within certain guidelines for conduct. There is probably little the government could not be involved in if it acted within general guidelines. The weakening of the private sphere by the excessive reduction in capitalism or private capital, however, destroys the delicate balance needed to assure a power base significant enough to counterbalance the power of the state. Thus, the metaphorical and symbolic function of economic discourse and the market process is weakened and as a result individual liberty is diminished.

Restricting government action to general rules not only provides a more fair and just format for the treatment of individuals but also serves to protect better the power base of the private sphere. General rules are more consistent with the dynamic process of the marketplace. Consequently, rules that establish safety standards or that require disclosure of standardized information along with price can be effective as long as individuals are allowed to exit or enter the market freely and as long as the market is able to set the price for the good or service in question. General rules are rules that establish or structure a particular market, such as the stock market, and are, in a sense, similar to the general rules of play that guide and inform conduct in a board game such as *Monopoly*. General rules are struck at the outset, and they apply equally to all participants who seek to enter or exit from market activity. General rules do not preselect winners or losers, as do specific outcome-oriented rules, but they do regulate the terms which might limit or constrain individuals and groups within the boundaries of socially acceptable conduct. This conception of government regulation is consistent with the classical liberal theory of law and economics.

In contrast to government regulation by general rules, specific outcome-oriented legislation can be devastating to the marketplace of urban life. The problem in the rental housing markets serves as an example.[8] Rent control is theoretically a means of assuring that housing is made available to people of limited incomes. An analysis of the effects of legislated rent controls reveals, however, a different result.[9] The rental housing market is a relatively competitive market with most landlords owning only a few rental units. For the owners of rental housing, ownership represents just one possible investment among numerous alternatives, such as stocks, bonds, money market funds, computers. The level of investment in rental housing and, thus, the supply of rental housing stock will be affected by the owner's rate of return on the investment. Rent control reduces not only the owner's rate of return, but limits the owner's ability to make quick cash flow adjustments in response to changes in market prices of input items such as fuel, repairs, and maintenance. Rent restrictions, therefore, provide an incentive to invest money in alternative activities and to convert rental housing units to condominiums and cooperatives that can be sold to higher income buyers. Because individuals respond to market changes such as rent controls, market reaction to such legislation is predictable. Sometimes, if the reaction involves decreasing investment in the production of rental housing stock, additional legislation may follow. Furthermore, if the legislature believes that market exit is undesirable, it might restrict conversions and divestment from rental housing, while simultaneously dictating guidelines for habitability, forcing reluctant landlords to keep up their property, even if rent controls have reduced the profits available to finance such activities.[10]

As a consequence of the perverse combination of laws designed to provide adequate housing for the poor, disincentives for investment can actually create or aggravate a shortfall of appropriate rental housing and may even contribute to the plight of the homeless.[11] Thus, the attempt to legislate more affordable rental housing may lead to more and more legislation as individuals respond to the original restrictions. Landlords retreat from rental housing to other housing markets first and then the restrictions on market exit accelerate their desire to avoid housing markets altogether.

Much of outcome-specific rule making can be attributed to the dynamics of special interest politics. The highly motivated people who seek protective legislation find little resistance to programs that assume private parties, such as landlords, are earning too much money. At little or no cost to the taxpayer, the state can force these private parties to provide the housing others want at the price they are willing to pay. Of course, many assumptions about private parties' ability to make so much money are unfounded. But in a society in which most people will have little reason to oppose pro-rent control forces or other special interests, it is certain that people will remain unmotivated as long as they feel someone else will be forced to pay for the program. We know, however, that this is a delusion because our thoroughly integrated economy means we all eventually end up paying for misguided policies, by way of inflation, unemployment, increased taxes, or the financial consequences of a large national deficit.

Consider again the example of rent control. State and local decision making in the rental housing market has nonlocal impacts. For example, the decision by New York City voters and legislators to protect current tenants from "unfair" rents, to the extent this creates a disincentive for investment and reduces the supply of rental housing, means that tenants who might otherwise live in New York City live in New Jersey, Connecticut, or elsewhere in New York State. This not only affects where people live but also affects the need for additional highway facilities, and it adds to traffic noise and air pollution in communities and states. Thus, the local decision to regulate rents has an effect on surrounding communities and states. To the extent that such effects lead to demands for federal revenue for interstate highways, mass transit, and other projects, there is revenue sharing by taxpayers nationwide.

The availability of federal revenue-sharing programs, urban and state grant programs, and tax incentives allows local communities to benefit their own residents at the expense of people from distant communities and states.[12] State and local governments know that the federal government will distribute funds to alleviate their "rental housing crisis," rejuvenate their dilapidated rental housing, or create tax incentives to offset local disincentives to investment in residential rental property. New York City, for example, can impose rent controls and otherwise establish disincentives for investment in rental housing, while offsetting many of the consequences of this action through federal intervention.

The federal government basically has two ways to generate the funds needed to assist state and local governments with housing problems.[13] It can raise revenue through taxes or it can add to the money supply by increasing the national deficit. Using the tax-based funding method, revenues raised from the national populace can be redirected to benefit the rental housing needs of any given local market, such as New York City. All taxpayers pay for tax incentives provided to investors in rental housing because the tax incentives require that public revenues come from taxing other taxpayer activities and investments.[14] In this way the tax laws are used to benefit investment in certain types of real estate. At the same time, the need for government revenue requires other taxpayers to make up for any resulting exemption from real estate tax revenue. Under revenue-sharing concepts, the federal government can, also, shift the receipts from one state to benefit another state, thereby making one state subsidize the rental housing policy of another. Ultimately, when federal funds are generated by increasing the federal deficit, all Americans pay for the negative effect on the value of the dollar and the national economy.

It is clear that state and local decisions concerning rental housing are significant for the whole nation. Under the current system of federal intervention, people from states without restrictive rental-housing regulations and rent control, such as Texas, are being asked to subsidize restrictive anti-investment policies in other communities and states. In many cases the policies they are indirectly subsidizing may be policies their own legislators directly considered and rejected. The local rental-housing regulation of New York City is made possible through a system of federal tax and revenue-sharing programs that can be used to offset the local disincentives for investment in rental housing. As long as such a relationship exists between the federal government and state and local governments, the residents of one state will continue to subsidize the economic policies of their sister states, and their sister states will have little incentive to change their rent control policies.

There are at least two levels of evaluation that emerge with respect to local rent control policies. First, rent control provides a major disincentive to local construction of new rental housing. Yet, if local governments consider this impact and the government wishes to enact rent control for a greater social purpose despite its negative effects, then this may rightfully be an issue of state and local concern under our federal system. On the other hand, this apparent state or local concern becomes a national concern in the second level of evaluation because state and local governments are using federal funds to offset some of the negative effects of their local policies. If they are not getting a free lunch, local governments are getting at least a substantially discounted lunch because local tenants have artificially low rents and local governments get federal subsidies to offset the negative effects of such a policy. The cost of the program is spread over a much larger population than receives the benefits. The negative effect of deficits or tax burdens have only a small impact on the tenant of a rent controlled apartment in New York City, although the tenant gets the full benefit of the program.

It would seem fair to conclude that if certain communities really believe in rent control, then they ought to be willing to bear the full cost of such a policy. At the very least, decision makers and the electorate should have full cost and benefit information available in order to evaluate and to justify such a social program. It is difficult, if not impossible, to make appropriate decisions when much of the information, such as the true cost of rent control disincentives, is buried under numerous cross-subsidies and formulations made possible by the magic of the federal purse strings. Even if nothing changes in the current practices of rent control legislation, residents of communities and states without rent controls should at least be made aware of the fact that they subsidize such policies elsewhere.

As the above analysis indicates rent control is a good example of the problem of outcome-specific legislation. Rather than create general market incentives that would favor a greater supply of housing or give direct voucher subsidies to those in need of housing assistance, the legislative process responds with piecemeal and outcome-specific attempts to favor specific and highly organized special interest groups. Such an approach is divisive and generally ineffective, as well as detrimental to the protection of individual liberty. It is, however, the exact type of behavior that would be expected in a situation in which state power becomes a free good subject to over-exploitation by those with access to its resources.

As I have tried to illustrate in this chapter, there is an important difference between a general rules approach and an outcome-specific rules approach to law and economics. The fundamental distinction between them may be understood as one of attitude, of outlook, or of presumption. The necessity for a discourse of general rules is important to classical liberal theory, however, because the form of social discourse, like the form of metaphorical social markets, is important; important because of the values and implicit ideological norms at work and promoted by the particular process in question.[15]

Chapter 9
Comparative Ideology

When the relationship between law and economics is considered in its broadest sense, it encompasses a variety of competing approaches. I have recently completed a book on comparative approaches to law and economics, and I will not repeat that discussion here.[1] It is important, however, that a comparative analysis be presented in order that the values and norms generated by alternative approaches to urban development can be appreciated.

The comparative approach to law and economics starts with the understanding that law is a derivative field of study; one's view of law and of legal institutions derives from one's view of economic relationships. This means that a person who has a marxist view of economic, political, and social organization will have a decidedly different view of law and legal institutions from a person who believes in free market capitalism. This understanding of law and economics incorporates, in a general way, Ludwig von Mises's view that all human action is economics.[2]

All human action involves the process of choice between competing alternative courses of action. Should I buy brand X soup or brand Y? Should I get a drink of water now or later? Should I eat pork or pasta? Should I continue to read this paragraph or should I glance away and scratch my forehead? When economics is understood as a form of discourse that addresses the basic questions of scarce resource allocation and the process by which choices concerning social organization are made, then one comprehends the endless variation of alternative ideologies. There are conservative, libertarian, liberal, marxist, and classical liberal economic perspectives, to name a few. Most critics of the combined efforts in law and economics have failed to appreciate this simple and fundamental point and have generally misunderstood the discipline as a purely conservative undertaking.

Chapters 1, 3, and 7 of this book articulated the basic values and norms promoted by the classical liberal construction of legal economic discourse. Applying this construct to law and legal institutions leads to a particular view of individual liberty, freedom, and human dignity. Having discussed those concepts, it is now important to contrast classical liberal values and norms with those generated by alternative conceptions of economic relationships.

This chapter further explores alternative visions of law and economics that consequently involve alternative conceptions of liberty. By shifting the conceptual and ideological framework of legal economic discourse from the classical liberal's reliance on the individual as the fundamental referential sign to a framework of communitarian or state values, different understandings of liberty are generated.

Communitarian (altruistic) and state-centered views of law and economics generally lead to conceptual frameworks of liberty that focus on the importance of groups, experts, and planners at the expense of the individual decision makers in the marketplace. They envision a different conception of the individual, the market, and empowerment, and they lead to what I identify as a conceptual "liberty of the community" or "liberty of the state."

These ideological distinctions are important because discourse on any particular construct in law and economics is governed by similar terms of dialogue. Yet these seemingly similar terms have dramatically different meanings. These differences are the result of a shifting framework for analyzing social problems. Each framework is supported by its own set of first principle assumptions concerning the nature of economic and political power. Because the social validation of any particular form of legal economic discourse has important consequences for the development of law and legal institutions, including approaches to urban development, it is important to have a basic understanding of the different values and norms generated by ideological and conceptual frameworks at variance with classical liberal theory.

Liberty for the community is a form of freedom or a perspective that considers the rights, benefits, and existence of the community as more fundamental than the individual. It is altruistic and communitarian in the sense that it asks the individual to be subordinate to the greater will and needs of the community. It emphasizes sharing, common goals, and mutual objectives rather than individualism or adversarial market competition. It does not see the greater benefit of the community as flowing inherently and naturally from the superior position of the individual and is, therefore, contrary to classical liberal philosophy. This perspective or notion of liberty can be identified with liberal, left, and marxist based ideologies.

These ideologies tend to visualize the world in terms of membership in groups or in terms of classes. Thus, they talk of women's rights and workers' problems rather than individual's rights or problems. The distinction is one of emphasis; the classical liberal recognizes that we do not live completely isolated lives but are social animals. Although we are individuals, we must live together with others.[3] Nonetheless, the classical liberal perspective is one that focuses on the individual at a primary level. The story of the world around us is the story of individuals with their own subjective viewpoints and experiences, although individuals may have similar opinions about certain issues. Consequently, the classical liberal can find more common ground between a poor underprivileged White child and a similarly situated African American child than he can find between people of the same race but different socioeconomic backgrounds. Still, the underprivileged White child cannot know what it means to be African American in the United States. Nor can the underprivileged African American child fully understand what it means to be "poor White trash" in a society that makes no excuses for White poverty.

In contrast to the classical liberal's individualist perspective, the concept of liberty for the community gives primacy to the group or class considered most relevant by the people leading the discussion.[4] This ideological shift away from the individual as the key referential sign facilitates the political deconstruction of traditional neoclassical economics because it challenges the very assumption that law should validate market choices, which are nothing more than the accumulated preferences of individuals. The community perspective seeks to validate collective values. It presumes that people are socially constructed by their community and that classical liberal theory is dehumanizing because of its focus on isolated and atomistic individualism. Ironically, however, the community, group, or class focus dehumanizes and alienates the individual by replacing differentiation with generalities that remind one of the problems of mass production. Once the communitarians depart from the individualist framework, they engage in a discourse of groups and, although the definition and identification of a group can change, it must always be more akin to mass production than to individual craftsmanship. The individual is, therefore, dehumanized and alienated to the extent that he or she is unwilling or unable to identify with the goals, plans, and ideas of others. Thus, the individual loses personal identity and is forced to find meaning and expression through people, groups, and institutions that exist separately and apart from him or herself.

The third and other conception of liberty that I refer to can be identified as liberty of the state. This conception of liberty views the individual as defined by the state and seeks to liberate and glorify the individual by enhancing and advancing the interests of the state.[5] The ideology of fascist Italy is the strongest example of this viewpoint, but it exists in lesser degrees in the philosophies of many right wing and conservative movements. Basically, this view requires the individual and the community, where the community is separable from the apparatus of the state, to subordinate their interests to the interests, identified by the state leaders, of the state.

For the fascist it was the state that defined a people, and it was the state that needed to survive in glory through history while individuals could come and go, live and die. To be Italian in pre–World War II Italy, the very definition of the Italian culture, for example, was inevitably linked to the state in fascist ideology.[6] Similarly, many conservative ideological perspectives of the present still use various versions of the nationalistic and patriotic undertones of the fascist philosophy. This is not to say that all conservative ideologies are fascist but to indicate that rightist ideology embraces aspects of the philosophy that was once so strongly crystalized in fascism.

In this world view the state must be given liberty to act against violators of its domestic law and to pursue its goals in the international arena. By shifting to this framework, the individual is again displaced as the key referential sign. A focus on state liberty allows one to reconstruct legal economic discourse in a way that validates authoritarian and dictatorial control over individuals and groups within the state. Consequently, conservatives often complain of media leaks and intermeddling by private citizens and groups who get in the way of U.S. foreign policy, even when such activities seem consistent with constitutionally protected liberties. In a similar way this perspective validates the activities of such people as Lt. Col. Oliver North. Such people act for the state and they are heroes even if their conduct violates the law. This philosophical perspective also requires the state to be strong internally, to have the power to exercise police power in an effective manner against those who might disrupt the internalized vision of state harmony. Conservatives who complain about the all too numerous restrictions on the right of police to search people and to use deadly force often appeal to such a vision. These same people tend to advocate the death penalty as an effective deterrent against crime as well. They argue that the death penalty can have a generally beneficial effect in assisting the state's police mission, while the question of the individual rights of the accused and the moral authority of the state to put someone to death is of secondary importance. As

Friedrich Hayek has noted, the problem of conservative ideology is that

[o]rder appears to the conservatives as the result of the continuous attention of authority, which for this purpose, must be allowed to do what is required by the particular circumstances and not be tied to rigid rule. A commitment to principles presupposes an understanding of the general forces by which the efforts of society are co-ordinated, but it is such a theory of society and especially of the economic mechanism that conservatism conspicuously lacks.[7]

Both the conception of liberty of the community and the conception of liberty for the state are statist in orientation because they seek to enhance the power of the state over that of the individual. While different methods may be involved in reaching their objectives, both approaches seek to use the apparatus of the state against the individual. Each conception of liberty also seeks to enhance and legitimize its power through transference, whereby individuals are led to believe that glorification of the group or the state brings glorification to the individual.[8] The Olympic Games serve as an example. When the U.S. hockey team won the gold medal at Lake Placid, it was a glorious moment not just for the team players but also for all Americans. Individuals could find glory, not in their own moral triumphs, but in the triumphs of the team and the state. Many college athletic programs accomplish the same thing. The residents of Indiana, for instance, are led to believe that all residents are glorified when the Indiana University basketball team, which bears the state name, is successful in out-of-state competition.[9] Many loyal Hoosier fans feel this, even if they never attended college. It is a feeling tied to state identification that is evident in the extensive and emotional coverage of the team by the media in the state's capital city. The coverage far exceeds the quantity and emotion afforded to the other two major universities in the state, Notre Dame and Purdue (Purdue being the other major state-supported university in Indiana). The ability to find individual identity through association with the state is an important part of the concept of state liberty, and the politicians who can successfully transfer that ability can do wonders for the promotion of the state and various statist ideologies.

Now that these three independent conceptions of liberty have been identified as part of varying ideologies, it is important to explore these ideologies within the context of current legal scholarship. For our purposes we will consider conservative, liberal, neomarxist, and libertarian perspectives and then comment on their relationship to classical liberal perspectives.

Conservative Theory

Conservative theory in the relationship between law and economics is similar to conservatism in other areas of political and philosophical discourse. The conservatives, led by Judge Richard Posner, offer a view of law and society centered around the status quo and around the maintenance of the free market system as a desirable *end* in itself.[10] Purporting to offer a neutral and objective basis for legal analysis, the conservatives reduce rights to numerical calculations and then proceed to balance countervailing claims by means of scientific equations. They argue that an efficient result will maximize wealth, and that wealth maximization produces the best attainable social arrangements. There are no inherent individual rights; rather, any result that is dictated by the pretentions of scientific calculation is used to justify the treatment of individual rights.[11] Thus, if one is down on one's luck, without a job, or without financial resources, one has no claim to any of society's resources unless those are provided out of charity.[12]

The conservative perspective plays into the age of science in that it purports to decide issues rationally and objectively without considerations of morality or of social norms that may run counter to its pseudo-scientific methods.[13] The statist tendencies of the conservative approach are furthered by an indeterminate and almost dogmatic reliance upon the outcomes they generate from the application of neoclassical economic methods to pressing social problems.[14] It is not the neoclassical model itself, but the indeterminate and almost dogmatic manner in which Posnerian conservatives employ the model as an end in itself, which causes problems for people concerned with individual liberty.[15] But to understand the problem of the conservative's use of the neoclassical model, one must first understand the assumptions upon which it is constructed. The assumptions of the model are sometimes attacked as unrealistic but are defended for their predictive qualities in assessing human behavior. For example, the model may not appear to have realistic assumptions, but if one uses it to analyze the impact on gasoline purchases as a result of a tenfold increase in the price of gas, it will accurately predict that people will make efforts to consume less gas than they otherwise would. The real attack on the neoclassical model, as used by Posner, centers on the question of the values incorporated into it, apart from any discussion of its realistic or predictive qualities.

To understand the value structure of the neoclassical model, it is necessary briefly to outline some of its major assumptions. First, it is assumed that people act in their own self-interest. Second, in the pursuit of their interests, people act rationally. It is this rationality assumption that allows the model to be predictive. Third, people have access to perfect (reasonably good) information. This assumption means that people have the knowledge necessary to act rationally in their own interests. Fourth, people and resources are assumed to be freely movable; therefore, people and resources will follow the uses deemed most valuable by the marketplace. Fifth, there are no artificial restrictions to entry into the market. The marketplace remains competitive because buyers and sellers are free to move in and out. Sixth, and finally, the current distribution of wealth and resources is taken as a given. Acceptance of the current distribution of income is an important assumption in the neoclassical model because the allocation of resources and rights derived from the model is determined by people casting wealth-based economic votes. In other words, to the extent that people cast their votes in the marketplace by spending dollars, the initial allocation of dollars will affect the outcome of the voting.

Each of the above stated assumptions incorporates certain values. These values need to be stated explicitly. First, although people are able to make rational decisions in their self-interest, it becomes a value to say that they should do so. This value reflects a determination that individuals rather than central planners should make the vast majority of life's daily decisions about the use of valuable scarce human and natural resources. It also presumes that these choices are in the aggregate the best choices for the society. Second, the notion that people have access to perfect or reasonably good information upon which to act rationally implies there is no economic or educational bias in the ability to process the information. The value expressed here accepts the current distribution of educational and economic resources that leads to disparate results in the processing of information by otherwise equally possessed human beings. Third, the ability to move freely implies a value judgment against the hardship claims of those who fail to uproot their families and relocate. It is a value judgment that dehumanizes the experience of relocating and treats people as inanimate objects. Fourth, free exit and entry into the market are presumed essential to competition, while the results of competition are presumed to be desirable. This means that the model values adversarial relationships. Fifth, and finally, acceptance of the current allocation of wealth and resources reflects a value judgment in favor of the process by which that allocation came about. It also reflects a value judgment that the current allocation is fair and equitable, or at least that there is no fair or equitable means of substantially improving or changing the current situation.

This brief description of the assumptions and values of the neo-classical model reveals important characteristics of the conservative theory of wealth maximization. Based on the assumptions and inherent values of the neoclassical model, the conservative approach to law and economics cannot be a neutral and objective method of inquiry. It promotes the validation of laws and legal institutions which favor people already in possession of a disproportionate share of society's political and financial power. Through the use of the wealth maximization concept, conservative ideology seeks to construct a legal economic dialogue which is closed to many individuals, and it fails to recognize that such a discourse is highly value driven. In contrast to classical liberal theory, which operates in conjunction with express value preferences for individual liberty, human dignity, and moral sentiments, the conservative theory of wealth maximization uses the claim to neutrality and objectivity as a sleight-of-hand to conceal and deflect criticism from its underlying value structure.

Although conservative ideology is free to embrace its own theory of law and economics, it should be faulted for not clearly identifying the underlying values and consequently the underlying bias that is a part of its perspective, which dresses up ideology in the academic regalia of neutral and objective scientific inquiry.[16]

A simple example will illustrate how conservatives can use Posner's theory of wealth maximization to easily manipulate prearranged results. Their use of the model is indeterminative and ideological rather than scientific. Consider the question of legalized prostitution and the Posnerian goal of answering a pressing social problem through the determination of efficient market outcomes that are allegedly free of moral influence and superior to any independent consideration of individual liberty and human dignity.

Posner uses the Kaldor-Hicks criterion as his wealth maximization principle. This principle allows "moves" to be taken (validates involuntary transactions) when the gain to one party exceeds the loss to the other party. Posner rejects Pareto efficiency, another common economic standard, because it permits moves only if there is a voluntary exchange where no party is made worse off as a result of the transaction. From this starting point we can discover the indeterminacy of the wealth maximization principle. On the one hand, the wealth maximization principle can be used to argue that prostitution should be legalized. Prostitution arguably represents a voluntary transaction between two consenting adults and, in addition to satisfying Kaldor-Hicks efficiency and the wealth maximization principle, it is a Pareto superior outcome, since its voluntary nature confirms that both parties are left better off by the exchange. On the other hand, it is just as easy to use the conservative wealth maximization method to include different variables or to give variables different weights, in order to reach the opposite conclusion. For instance, the negative effects of prostitution on the harmony of family life or the estimation of increased street crime as a result of prostitution can all be argued to offset economically and socially the value of permitting prostitution.[17] Thus, whether the theory's scientific results favor or disfavor prostitution depends on the conservative philosophy used for support. The indeterminacy of such a theory is, therefore, significant because it undercuts the pretensions of the model's ability to generate scientifically "correct" answers to complex social and legal issues. As a result, the key to understanding the value of the conservative theory of law and economics is the same as understanding the econometric forecasts for economic growth, inflation, or the price of oil. The outcomes generated by these models are dependent upon and limited to the variables considered and the weight given to each variable.[18] Consequently, when all scientific pretentions are set aside, the results of conservative approaches to law and economics are to be found in conservative ideology rather than in the science of mathematical deduction.

The discourse of conservative approaches to law and economics is one that favors the liberty of the state and conservatively minded groups. It does this by applying a seemingly scientific and individualistic market model of economics (neoclassical economics) to the resolution of pressing social problems. Yet in the process it fails to take account of the humanistic principles of economics first set out by Adam Smith.[19] Unlike Posner's wealth maximization construct, Smith's philosophy of law and economics includes a recognition of natural rights, human dignity, and certain welfare rights for all members of society.[20] When Posner says that people without resources or people who are born "feeble-minded" have no claim to any allocation of social resources, he is simply stating propositions contrary to the humanistic work of Adam Smith.[21] Similarly, when Posner asserts that slavery can be justified on efficiency grounds, as wealth maximizing in certain situations, he is speaking of a non-Smithian and non-classical liberal interpretation of the economic marketplace.[22]

The discourse of conservative law and economics is a discourse of exclusion. Despite the various moral value choices assumed by the use of a neoclassical economic model, the practitioners of Posnerian law and economics engage in a dialogue of efficiency that is made to appear as a purely factual determination. Efficiency and wealth maximization are, thus, presented as principles intended to invoke an element of science. As a result, such discourse is made to appear more natural, more objective, and more determinate. But, as has been explained, this is not the case. The facts themselves are a matter of subjective interpretation and they are submitted to an indeterminate mode of economic analysis that itself rests upon certain assumptions and value judgments.[23] Wealth maximization and efficiency language are used, therefore, to marginalize and extinguish our conscious participation in moral and humanistic decision making.

Once the conservative construct of law and economics is accepted, the legal conversation is transformed into a collection of facts and fact determinations. If one considers the problems of surrogate motherhood under wealth maximization methods, for example, one must undertake a factual determination of the costs and benefits of such legal arrangements. At the same time one is permitted to avoid the underlying and difficult questions about women's roles in society and the ability of women to engage freely in exchanges of this type.[24] One never needs to consider how the market and law have historically treated women.[25] In a similar way, wealth maximization discourse can ignore the issue of whether African Americans or Hispanics, for instance, have anything to exchange in the marketplace. If a voluntary contract becomes a matter of dispute, conservative ideology requires us to consider the relevant facts of the bargain. The discourse of wealth maximization validates voluntary contract transactions without asking whether some people have been systematically deprived of an opportunity to acquire the wealth necessary to bargain voluntarily.[26] In this way Posnerian approaches to law and economics deprive certain individuals of the opportunity to participate in the market. These approaches are conservative because they are grounded in and continue to promote values biased in favor of prior distributions of wealth, power, and resources.

As illustrated above, the conservative approach to law and economics embraces its own form of discourse. This discourse is not objective or neutral but is instead subjectively constructed to promote conservative values and assumptions concerning the individual, the community, and the state.

Liberal and Left Communitarian Approaches

In contrast to the conservative approach, liberal and left communitarian approaches are more openly subjective (less scientific). Both liberals and left communitarians, however, are in accord with conservatives, such as Posner, when they rejected the concept of an individual's natural or inalienable rights. They tend to argue that such conceptions of the individual stand in the way of progress on social welfare programs because too often those conceptions are used to protect the wealth, resources, and position of people in power.[27] Both groups would criticize conservative theory for its status quo validation of prior distributions of wealth, resources, and power. The conservative emphasis on the protection of private property rights is the legal context in which this disagreement is most often played out. In addition to their rejection of natural rights, liberals and left communitarians might generally be viewed as placing a great deal of value and confidence in the public or state side of the checks and balances model.

In this section of the book a brief discussion of these alternative approaches will be offered. While not meant to be all-inclusive, this inquiry should provide sufficient background for further discussion.[28] It will be helpful to consider each approach separately.

The liberal perspective can generally be viewed as replacing natural rights with a requirement of equality of treatment[29] and resolving conflicts of competing claims on social resources by appeal to the political process rather than the market process. The state, on behalf of the community, can take whatever actions it desires, but in so acting it should be limited by a political requirement to treat all people equally. The requirement for equality of treatment is deemed necessary to assure protection for individual rights since a democratic political process assures broad-based participation. Theoretically, therefore, no group should seek an aggressive measure against another group because of the potential for retaliation. In this manner the process protects people through the restraining first principle of treating everyone equally. The difficulty arises, however, as soon as it is realized that biologically and environmentally individuals are not equal—not merely fungible members of a group.

In the liberal conception, the state pursuing community goals can legitimately do whatever it wants. The political process is supposed to protect the individual, but there are no natural rights limitations on the activities the state can undertake. Thus, individuals may have their rights reduced by the state as long as there is an element of equality in the process of reduction. Although this conception may have some initial appeal, it is clear that it ignores the dynamics of special interest influence over the political means. Furthermore, it puts entirely too much power into the hands of those that operate the machinery of the democratic process. In essence, the liberal approach elevates the myth of democratic institutions to the level of legitimizing those actions of the state directed by a liberal statesman. In this way it is like the Posnerian conservative who elevates and legitimates efficiency and the market process without regard for the natural rights of individuals. The difference between the two theories is, in essence, a matter of one theory putting complete faith in the private market process and the other theory substituting a public political process for the market. Each process serves its own constituency, but neither is fundamentally concerned with the rights of individuals.

The liberal conception of law and economics is consistent with the typical statist formulation of empowering the right people, in the right places, with the right resources. The private sphere in our checks and balances model is played down and diluted because it offers a challenge to the "superior" planning power of the liberal statesman who is able to understand what is best for the community. The desired outcome of equality in liberal theory is achieved through a personal political process and not left to the impersonal operation of an unmanaged marketplace.

The discourse of a liberal approach to law and economics is, therefore, one that favors a liberal state and the programs of liberal groups. It is not a discourse of individual rights that are inalienable or protected from intrusion by the state. Rather, liberal discourse involves the transformation of a natural rights dialogue into a dialogue about political power. In this sense one's rights become contingent on the political process, and the political process is guided by a liberal dialogue in which the presumption is that all people are entitled to an equal share in all scarce resources and in the exercise of political and economic power. Anyone asserting a right to a greater distribution in their favor has the burden of justifying such an unequal outcome.[30]

Bruce Ackerman has written extensively on liberal theory in law and economics and he identifies this liberal form of discourse as a *neutral dialogue*.[31] In his neutral dialogue there are three key components. First, there is a requirement of *rationality*. Rationality requires anyone seeking an unequal distribution of resources to justify that objective by engaging in a persuasive philosophical dialogue. Second, there is a requirement of *consistency*. Consistency requires that the reasons offered for the unequal distribution of resources be consistent with the justification. An example might be the request for Whites to control more resources than African Americans, because the justifying argument that Whites are superior to African Americans is inconsistent with the liberal principle that all people are created equal. Consequently, the effort to justify a greater distribution of wealth and resources for Whites fails the test of a neutral dialogue because it is inconsistent with a fundamental principle of equality. Third, there is a requirement that the dialogue of persuasion be *neutral*. Neutrality requires that claims made for validation of an unequal distribution of resources cannot be legitimized on the basis that the superior resource or power-holder has a better conception than others of the social good. Similarly, one cannot justify an unequal distribution by appealing to an intangible higher source, such as God or divine revelation. Neutrality would rule out such justifications as a parent telling a child they must do or refrain from a certain act because the parent says so, or that certain conduct should not be engaged in because it is a sin and is not how God wants us to act.

Ackerman's neutral dialogue exemplifies the liberal approach to law and economics discourse. It sets the discussion of resource and power allocation within a conceptual framework that leads to a different vision of society from that which would result from conservative or classical liberal approaches. The liberal economic discourse presumes equality of outcome, a rejection of natural rights, and a rejection of neoclassical economic market justifications of resource distribution, and it elevates the political process to center stage in resolving pressing social problems. Furthermore, the liberal economic discourse incorporates the assumption that experts are best able to understand and address pressing social problems. Ackerman's conception of legal economic discourse, emerging from the context of the Great Depression and the New Deal, shifts the ideological framework away from Chicago School and Posnerian economic analysis and delivers us into the Keynesian world of market failures, insurmountable transaction costs and externalities, and the need for liberal intervention and management of social institutions for the common good.

The more critical or left communitarian views of liberalism tend toward a socialist or neomarxist ideology.[32] At the outset it should be stated that I consider socialists to differ from marxists in the way they treat private property more as a matter of form than as a matter of substance. Socialists, for instance, allow ownership of private property in many instances, but they undercut the power base implications of such capitalist ownership by taxing extensively and by regulating out of existence the separateness required to make the private sphere a counterbalancing power source to the state. The marxists, on the other hand, seek communitarian ownership and are more clear about the consequences of their philosophical vision. They would like to place ownership of the means of production in the community, represented by the state, and thereby eliminate the power base of the private sector. This dilution of capitalism and private property has implications for the counterbalancing power source conception of the public and private spheres as set out earlier. A shift to a highly socialized or marxist view of economic relationships inevitably fulfills the liberal tendency toward public rather than private determination of resource allocation.

The practical implications of a left communitarian or neomarxist view is clearly a strongly statist ideology with emphasis, in our checks and balances system, almost exclusively on the public or state sphere. Under this system of analysis enlightened individuals with the expertise for properly managing the vast array of public goods and resources are by necessity required to run the state in a way that will best serve the needs of the people they represent. This requires an ability to both know and implement the best decisions for everyone in the society. Since it is clearly impossible to do this on an individual basis, the state tends to act in terms of generalities, and thus must fulfill by its action the ideological vision of class consciousness as opposed to individual self-realization. Since the state controls most, if not all, significant resources in these systems, it is very difficult to move the state in any direction that might be contrary to the vested interests or ideological agendas of the people in power.

The discourse of a left communitarian or neomarxist view of law and economics supports views that are fundamentally different from those of classical liberal theory. In law, this form of discourse is the primary construct of the Critical Legal Studies (CLS) movement.[33] One of the primary objectives of CLS scholarship is demonstrating the indeterminacy of other approaches to law, such as Posner's conservative theory of wealth maximization. The focus on indeterminacy is meant to reveal existing law and institutional structure as contingent and socially chosen. From this fundamental platform CLS proceeds to demonstrate the bias in our process of social choice and that this bias reflects class struggle and exploitation. Law and legal discourse, as presented in other ideological constructs, is envisioned as an attempt to make current social, economic, and political arrangements appear natural and, therefore, legitimate. I do not believe, however, that a showing of indeterminacy supports the reconstruction of society in left communitarian or neomarxist terms. The proof of indeterminacy only illustrates the need for a persuasive dialogue concerning the desirability of the alternative values generated by conflicting forms of discourse.

The task of CLS is to unmask the current legal order and to raise a new consciousness concerning the political choices confronting society. CLS argues for a more altruistic and public orientation to law and economics discourse that is possible only by one's freedom from the atomistic constraints of the individualistic and self-interested value structures of exploitative capitalism.

Left communitarian and neomarxist discourse focuses on the difference between *rules* and *standards* in legal argument.[34] Rules are generally portrayed as individualistic and formalistic. In contrast, standards are thought of as altruistic and context-sensitive. It is argued, for instance, that rules of contract formation are formalistically applied to uphold bargains between contracting parties without one's ever having to consider the context of the bargain itself. The rule-oriented lawyer, according to CLS, merely searches for compliance with rules, such as offer and acceptance, but never has to question the relative strength or weakness of any one party to the agreement. The rules, in other words, allow one to endorse or validate bargains as entered into freely without one's considering the implications of potentially exploitative power situations. Standards, on the other hand, require one to set aside a concern for formalism and ask one to consider the context of the transaction. Did one party have more education, more wealth, or more social, political, and economic power than the other? Was one party a member of a minority group with a history of exploitation and subjugation by the other participant's group? These additional factors need to be considered under a standards approach and allegedly play little or no role in a rule-oriented approach.

Rules, in contrast to standards, are socially chosen criteria for legitimizing socially biased arrangements. The rules are created for the benefit of people already in power and they serve as a means of justifying and retaining that power. The rules of contract law, for instance, favor people with something (wealth) to bargain about.[35] These rules formalize and legitimize the possession and transfer of property and wealth to the continued disadvantage of those with less power or resources. CLS scholar Mark Kelman puts it this way:

[O]ne can deny that one's attitudes about others are painful or contradictory if one believes that one has established categorical bases [rules] for dealing with them, for distinguishing benevolent interaction from exploitative attacks. . . . Rules are associated with distancing and role playing; the bureaucrat need not listen as long as he does his job, gives you your due. No one can demand anything but compliance with present rules; conversation and explanation of one's conduct are avoided, for it is easily ascertained whether one has done all he must, one can shut up those who ask for explanation—a rule's a rule, don't complain to me. Ongoing attempts to reassert the coherence and comprehensiveness of doctrine, of whatever web of legal rules purports to describe social relations, are part of a collective effort to pacify and reassure us that we have been delivered from existential tragedy. Rules are the opiate of the masses.[36]

Thus, to engage in a left communitarian or neomarxist form of discourse on law and economics is to promote values which are antagonistic to traditional neoclassical economics and classical liberal concerns for the individual. The difference between the left communitarian or neomarxist view and that of liberals is one of degree. The neomarxist critique of CLS calls for a complete deconstruction of current social arrangements followed by a reordering of public and private values. This differs from liberal discourse, which tries to work within the general constraints of society while advocating a redistribution of power and wealth. These values are inherent in the form of discourse, and once one accepts the parameters of this discourse, as is true of alternative constructs as well, the form of law and legal arrangements becomes substantially different from how it might otherwise be under an alternative ideological approach.

Libertarians

Finally we come to the libertarian perspective. Unlike conservatives, liberals, and the left communitarians, the libertarians put a great deal of emphasis on the private sphere in our checks and balances model, and, like classical liberals, they are suspicious of the exercise of state power.[37] They believe that private sources of power must be available to keep the exercise of state power under control and within reasonable boundaries. Libertarians tend to recognize that individuals are the relevant reference point for liberty and they tend to view these individuals as having certain natural rights or certain inalienable rights that vest each person with personal autonomy. The libertarian view, like that of classical liberalism, is essentially an anti-statist philosophy and in this regard stands in contrast to the other views discussed in the earlier parts of this chapter.

Libertarians tend to speak of the state of nature and of the minimal state. The state of nature defines the original framework that gives rise to private ownership.[38] In the original state of nature people freely roam the earth, and it is through individual hard work that certain resources, such as wild game, trees, or minerals, are brought under control and put to use. It is the application of labor and the natural right to the fruits of one's labor that justifies and legitimates the emerging concepts of private property and of individual rather than state ownership.

The recognition of private property rights is said to create natural incentives for people to create valuable goods and services and leads to an environmentally sound allocation of scarce resources. Libertarians, for instance, might argue that the problem of overgrazing certain natural resources, such as air and water, is due to the lack of private property rights. If air and water rights could be assigned and exchanged in a private market, there would be a system for allocating their use. As demand increased, prices would rise, and there would be a mechanism for reducing the potential for overgrazing. Of course such a system would mean that the resources of air and water would not be free, and some politically motivated groups would be upset. These resources, however, are not free anyway. Because of overgrazing we all pay with such unpleasant externalities as pollution and shortages. It is only the appearance of cost-free resources and not the reality of use without cost that is evident when no private rights are attached to such resources.

A key element of libertarian philosophy is the conception and role of the state. Libertarians attach a strong moral claim to the foundations of private property and the free market process for the allocation of private resources. Within this framework they recognize a legitimate role for government bounded by what they often refer to as the minimal state.

The libertarian conception of the minimal state is effectively argued by Robert Nozick, who basically asserts that the conception or limits of the state are found by reference to the state of nature.[39] This is to say that in the absence of an organized state, individuals will, nonetheless, find it beneficial to organize or mutually agree to be bound by obligations for certain services. An example might be to provide for the public defense, or that some members of the community would specialize in protecting the group's necessary work and food production from the encroachment of roaming warriors or other villages. This type of arrangement, leaving others to tend to the production of goods and services, would be so beneficial that it would naturally arise out of the state of nature. This arrangement then becomes the ground for arguing that such services as public defense and others that would arise only in the natural order of things help define the minimal state, and it is this notion of the minimal state that should be translated into the organized state.

Richard Epstein makes a good argument for incorporating a libertarian view of government and the United States Constitution into his legal scholarship. But Epstein's book *Takings* illustrates a significant point of departure between libertarian theory and the approach to classical liberalism developed in this book.[40] Epstein makes powerful arguments in favor of individual liberty and private property, but he then dismisses everything since the New Deal as both inappropriate and unconstitutional. In contrast, it seems that a classical liberal might not reach this conclusion. The classical liberal might first ask, what are the rights of a human being in a given society? And, in a rich and affluent society, such as late twentieth-century America, it may seem that many of the aspirations of the New Deal could be compatible with classical liberal conceptions of individual liberty and human dignity. Certainly, the idea that individual liberty and human dignity require access to shelter, food, and medical care would be within the classical liberal philosophy. The classical liberal would, thus, envision a greater role for government than would the libertarian. The libertarian might be said to envision too narrow a view of the public sphere in our checks and balances system. The view might be so narrow as to result in a social order as disharmonious as that offered by the extreme statists. The entire purpose of the state, after all, is to counterbalance the private sphere with the public sphere, and only in the emergent equilibrium of this balance can individual liberty and human dignity emerge and encompass the greatest measure of personal autonomy and human worth. In classical liberal terms, the enhancement of individual liberty is found by borrowing from the competitive market metaphor in neoclassical economics. It is the presence of effective counterbalancing power sources that best protect individuals, and consequently a social order dominated by private coercion can be as harmful as one dominated by an overly powerful state apparatus.

In this discourse of libertarian law and economics, individual rights are paramount.[41] Like classical liberal theory, libertarian ideology denies the absolute power of the state and engages in a dialogue concerning the appropriate limits of state power and the meaning of natural rights. Natural rights, in essence, provide the theoretical foundation for asserting an inherent limit to state power. Epstein addresses the issue of natural rights in the following way:

> [T]he political tradition in which I operate . . . rests upon a theory of "natural rights." . . . Whatever their differences, at the core all theories of natural rights reject the idea that private property and personal liberty are solely creations of the state, which itself is only other people given extraordinary powers. Quite the opposite, a natural rights theory asserts that the end of the state is to protect liberty and property, as those conceptions are understood independent of and prior to the formation of the state. No rights are justified in a normative way simply because the state chooses to protect them, as a matter of grace. To use a common example of personal liberty: the State should prohibit murder because it is wrong; murder is not wrong because the state prohibits it. The same applies to property: trespass is not wrong because the state prohibits it, it is wrong because individuals own private property.[42]

In many respects the libertarian approach to law and economics is similar to and compatible with classical liberal theory. It uses the individual as the key referential sign, values natural rights and individual autonomy, and supports a market-oriented society that respects and protects private property. Libertarian theory is consistent with free market capitalism and with the basic values expressed in neoclassical economics. Likewise both approaches would reject the conservative market discourse of Posnerian wealth maximization because it rejects natural rights and allows the state to trample over individual rights in the name of a subjective pseudo-scientific quest for efficiency. Libertarian theory ignores, however, the classical liberal demand for social equilibrium between competing sources of public and private power.

Unlike classical liberal theory, libertarian theory is generally incompatible with discussions of welfare rights and human dignity. Libertarian discourse is constrained by a rigid conception of private property rights and is thereby rendered relatively weak as a tool for accomplishing a structural redistribution of scarce social resources.[43] Classical liberal theory, on the other hand, recognizes a welfare rights position as part and parcel of an understanding of the full scope of individual liberty in the context of a social community. Building on the original work of Adam Smith in this area,[44] classical liberal theory defines individual liberty as embracing a concept of human dignity that requires certain welfare transfers to be made in order to protect every individual's opportunity to participate in both the economic and political dimensions of society.

Classical Liberalism Compared

Classical liberalism is unlike any of the other theories that have been discussed.[45] It alone seeks a process of public and private balance for the purpose of ensuring individual liberty, for it is from the give and take of counterbalancing power sources that the broadest base of people and ideas will be allowed to coexist. In addition, classical liberals continue to support Adam Smith's dualistic conception of the relative and nonrelative nature of individual liberty and human dignity, while embracing a requirement for market participation by all individuals. The requirements of human dignity mean that we cannot legitimize the tragedies and hardships of individuals by cloaking them in the language of protecting private property rights or of following the natural consequences of a market process that should be protected for its own sake. Similarly, classical liberals cannot allow statist pretensions of the public good to run roughshod over the private rights and property of the most productive members of the society. The classical liberal must reject the libertarian notions of the minimal state and must instead seek to define a state that serves as an appropriate counterbalance to private coercion such that the resulting society works as well for the individual as competition in the commercial marketplace works for the consumer.

By following the philosophy of Adam Smith, classical liberals recognize the need for moral judgment in law and social policy in order to protect individual liberty.[46] By pursuing the protection of individual liberty through social cooperation, the classical liberal is willing to restrain certain individual conduct by implementing general rules through a process that respects the human dignity of each person. Furthermore, the classical liberal envisions an affirmative role for government action when there is a significant social purpose involved, such as the protection of basic human dignity by providing food, shelter, medical care, and education. Government action is also called for when the private market is unlikely to provide these goods and services without government intervention, such as when the intended recipients are poor and have no purchasing power to command the attention of private suppliers.

Classical liberalism is a philosophy that does not believe in capitalism or the free market for its own sake. Rather, it is a philosophy that puts paramount value on freedom and individual liberty as the ultimate objective, with capitalism and the free market identified as the best means for achieving and maintaining that objective. This philosophy is also not constrained by the status quo problems of conservative wealth maximization theory because it believes that the capitalist ideals and the fulfillment of individual liberty have not yet been achieved. Consequently, all law and social policy claims that seek justification on the basis of prior or current political and economic arrangements, or which are based on the renditions of neoclassical economic analysis, are subject to critical review in light of the moral imperative to protect and advance freedom and individual liberty.

In classical liberal philosophy, concerns for economic efficiency are distinctly secondary to concerns for freedom and individual liberty. Milton Friedman, a longtime spokesperson for classical liberal philosophy, has expressed this opinion for years. As long ago as 1962, when his book *Capitalism and Freedom* was first published, Friedman argued that capitalism was a necessary but not a sufficient basis for freedom.[47] In other words, capitalism could not be the ultimate objective because capitalism itself does not assure freedom. More recently, in a 1987 article, Friedman said:

A free society, I believe, is a more productive society than any other; it releases the energies of people, enables resources to be used more effectively and enables people to have a better life. But that is not why I am in favor of a free society. I believe and hope that I would favor a free society even if it were less productive than some alternative—say, a slave society.

I favor a free society because my basic value is freedom itself.[48]

These views are consistent with the views of another great contemporary classical liberal philosopher, Friedrich Hayek.

Hayek, like Friedman, seeks to protect individual liberty from the coercive interference of others, including the state.[49] For Hayek, spontaneous social order is only possible in the capitalist society and, therefore, capitalism allows for the greatest sphere of individual autonomy.[50] He believes in the free marketplace and in a maximum of individual autonomy, but he also acknowledges that the expression of freedom sometimes requires the government to protect basic liberties. Such action is permissible, it seems, if it proceeds by general rules and is otherwise consistent with concerns for human dignity and liberty.[51]

In classical liberal theory, therefore, economics provides a tool and a guide to the critical evaluation of law and social policy. It provides means for analyzing alternative approaches to social policy that enhance ordinary legal analysis. The economic model, however, is no substitute for individual moral judgment. The classical liberal does not delegate or obscure difficult moral questions with simplistic and formalistic concepts, such as wealth maximization. Rather, the classical liberal engages in an ongoing dialogue designed to further freedom by offering the concept of individual liberty and human dignity as the bedrock values of social cooperation. Furthermore, through this dialogue, classical liberals seek to influence and establish the general rules of social morality, which are, as Adam Smith said, "ultimately founded upon experience of what, in particular instances, our moral faculties, our natural sense of merit and propriety, approve or disapprove of."[52] In this way, moral judgment remains an important part of the classical liberal theory of law and economics, and classical liberal philosophy provides a constructive basis for aiding lawyers in the process of social evolution.

By engaging in moral discourse, the classical liberal is not asserting a special knowledge of a given set of natural rights. Rather, classical liberal theory posits natural rights as an important element of discourse in a system of individual liberty. Natural rights consist not of a God-given list of specific rights; instead natural rights emerge from individual and group experiences that continually enhance and validate changing norms concerning human dignity. In this way the classical liberal commitment to moral dialogue is a commitment to opening rather than closing conversation. It is likewise an ideological guidepost for directing legal economic discourse down a path that rejects the notion of an all-powerful state. Natural rights and morality serve, therefore, as signs in the semiotic sense that they structure the content and ideological substance of a particular form of discourse.

As signs, rather than the product of divine revelation, morality and natural rights allow classical liberals to promote more public regarding activity than libertarians. Likewise, classical liberals are unconstrained by the pseudo-science of Posner's wealth maximization principle, which continually seeks to disempower the least powerful members of our community. Classical liberals, for example, are therefore able to support many government programs, such as a guaranteed minimum income, public education, job training, and housing.[53] Their methods for achieving these goals, once the moral objective has been determined, would be consistent with information provided by standard market analysis.[54] For instance, a concern for providing an adequate supply of low-income housing would not lead the classical liberal to suggest such economically destructive policies as rent control or the construction of so-called public housing.[55] To the contrary, the classical liberal would reject rent control on the grounds that basic economic analysis reveals that it hurts rather than helps the poor by discouraging the production of rental housing.[56] Similarly, public housing in the form of government-controlled projects would be rejected because a government monopoly of low-income housing would be less beneficial to the poor than housing vouchers that could be used by tenants to find reasonable housing in the market.[57] In this way the classical liberal attempts to blend moral judgment and normative social values with the powerful analytical tools of economics. Economic models, however, cannot be treated as godlike structures and they must ultimately be subject to a principled analysis of what it means to be human.

Classical liberal discourse concerning law and economics incorporates its own set of values. The discourse is individualistic and promotes a free market approach to social organization. Natural rights and human dignity play an express role in the classical liberal dialogue. Classical liberalism embraces a metaphorical and symbolic understanding of economics as a form of discourse and that requires constant attention to matters of morality. Counterbalancing power sources serve as the cornerstone for the metaphorical use of economics, and it is through competition that freedom, creativity, and spontaneous social order are furthered. Conscious of past distributional bias and never willing merely to incorporate the outcome of "scientific" approaches to economics, the classical liberal theorist must always engage in a persuasive discourse regarding the fairness, reasonableness, and appropriate value consequences of suggested approaches to pressing social problems. Classical liberalism promotes, therefore, a process for understanding and talking about law, legal relationships, and legal institutions that is different from that offered by other ideological approaches.

The alternative ideological approaches to law and economics, discussed in this chapter, are important because they have real and practical consequences. The ideological framework in which one thinks about and implements law has an effect not only on the structure of legal discourse but also on its content. Basic assumptions about the roles of the individual, the community, and the state vary as they do between the alternative schools of thought, and one's view of law and legal institutions is likewise varied. Notions of property, contract, free choice, reasonableness, fairness, and justice are completely contingent upon the ideological framework used to evaluate law and society. Where the conservative sees complete social justice and legal harmony, the left communitarian and neomarxist are likely to see illegitimate hierarchy and exploitation by a powerful group over a disempowered group: instead of social justice and legal harmony, there is injustice and disquieting legal acquiesence.

Law and the structural institutions related to it are contingent upon validation within a particular legitimizing theory. Consequently, the predominance of one form of legal economic discourse over another will lead to the validation of one set of legal arrangements rather than another. Similarly, the study of the legal relationships endorsed by a society to accomplish such ends as urban revitalization and development will reveal a tendency to validate particular aspects of one theory of law and economics at the expense of another. Thus the reader should be prepared for the critique of current approaches to urban development that follows in Part II. First, however, let us turn to a brief discussion of the first principle basis upon which alternative ideological approaches seem to rest.

Chapter 10
First Principles and the Concept of Faith

As with a belief in God, Christ, Buddha, Zeus, dialectics, evolution, or creation theory, a belief in the workings of a free marketplace or in some dimension of natural rights or human dignity requires a belief or faith in first principles. No matter how much one tries to make the unknown knowable, there will always be a gap. Convincing arguments, theories, and proofs can be offered, but, fundamentally, every conception of what we are and how we relate to the universe around us is a theory or conceptual metaphor.[1] Consequently, every outlook requires a first principle or series of first principles as a foundation. The only realistic support for the internalized validity of such first principles are faith and experience.[2] The frontiers of faith can change over time as we learn more about our world, but the concept remains because there are still unknown questions behind every new fact. The exploration of space, for instance, has helped to tell us more about our world than we could theorize when we were earthbound. Nonetheless, we can still only speculate about the more profound questions of our origins and our future.

When one engages in legal economic discourse concerning alternative theories or ideologies, one engages in a battle of often unspoken and implicitly assumed first principles of faith. Although we might be right or wrong in our arguments when we claim they logically flow from an internally consistent set of first principles, it is impossible to determine right or wrong between competing perspectives. Instead we are forced to consider the values, persuasiveness, beauty, harmony, or power of explanation contained in each vision. As a result, we may view some conceptions or ideological visions as more convincing, more informed, or better than others. But what we are really saying is that we find the first principle claims of one theory, or the values they promote, to be better as a matter of our own personal faith or subjective experiences than those first principles or values offered by other perspectives.

It is important that we learn to identify and confront the underlying first principles of the rhetoric and actions that occur in the society around us. Only by getting at the heart of the real underlying dispute of first principles can we begin to have a constructive dialogue about our past and our future. The abortion/right-to-life issue is an example. The real matters of debate in this controversy are the questions of what is life, when does life begin and end, and by what means? These are incredibly complex issues. It seems fundamental that if one believes human life begins at conception, one will have a dramatically different view of the abortion/right-to-life issue from if one believes that life begins at birth or at some developmental stage between conception and birth. The problem with the debate is that we have allowed lawyers and others to distract our attention from the real issues. Instead of talking about the issues of life raised above, we speak of privacy rights and personal autonomy as if they were separate from the underlying questions. Although this may be politically expedient, it distracts the social dialogue from the real gravity of the issue.

Similarly, the basis or framework from which one departs on these underlying issues can have consequences in outcome that favor one politically active group over another. The difficulty with the political rhetoric behind pressing social problems is that it frequently masks the connection between the decision being made and the underlying first principles that support those decisions. In this respect the problems of urban development and revitalization are no exception. Politicians speak of public entrepreneurship instead of urban socialism not because there is a significant distinction, but because public entrepreneurism is a phrase that seems to invite little or no consideration of normative values or first principles that might be contrary to accepted notions of individualism and free market capitalism. In this respect law has distracted attention from the real problem of urban development and revitalization efforts in the same way that it has obscured the true complexity of the abortion/right-to-life debate.

Underneath the many legal approaches to urban planning, land use, and finance are a series of critical values and ideological views based on important first principles. By analyzing these various legal arrangements much can be learned about the ideological visions of the proponents of emerging trends in urban development and revitalization. It is clear, for instance, that a statist-oriented socialist will have a different method for approaching urban planning from that of an individualistic, *laissez faire* capitalist. Consequently, it is important to analyze current urban practices to see what they reflect about the nature of our social, political, and economic evolution. At the first level of analysis one needs to be more informed about the ideology reflected in the legal arrangements of a given community. At a second level of analysis one needs to make a normative decision about the wisdom of pursuing one ideological vision rather than another.

For the first level of analysis, I seek to unmask the reality behind the rhetoric of urban development and revitalization efforts. Regarding the second level of analysis, I posit classical liberalism as the best way to promote certain ideas and normative values.

When the concern for human dignity, individual liberty, and participative interaction between the public and private sectors of our checks and balances system is considered paramount, the classical liberal approach seems to provide the best philosophical framework for considering the proper arrangements for our social, political, and economic evolution. If one finds the values of individual liberty, human dignity, and a counterbalancing system of checks and balances within a framework of general rules and principles to be supportable, then one should prefer the classical liberal approach to these problems over that of other philosophical visions. Thus, in absolute terms it is not the claim that classical liberalism is the only true or correct philosophical vision, but rather that classical liberalism is the best method for promoting certain values, such as individual liberty. If one were committed to a conception of liberty of the community group or of liberty for the state, the best philosophical vision for promoting these values would be decidedly different from that offered by classical liberalism.

Part II
The Urban Development Context

Chapter 11
Planning and Serfdom: The Police Power

Thus far much of the discussion has been general. Now it is time to clarify some of these issues by application to one important area of inquiry, an area that although limited in scope is, nonetheless, a microcosm of society. Urban development and revitalization efforts are the points of departure for making specific observations about the state of our society. In looking at urban revitalization efforts, one can separate the analysis into two areas. The first area of inquiry involves what was called earlier the police power of the state and requires us to consider the evolution of urban planning and zoning. The second area of inquiry involves what was referred to earlier as the power of the purse, and this involves consideration of the various ways the state can undertake wealth transfers in an effort to promote desirable projects and plans. Each of these methods of affecting the urban landscape involves the allocation of resources through the political rather than the economic means.

The history of zoning and planning in America can be divided into three broad phases or periods. The first phase involves the domination of the private sphere over the public sphere in the areas of urban growth and land use. The second involves the evolution of general rules and regulations governing the scope and direction of urban growth and land use. The third concerns recent trends in outcome-specific planning and land use management.

It would be historically inaccurate to say that there was ever a time in America when zoning or land use planning did not exist.[1] Even the earliest colonial towns and cities evidence a certain degree of planning and regulation. It would be a mistake, however, to believe that early colonial attempts at land use management were pervasive. Certainly the expansion of the American frontier left a great deal of room for individuals and private groups to influence and direct the growth and development patterns of community life. The foundation of land use devices in the common law concepts of restrictions, reservations, easements, and other such formulations played a major role in early efforts at land management. But these were typically exercised by individuals in the private sphere and motivated by personal aspirations.

Although private methods of land use planning were predominant in the earliest period of our country, such methods have not yet completely vanished. Even Houston, Texas, with its dynamics and size, finds itself governed to a great degree by a complex weave of private property arrangements.[2] As the fourth-largest city in America and the last major city without a comprehensive zoning and planning code, Houston is a unique case. Supporters of private property arrangements consider Houston an excellent example of how individuals can effectively and efficiently arrange land use controls without the excessive interference of government regulation.[3] On the other hand, Houston remains an example of congestion, incompatible land use, and urban sprawl for those who see the city's failure to adopt strong public involvement in zoning and planning as a mistake.[4]

The second phase in American land use management focuses on the *Euclid* decision by the United States Supreme Court.[5] In that case one sees the emergence of zoning by general rules and regulations. Under this general conception of the zoning and planning process, the public became active in establishing general zones of land use within the community. A local zoning and planning board might designate, for example, certain sections of a community as places for industrial use, commercial use, or multifamily residential or single family residential use. The purpose of such designations was to use police power to manage land use in the best interests of public health and safety. Industrial activities, for instance, involve heavy traffic, large trucks, loud noise, and possible extensive dust and air pollution. Although such industrial activities are entitled to access within the community marketplace, they could be potentially problematic for children, schools, or residential activities. Thus, while it was apparent that industrial activity could mean jobs and economic prosperity, it was also realized that the community, as a whole, would be better served by separating various land uses.

Significant features of the general approach to zoning and land use planning are, first, the ability to enter a zone as a matter of right so long as intended use is compatible with the general zone requirements; and second, the ability to put higher ranking uses within lower ranking zones despite the inability to do the opposite.[6] The access to a general zone as a matter of right is significant because it means that urban planners must act initially with a general concern for public health and safety. A general zone requires considerations and guidelines that can leave an area open to a considerable degree of private choice in determining the best uses for the land in question. For example, an industrial zone may have guidelines on the amount of noise, air and water discharge, parking facilities, trucking activity, and use of heavy machinery. But any number of activities—including such enterprises as a building supply and concrete manufacturing operation, an appliance manufacturing business, a chemical company, a ship building company, or a musical instrument manufacturing operation—might be brought into the zone. As a matter of right any specific use that falls into a general category has a right to access. This approach leaves a substantial degree of latitude in the private sector, while simultaneously giving the public sector the power to direct so-called incompatible uses in an effort to create a safer, healthier, and more harmonious living environment.

The second feature of the general zoning approach is the ability to bring a higher ranking use into a lower ranking use category.[7] For example, a single family residential use would generally be given a higher use ranking than that designated for an industrial zone. Consequently, an industrial use could not be placed in a residential zone, although many communities might allow the higher ranking use, the residential use in this example, to be placed within the lower ranking industrial zone. This arrangement can be useful because it puts at least a partial check on zone determination by allowing individuals to decide how threatening certain types of land use activities are to their health and safety. A balance of sorts between the public and the private spheres in the use and management of valuable land resources is facilitated.

Although *Euclidian* zoning has not been without its critics, it is a form of zoning that puts emphasis on land use management by general rules. A general rule approach may at times be rigid or less flexible than some other form of land use control, but it is a method that emphasizes the ideological benefits promoted by classical liberal theory. A system of land use control that operates primarily from a general rules approach is ideologically better, in classical liberal terms, than a more discretionary system. One must remember that many people criticize democratic forms of government as hopelessly inefficient, yet it is precisely the inefficient elements (checks and balances, for instance) that best preserve the higher values of liberty and freedom. Similarly, although a general rules approach to land use control and management presents certain problems, the inherent limitations of a predominantly general rules approach is precisely the structural process that best preserves a balance between the exercise of public versus private control of property.

The third phase of outcome-specific planning evolves out of the general approach. One of the earliest methods of outcome-specific planning involved the power to grant variances for particular uses and individuals, thus allowing specific alternatives to the general zoning scheme.[8] As a check on the potential abuse of issuing discretionary variances, most zoning codes required the holding of public hearings before a variance could be granted. This requirement greatly politicized the zoning and planning process at the specific personal and project-oriented phase of a building request. Although previous hearings on the approval of a general zoning and planning code would also be political, they would be restricted to general rules and guidelines as a result of planning in advance of specific project requests. Moving from the general, before-hand determination of permissible uses to the issue-specific request for a variance resulted in the evolution of greater control over the community by people involved in the political process. This enhanced their ability to exercise the political means on behalf of specific political or ideological objectives. As a result of this process, emphasis shifted from general principles to a situation of status whereby one's influence in political circles became more useful or important than one's claim as a matter of right.

Variances are not the only example of the politicization of the zoning and planning process. Others include the increasing use of Planned Unit Developments (PUDs), the use of special districts, and the project-specific approval process for developments with significant local or regional impact. Each of these planning devices requires specific approval of projects on a case-by-case basis with negotiated agreements between the private parties and the public officials regarding the exact scope and nature of a permissible undertaking. The public sphere has now positioned itself as the planning expert over that of the private sphere. Getting either a variance or an approval for a specific project that falls into one of these individual review/approval processes now requires a great deal of political maneuvering.[9] Projects must be modified and located to be within the specific vision of city planners. Furthermore, extractions are often required, such as requiring a builder to repave city streets on each side of his or her operation, requiring an office building developer to purchase land elsewhere in the city and donate it for public park purposes, or requiring funds for housing projects or school-building purposes. Sometimes these requirements are an express part of getting a project approved. At other times they are simply the wise choice of developers seeking the vote of a planning board member who needs a public project, such as a small community park, in his or her district.

Some of these linkage programs are formalized in zoning requirements, such as in San Francisco and Boston, and they are useful for the political process in two ways.[10] First, by requiring the developer to modify plans and through extractions to offer other contributions for roads, parks, schools, or low-cost housing, the politicians demonstrate their power to affect the private sphere. Whether or not this power is exercised to the long-term benefit of anyone in particular, it does send a clear and persuasive message; the impersonal marketplace of decision making is subordinate to the personal status-oriented sphere of the state. Second, extractions serve as a way to finance state-approved projects without having to go to the public with a direct tax increase. Thus it appears that a political agenda is financed for free and it is hard for individual taxpayers, other than the few from whom wealth transfers are extracted, to get upset. These two consequences of the extraction or linkage process enhance the power, resources, and the perceived prestige of politics. The often unmentioned costs of such programs, in addition to their negative impact on the operation of the private sphere, are indirect costs and consequences for the residents of affected communities.

Extraction and linkage programs are a tax on specific types of activities. By focusing this tax on the activities of major developers, politicians avoid a public backlash because the general public is likely to display little if any sympathy for making developers pay their "fair share." But these developers must deal in a competitive marketplace. And, although a few politically connected developers will still find these arrangements profitable, the artificially increased cost of real estate development will cause many marginal developers to consider relocating their projects, if not dropping them altogether. In either case, however, the increased cost of development will have to be passed on to the public in the form of rent increases or higher unit sale costs. This means that goods and services associated with these buildings and real estate projects will become more costly, and the community will pay an indirect tax by having a higher cost of living. The indirect tax is, however, more politically viable than a direct tax on the public because it is harder to quantify and because politicians can blame the higher cost of living on the private sphere. Consequently, the politicians can assert reasons for allowing an expansion of the political means so that developer costs and profits can be kept in line.

Increasing the political control and management of urban planning seems to raise little concern with the general public. Examples of public waste, mismanagement, and overcharging, as illustrated by the Defense Department, are apparently ignored on the grounds that failure in these situations is merely a result of not having the right people in the right places with the right resources—the situation is rhetorically manageable whereas the private marketplace is by definition unmanaged. Apparently the same views are held about the political management of the urban environment.

The other problem that is enhanced in our third and current phase of planning and zoning is the ability to use the planning and zoning process for the exclusion of politically unpopular or disenfranchised people. While this is always a potential issue for planning and zoning, it is magnified in the outcome-specific phase. The problem here is that politically connected groups can use the political means offered by the planning and zoning process to achieve financial and discriminatory outcomes that would not be possible in a more impersonal and balanced setting. The upper middle-class residents of Palo Alto, California, for instance, have witnessed tremendous financial rewards as a result of implementing zoning restrictions that require large lot sizes and the maintenance of open space.[11] Although many people want to move to Palo Alto, the current residents have excluded them and have done so in a way that assures current owners of greatly increased property values. Similarly, communities have been known to zone multifamily residences, especially apartments, for one- and two-bedroom capacity to assure a minimal impact on the cost of school construction, while at the same time seeking to increase the tax base by allowing more income-earning residents to enter.

Zoning has become a powerful tool in the exercise of political means and it can easily be used to exclude the poor, people with large families, and the disenfranchised. But rather than try to unravel the process and reduce the power of the public sphere, the latest developments in this area include an emphasis on further planning and land use management. Just as the implementation of rent controls led to further regulation to restrict the exit of landlords from the rental housing market, so too have the negative implications of increased zoning and planning power led to a statist outcry for more, rather than less, planning. The lastest irony in urban planning is the concept of inclusionary zoning.[12] In inclusionary zoning the state tries to plan and manage the inclusion of individuals and groups into communities in which previously they have been systematically excluded by the efforts of state-sponsored planning and land use management. Rather than learning from prior mistakes, believers in pervasive statist planning seem endlessly fascinated with the need for more rather than less state involvement in urban life.

One final method of state police power that must be considered in the context of planning and zoning is the exercise of the takings power to transfer private property from one party for the benefit of another.[13] These eminent domain actions, also known as condemnation proceedings, can be used to carry out an urban development and revitalization program.

Through condemnation the city can assist the developer in several ways.[14] First, condemnation provides a mechanism for acquiring property at public expense by compensating the involuntary grantor. Once the city acquires the property, it then can make the property available to the developer at a below-market cost, or at no cost. Second, condemnation proceedings allow the city to eliminate any hold-out problems when parcel assembly involves the acquisition of valuable property rights from more than one owner. The hold-out problem and parcel assembly are particularly troublesome for large-scale projects in downtown centers. The urban setting often means the involvement of numerous fee ownership interests, leasehold estates, easement rights, air rights, and other rights. The large-scale urban developer, therefore, is greatly assisted by a reduction in the cost of coordinating numerous voluntary exchanges for these valuable development rights and is also able to avoid the blackmail prices and "won't sell at any price" problems of hold-out owners.

To understand better the problem of the hold-out seller and the blackmail price-setter, one need only consider two stereotypical examples. The typical hold-out seller is an elderly person who refuses to sell his or her home because he or she has lived there for a lifetime and does not want to move. The typical blackmail price-setter is a speculator who wants to sell the property as the last parcel necessary to complete the real estate puzzle. By selling last, the blackmail seller seeks a purchase price that not only covers the value of the property, but includes a premium for its being the last necessary parcel to complete the property assembly. The blackmail price, therefore, is an attempt to take advantage of the buyer's prior costs in acquiring the other parcels. The blackmail price thus would not reflect the value of the parcel itself, but the parcel's value to the planned project.

In an urban setting, with many small lots and multiple owners of easements, one is likely to confront either the hold-out or the blackmail seller when undertaking a major real estate project. The private developer may not be able to convince all hold-out sellers to change their minds. As to blackmail sellers, the developer will have to either pay higher prices as a cost of doing business or expend resources to hide the assembly process and to keep full information away from necessary sellers. All these considerations add to the cost and risk of completing a major downtown real estate project, but, to a certain extent, this cost can be reduced or subsidized by transferring it to the city.

The city can use its condemnation powers to acquire the private property of the potential hold-out or blackmail seller. In addition, the city can acquire the property at a price that reflects the fair market value of the parcel itself, rather than an inflated blackmail price. After acquiring the property from the private owners, the city can transfer it to a selected developer to complete a project desired by city planners.

Not that long ago, the condemnation powers of the state were limited.[15] A taking of private property was permissible only when a public purpose was served. Traditionally, such public purposes were generally clearly understood to be *public* in the sense that they were fundamental to the purpose of government and involved the types of projects not provided in the private marketplace. Examples of such public projects included the taking of private property for building roads, schools, parks, and water management facilities. Today, however, the jurisprudence of takings law allows a taking of private property even when it is to be transferred to another private person.[16] Furthermore, the person receiving the property can engage in a for-profit activity using property that has been transferred not through the intervention of a private market of exchange, but through the condemnation powers of the state.[17]

Many of the urban real estate projects undertaken in this new era of takings jurisprudence are difficult to relate to the purpose of government in a free society because they include shopping centers, restaurants, hotels, and office buildings. Despite the nature of these projects, the courts have permitted the state to exercise its power of eminent domain. The only apparent requirement is that the city officials must state that the project will ultimately benefit the public. With so flimsy a test of public purpose, it is difficult to imagine a politician who could not justify almost any taking of private property. The real or substantive message from the courts seems to be that these matters are for the political process. As a result political means are further enhanced, and the rights of the individual vis-à-vis the political process and the state are further eroded.

This brief discussion of the general evolution of planning and zoning in American urban life reveals that we have lost touch with the essential balance and harmony of the relationship between the private and public spheres in a free society. It also shows a breakdown in our understanding of the values we proclaim when we speak of individual liberty, freedom, competition, and the marketplace. Though we may speak of these ideas, we have accepted a belief in planning and in the notion that "many led by a few" can better coordinate the direction of individual activity. The problem here is not merely that we have accepted the supremacy of the state in the area of urban development and revitalization. In the process of accepting state planning in this area of our life, we have learned to accept its expansion into other areas as well. Thus the pervasiveness of the welfare state expands, as we continually create and validate more examples of its apparent legitimacy.

Chapter 12
Planning and Serfdom: The Purse Power

Urban development and revitalization are a complex problem, even for cities lucky enough to be experiencing a renaissance of broadly based economic, political, and social renewal. Revitalizing many aging American cities requires a tremendous expenditure of public and private resources, and revitalization does not merely mean arranging funding for a new downtown office building. A lone office building, or just about any other specific real estate project, is by itself insufficient to revive the lifeblood of a city facing industrial and commercial decline, deteriorating and neglected housing, shrinking or vandalized recreational land use, and a crumbling infrastructure. Revitalization efforts must be broadly based and must integrate the need for enhanced infrastructure with the need for restoration or new development of commercial, industrial, and residential facilities. This integration must be accomplished while preserving recreational and artistic amenities sufficient to offset the dissipating influences of the less congested lifestyle available in the urban fringes.

The size and scope of necessary revitalization efforts for many cities pose monumental policy questions. First and foremost among these is a choice of whether urban planning efforts should strive for outcome-specific results or merely a general political, economic, and legal environment conducive to revitalization. In other words, in the context of a dynamic, multi-urban national economy, can local politicians and urban planners be expected to select and promote the best revitalization plans on a project-by-project, neighborhood-by-neighborhood basis, or are revitalization efforts best realized by creating a foundation for market-directed revitalization based on an enhanced free flow of capital, technology, labor, and ideas? Before answering this question, one must analyze the co-financing arrangements currently facilitating urban renewal.

For purposes of general discussion, the current offerings in public/private partnerships and co-financing programs can be grouped under two major headings: first, acquisition, development, and construction assistance (ADC assistance), and second, tax-related assistance.[1] These two broad categories are neither definitive nor mutually exclusive. Rather, they are designed to facilitate a quick and shortened discussion of the nature of co-financing programs before I address the more complex issues pertaining to their use.

ADC assistance programs involve both direct and indirect methods of co-financing particular revitalization projects. The major subcategories of ADC assistance require public and political involvement in making direct loans or grants, sharing acquisition or land improvement functions, undertaking provisions for collateral-support structures and services, and using condemnation powers to affect parcel assembly.

Making direct loans to a real estate project places the city in a role similar to that of a more traditional commercial lender. The city uses public funds to help finance a project to be developed by a private developer whom the city selects. In return for carrying part of the costs of the project, the city, like other commercial lenders, requires a return on the loan, which it may receive by taking a percentage of the income the property generates, such as a percentage of the rent in an office building or retail center. In addition, the city may have the right to share in the property's future appreciation, in the same manner as a commercial lender would exercise an equity kicker option in a commercial loan. In this way, the city shares in the project's potential income flow and equity appreciation while also hoping that the project itself will spur additional city revenues by increasing job opportunities and property taxes.

In a time of governmental austerity, grants are becoming less reliable as a source of revitalization funds. Nonetheless, they have played and continue to play an important role in co-financing real estate projects. Major grant programs generally rely on federal funds made available for local projects. Various cities apply for limited grant or subsidy money on the basis of specific, project-oriented guidelines. These guidelines typically require evidence that the proposed development will provide housing or jobs for a certain number of low-income people or that the grant will be an essential element in the renewal of a blighted neighborhood. Through the grant process, local city politicians aid private developers on qualified projects by combining local resources with funds from the federal government.

Grant programs generally do not require a sharing of income or equity appreciation between the public and private parties, but do carry restrictions limiting the profits the private developer reaps. For instance, a private developer may receive a grant or other federal assistance to construct low-cost rental housing, but may then be restricted in the amount of rent that he or she may charge.

Public sharing of acquisition or land improvement functions can take several forms. The city can voluntarily purchase desirable land for a project and then, as owner, structure long-term lease provisions that reduce the private developer's overall project costs. Alternatively, the city might acquire voluntarily the property and then arrange a sale of the fee ownership to the private developer, either on an installment contract basis or by sale with a purchase money mortgage with terms favorable to the developer; terms that extend payments and allow for low nominal interest rate equivalents amount to favorable subsidies. In yet another variation of this scheme, the city might acquire the land and undertake basic site improvement, such as removing existing undesirable structures and upgrading sewage and utility service facilities, before turning the property over to the developer. This process allows the city to subsidize the private developer with public resources by undertaking activities to complete the project that otherwise would be required of the developer.

By providing for collateral-support structures and services, the city indirectly subsidizes the private developer's construction of an approved project. The best and simplest example of this activity would be when the city agrees to construct a multilevel parking garage adjacent to the site for the private developer's hotel, office building, or retail center. In this way, the developer acquires the construction of a necessary amenity, but at no personal expense, while the city provides a significant subsidy to the private developer in exchange for the developer's commitment to the approved project.

Finally, the city's condemnation powers can be used to assemble a parcel sufficient for project development. Here the takings power, discussed earlier, is used in combination with the purse power because the state can take private property and transfer it to an approved developer as a way of subsidizing the cost of the developer's project.

Tax-related assistance is also a major part of co-financing efforts to revive urban centers.[2] The major subcategories of tax-related assistance include the following: tax abatement, enterprise zones, tax increment financing, and bonds.

Tax abatement schemes are attempts to lure specific businesses or construction projects to a city by means of a scheduled reduction in real property taxes and other local service fees and tax assessments. In exchange for the city's concessions on taxes, the incoming business or project developer agrees to operate its facility for a given period and attempts a favorable impact on local job creation and a long-term enhancement of the local tax base. The trade-off involves a short-term city subsidy to the private enterprise in exchange for a less than certain long-term benefit of greater local job opportunities and eventual additions to the city coffers as the abatement period is phased out.

Enterprise zones, in a sense, are nothing more than better structured approaches to tax abatement. The enterprise zone concept has been used and promoted with varying success in Great Britain and the United States. Enterprise zones take on an attraction superior to that of most simple tax abatement schemes because they combine nonlocal subsidies with local incentives. Usually, to qualify as an enterprise zone, a designated city area must have certain levels of high unemployment and urban blight. Once the guidelines for qualification are met and enterprise zone status is established, a qualified investor or employer, who moves to or expands his or her operations within the zone, is eligible for favorable tax treatment. This favorable tax treatment subsidizes investment in the enterprise zone vis-à-vis other areas unable to offer similar reductions in tax obligations. In essence, the operative goal of using enterprise zones is to reduce a substantial element of business cost—tax liability—in exchange for business investors' investing in the locations and within the guidelines prescribed by the government. One question about enterprise zones is how much they foster new investment and new job opportunities as opposed to shifting business from outside to inside the zone.

Tax increment financing (TIF) is another new co-financing method currently used to facilitate urban redevelopment projects. This method allows the city to raise revenue through offerings in the bond market. The revenue from the bonds then can be used to assist a private developer in completing a desired project. The source of revenue the city will use in retiring the bonds is the anticipated incremental increase in ad valorem taxes generated by the presence of the new project in the downtown area. In other words, the city, having designated the appropriate location for its project and having selected a developer, floats a bond issue to finance the project. The issue is backed by an expectation that the new project, in fact, will stimulate significant economic activity so that tax revenues from the area will increase enough to carry the cost of the bond obligation.

A final tax-related assistance program involves the use of industrial development bonds (IDBs). IDBs have been used to encourage the development of both industrial and commercial projects. Like TIF schemes, IDBs rely on the city to issue a municipal bond. Qualified IDBs receive tax-exempt status and, therefore, allow the city to generate money for acquisition, development, and construction activities at a lower cost than if the private developer had to secure these financial resources from private lenders. Thus, the city can assist the developer by offering lower cost terms of purchase, lease, or financing than would be available without the tax-related subsidy. The funds to repay the IDB are not generated from incremental increases in the local tax base, as with TIF, but instead come from the project itself in terms of a share in the income the project generates.

The best example of an arrangement allowing the city to share in the income generated by an IDB project is a downtown commercial use, such as a shopping center or an office building. Instead of selling the property to a private developer, the city can use its IDB-supported acquisition of the land to structure a long-term ground lease with the developer. In this arrangement, the city acts as ground lessor and the developer as ground lessee. The IDB's tax subsidy allows the city to arrange the developer's lease terms at a very favorable rate. The city can then pay off the IDB through the rental income flow under the ground lease, which may include provisions for additional rent percentages keyed to the success of the project.

This brief overview of both ADC and tax-related assistance efforts illustrates the broad nature and flexibility of co-financing alternatives.[3] The ideological implications of such efforts and a normative evaluation of these methods are important concerns of this book. We must not merely ask whether these arrangements lead, ultimately, to the construction of new assets for an urban community. Rather, we must ask how the means selected to achieve this objective effect the very structure and content of legal discourse.

The critique that follows is meant to illustrate the ideological significance of emerging trends in urban revitalization efforts. It is a critique that asks the reader to consider the underlying values that are being transformed in order to achieve certain localized benefits.

Chapter 13
Indianapolis: Example of Renaissance and Counter-Renaissance in Urban Life

Having described the nature of co-financing activities and discussed some of the major legal issues associated with these activities, I will now consider how Indianapolis has used a number of police power and purse power techniques to foster its own renaissance.

Indianapolis is a city of approximately 1,200,000 people located in central Indiana.[1] The city comprises 84 percent of Marion County's population, and the city and county share a primarily merged government structure.[2] As in most midwestern cities, manufacturing industries traditionally have played a major role in the Indianapolis economy.[3] In the 1970s and early 1980s Indianapolis experienced a serious decline in its commercial and industrial base.[4] The experience in Indianapolis was similar to that of many other cities in the nation's Rustbelt.[5] Between 1970 and 1980, Indianapolis lost about 45,000 residents, and from 1979 to 1982, Marion County lost 35,000 jobs in the private sector.[6] Despite this decline, Indianapolis continued actively to pursue downtown investment and a redevelopment strategy based on construction of amenity infrastructure and sports facilities.[7] As a result, between 1974 and 1986 approximately $1 billion were invested in sports facilities and related downtown projects.[8] The downtown business district alone had some forty office, retail, hotel, and housing projects planned or completed in the last ten years.[9] This revitalization activity shares a common denominator—the city's willingness to engage in and foster public/private partnerships.[10] As a result, Indianapolis presents an opportunity to examine current real estate development and financing techniques in practice.

Through various public/private arrangements, the city of Indianapolis has become developer, equity partner, or landlord for a number of major downtown projects.[11] Its redevelopment ventures have put millions of dollars of taxpayer money at risk in real estate projects.[12] These projects, although intended to revitalize the city, are not charitable ventures, but investments in potentially profit-making activities. The success and profit of these projects were not assured, and, in fact, most have provided marginal profit to the city at best.[13] Only after an initial period does the city expect to see any major returns on its investment. Any anticipated returns, of course, are subject to the risks of the general real estate market and to the marketing and management risks for each individual project. Early returns on several projects are indicating financial difficulty for the city. Table 1 illustrates the problems associated with some of the city's major investments.[14] The structure of these public/private partnership projects can be understood more easily by considering typical arrangements. A few illustrative projects are therefore described in Table 2.[15]

Indianapolis's co-financing activities reveal more than a willingness to take risks with public funds; they reveal that these activities can be highly advantageous to select developers. The city has selected, for example, a single developer for at least two major office buildings, a downtown hotel, renovation of a theater and ballroom, and a downtown shopping store. The same developer is also involved with Market Square Arena where the Indiana Pacers play basketball,[16] and is behind the city plan for $400 million in construction for a downtown shopping mall that would encompass 1.9 million square feet of new and existing office space and would cover a two-and-a-half block area.[17]

The city is joining forces with this developer to assist in the down-

TABLE 1. Net Losses for Public-Private Projects (in Thousands of Dollars)

Project	1989	1988	1987
1. One North Capital Building (offices)	546	465	436
2. Two West Washington (offices)	828	255	1,001
3. Claypool Associates (hotel and shops)	not available	4,400	6,050
4. Union Station Associates (retail)	not available	1,529	1,633
5. B&D Associates—Union Station (hotel and parking garage)	1,356	1,096	1,160

TABLE 2. Co-Financing in Indianapolis

Project	City Role	Terms of Contract	City Income
Indiana Theater	fee owner and lender of $1.5 million for renovation	6% interest for 35 years	50% of profits from theater, plus annual rent of $30,000 and 4% of net income from the theater restaurant
Merchants Plaza (offices and the Hyatt Regency Hotel)	city floated $4.5 million in bonds to buy and prepare land, which it owns and leases	60 year ground lease	$360,000 annual rent and 5 to 7% of gross revenue over $10 million
One North Capital (office building)	lender of $3.2 million for construction	6% interest for 35 years	50% of profits
Two West Washington (offices and shops)	lender of $1.2 million for renovation	6% interest for 35 years	50% of profits
Embassy Suites (hotel and shops)	lender of $6 million for construction	interest free for 30 years	$400,000 annually and 25% of net cash flow
Union Station (hotel and retail center)	fee owner and lender of $4 million for renovation	6% for 25 years plus rent	annual rent of $200,000 to $290,000 and 50% of net cash flow

town mall project. Its assistance includes an initial outlay of $4.5 million to purchase property and for preliminary construction work to enhance the site.[18] The city also will purchase the necessary property for the mall from current owners or, alternatively, use its power of eminent domain.[19] Additionally, the city plans to seek federal grant money for the redevelopment project and to provide a package of state and local tax incentives valued at approximately $200 million.[20] As a result, the developer will be able to construct a major downtown mall and use substantial public resources to leverage its investment. With city co-financing the developer will be able to share in the profits of a $400 million mall. Despite sharing profits with the city, the developer stands to reap substantially more profit and prestige as a proprietor of a $400 million mall than as a proprietor of a much smaller mall. The city's co-financing position will also enhance the ultimate chances of the project's success because the city will have an incentive to promote the mall by providing free advertising and good will for the developer. In addition to the projects outlined, Indianapolis has used a wide variety of zoning and co-financing techniques, including tax increment financing,[21] tax abatement,[22] and the full range of ADC assistance[23] in its redevelopment efforts. As a part of its co-financing technique, the city has succeeded in incorporating federal and state assistance programs into its own redevelopment efforts.[24]

Indianapolis's best example of the incorporation of nonlocal monies into a co-financed project is Union Station, which opened to the public at the end of April 1986.[25] The Union Station project involved a $65 million renovation of the old downtown train station built in 1888.[26] In 1986 the station reopened as a hotel and retail complex with more than 100 restaurants and stores and a 276-room Holiday Inn.[27] The project, which opened amidst much fanfare, including live television promotions on NBC's *Today Show*, brought praise to local city officials and to the primary private developer.[28] The project required the city, as owner of Union Station, to lend $4 million to the private developer at below-market interest rates.[29] In addition, the financial viability of the project depended on the availability of federal assistance. The project consumed $16.5 million in federal money, of which $12 million were a grant for mass transit, even though Union Station in its present form has very little to do with mass transit.[30] Additional federal assistance was provided in the form of a 25 percent historic preservation tax credit that allowed developers to recoup one out of every four dollars they put into the project.[31] As a result nearly 50 percent of the project cost for Union Station was paid for by the public rather than by the private developer.

In addition to relying on its police and purse powers to plan and manage the Indianapolis urban landscape, city planners have used police power to effectuate outcome-specific zoning. The city designated the downtown center as an area requiring virtually project-specific approval and negotiation for all development activity. Consequently, projects and developers who are not connected to the political visions of the city leaders can be easily disapproved. And, when current property owners sought to maintain their downtown store and building locations to compete with the city's proposed shopping mall development plans, the city used its power of condemnation to eliminate effective dissent.[32] Furthermore, the city used its zoning power to reduce and prohibit development in some corridors of the city.[33] This action helped reduce private developer choices and forced more people to consider the city's agenda for downtown.

The "state capitalist" programs of Indianapolis's movers and shakers are signs of changing times in the heartland of America. Local business leaders boast in national magazines of the fact that nothing gets done in the city unless they are behind it.[34] Furthermore, the local newspaper, the *Indianapolis Star*, conveniently withholds anti-development news stories from publication until after crucial votes are taken.[35] After-the-fact publication apparently allows the paper to say they covered both sides of the issue even though only mostly favorable information gets noticeable prior circulation.

In addition to these political means, the city has successfully enlisted the support of Indiana University and one of the nation's wealthiest private foundations, the Lilly Endowment. There is evidence that Indiana University has provided an excellent vehicle for aiding the city in its urban planning efforts.[36] When a poor African American neighborhood stood at the doorsteps of downtown, the university and the city combined efforts to eliminate urban blight by selecting that very neighborhood as the location for major university expansion. Since the 1960s the university has continued to provide a major source of "off-budget" development for the city. When Indianapolis, prompted by the Lilly Endowment, decided to build a reputation on sporting facilities, the Indiana University campus was selected as the site for major track and field facilities and a magnificent olympic quality natatorium, despite the lack of any significant student sporting activities on campus.[37] Indiana University college athletics occur some fifty to sixty miles to the south on the Bloomington campus. In addition to these subsidies for the city, the university also undertook responsibility for a major hotel and conference center. It was primarily envisioned as a facility to complement sporting activities and other needs of the city while also available for university functions for those few on-campus departments that could afford some of the highest rates in the downtown area. Despite efforts to funnel university and community business into the hotel and conference center, financial short-falls have made it necessary to raise student fees to cover the university's share of debt service on the project.[38] All of this construction activity is a complement to city development efforts and it stands in stark contrast to the slow pace of expenditures on new buildings and resources for academic purposes.

The Lilly Endowment is said by some critics to be "painting Indianapolis Lilly White." By some accounts, this is not totally inaccurate. Much of the revitalization efforts of Indianapolis have been focused on results that benefit the White upper and middle classes. Extensive government expenditures for upscale housing, shopping, sports, and tourist attractions cannot be said to benefit the poor of the city.[39] The Lilly Endowment, the not-for-profit arm of the only major corporation in Indianapolis, and its directors are among those that have great plans for the city's future. Much of the focus of downtown development and university expansion over the years has been directed by the political and financial power of the Lilly Endowment, an endowment of over $2 billion that has spent approximately 44 percent of its giving in Indianapolis.[40] That much money can pull a lot of political weight in a town like Indianapolis. Although there may be nothing sinister in this symbiotic relationship, it does raise certain questions about the role of public and private parties in urban revitalization efforts.

Recent news reports have raised further questions concerning the activities of the various public/private partnerships undertaken in Indianapolis.[41] Spearheaded by seed money from the Lilly Endowment and augmented by various private and public resources, many Indianapolis real estate projects owe their existence, not to the work of an elected body, but to the behind the scenes efforts of the City Committee. The City Committee was apparently established in the late 1970s and only became public in 1989.[42] The Committee was an exclusive club with membership by invitation only; it included only one Black member and no women.[43] Women were intentionally excluded because they would interfere with the male activities of the committee.[44]

The City Committee consisted of about thirty successful male executives, and their task was to plan the future of Indianapolis without exposing their role or presence to public scrutiny.[45] By design or by mere coincidence, the members of the City Committee were the politicians, Lilly Endowment officers, real estate developers, contractors, bankers, lawyers, and other professionals who eventually became primary actors in receiving, directing, and managing various public/private enterprises.[46] The City Committee planned city development projects and then apparently passed its plans on to official public entities to make the recommendations and carry out the city programs. Evidence revealed questionable connections between various movers and shakers, their public political counterparts, and the various projects undertaken by the city.[47] Although public funds were used to subsidize and promote a wide range of projects in Indianapolis, many of the benefactors of these undertakings turn out to have been on the planning, management, or oversight boards of the City Committee and the public entities acting with authority over the projects.[48]

The dangers of such public/private cooperation seem evident. It destroys the appropriate balance between public and private power sources and thereby destroys the creative process and the environment for freedom. The separation of the public and the private sphere is important and the cooperative arrangements of private interests seeking to employ the power of the state should be avoided. As Adam Smith noted more than two hundred years ago, with reference to groups similar to the City Committee, "People of the same trade seldom meet together, even for merriment and diversion, but the conversation ends in a conspiracy against the public."[49] Furthermore, Smith warned the public to be suspicious of recommendations from private business interests seeking to enlist the support of the state. Smith said, such recommendations

come from an order of men, whose interest is never exactly the same with that of the public, who have generally an interest to deceive and even to oppress the public, and who accordingly have, upon many occasions, both deceived and oppressed it.[50]

Indianapolis, in the context of all that has been said, is, therefore, a most intriguing city to focus upon in a study of the rise of statist ideology in American life. In the midst of what is deemed by many to be the cornerstone of rugged individualism, conservative republicanism, and the "can do" rhetoric of free market capitalism, stands Indianapolis—monument to central planning and state ownership. The irony of it all is lost in the echoes of city boosterism that overwhelms the voices of the displaced homeless and unemployed.

It is also interesting to note that a key to Indianapolis boosterism and a proclaimed major accomplishment of city planners was the successful relocation of the Colts football team from Baltimore. So important was the perceived need for a city team that city planners undertook the building of a domed stadium before any team was under contract to locate in Indianapolis.[51] In getting the Colts to relocate from Baltimore, the city built a first-rate training center leased to the Colts for one dollar a year, and the city has guaranteed the sale of 40,000 of the 60,000-plus seats available in the Hoosier Dome for home games.[52] As a result of the city guaranteed ticket sales and the subsidy of the training facilities, the Colts organization is very profitable. In fact, the guarantee of ticket sales would have allowed the Colts to make a profit even during the player strike of 1987.

The Indianapolis Colts serve a political function as well by giving the residents of Indianapolis a basis for local identification. Some hope that this identification will stimulate local pride in much the same way that the Olympics enhances national pride and university athletics fosters collegiate pride. The political success of such programs is based on transference of identification, a process that reduces or eliminates individuality by focusing identity on crowd participation. The dynamics of crowd participation gives one an identity anchored not in the self but in the university, the city, or the nation symbolically represented by the contestants on the field. Consequently, it makes the centralizing of a political agenda more feasible because people learn to identify with the goals, aspirations, and objectives of the home team. They are led to believe that the success and glorification of the home team is equivalent to the success and glorification of the self. In this way the residents learn to cheer for the home team and to support the home team's political agenda; they no longer see themselves as individuals in the crowd, nor do they promote individualism on the political scene. This anti-individualist perspective is further reinforced by political rhetoric that erroneously equates individualism and self-interest with selfishness—a trait politicians seem to find lurking behind all the evils of programs and ideas they oppose.

As this brief discussion illustrates, the activities of Indianapolis represent substantial financial undertakings for a community of its size and reflect the increasing drift toward statism in our society. The public is being asked to pay for these undertakings through a variety of direct and indirect local, state, and federal tax arrangements. Furthermore, although some believe the successful completion of new office buildings and shopping centers and the acquisition of the Colts are great achievements for the city, it is hard to understand how such functions can be perceived as the legitimate role of government when thousands of people in the city are homeless and unemployed. The thought of government power and tax dollars being used to acquire a football team, a Saks Fifth Avenue department store, and luxury waterfront apartments seems to be contrary to the down home and traditional values of Indiana folklore.

Such activities underscore a new legal discourse that is different in structure and content from either past legal and economic arrangements or current political rhetoric. The blurring of public and private activities and resources has led to an ideological transformation of the underlying values at work in the organization of law and legal institutions within the urban community. Joint investment, promotion, management, and profit-sharing between the public and private spheres of our checks and balances system is only possible in a society that has rejected, in a fundamental way, the values of classical liberal theory. This ideological position is harmful to the preservation of individual liberty and spontaneous social order. Moreover, the normative thesis of this book asserts that the loss in creative process, spontaneous social order, and individual liberty from such an ideological transformation far outweighs the short-term gains in brick and mortar that have accumulated in Indianapolis and other cities across the country.

This critique of current approaches to urban revitalization is difficult for some people to understand. It is easy for them to see the new buildings that have resulted from such activities and they understand as rational the public choice process that leads political groups to elevate discrete short-term objectives over that of the less defined and long-term interests of the general public. The point of the critique, however, is that dollars and cents, and bricks and mortar, do not tell the entire story. Important ideological values must be transformed in order to validate the emergence of the complex interrelated legal and economic arrangements of public/private partnerships engaged in the cooperative efforts of urban revitalization. These new legal and economic relationships are illustrated by the activities in cities such as Indianapolis.

While various economists might argue over the materialistic loss or gain from such urban development projects,[53] the argument here is that the transformation of the structure and content of the legal economic discourse has a real and detrimental effect on the humanity of the society in which we live. It is a criticism of the process by which certain ends are achieved, or perhaps more aptly, of the process by which certain ends are validated as the appropriate aspirations of social achievement. This book asks, by way of analogy, not only whether Mussolini made the trains run on time but what values and norms were displaced in order to achieve that end. One must ask not merely whether Indianapolis produced new buildings or acted in accordance with rational conceptions of public choice theory, but whether the actions of Indianapolis promote a society that is good for the human spirit and the promotion of individual liberty, creativity, and spontaneous social order. In the context of classical liberal theory, the answer to this inquiry must be that Indianapolis has proceeded on a path inconsistent with individual liberty, even if it has produced some tangible and material products that are valued by particular groups or special interests within the local community.

Chapter 14
The Politics and Economics of Urban Development

In the context of urban development and revitalization, special interests employ the political means to aid current, established urban centers at the expense of suburban areas, emerging cities, and urban areas with less political clout. Political means involve, of course, the police power and the purse power. As previously described, both involve the use of public funds and resources to promote specific, politically approved projects in designated locations. Cities such as Indianapolis, for instance, are able to encourage real estate development in their downtown centers by subsidizing the cost of projects. These subsidies reduce the cost of investing in Indianapolis relative to investing in an unsubsidized area or project. In this respect, public resources, which essentially are private resources captured by the government for its own use or allocation, are used to assist one special interest group—the city of Indianapolis and its key constituents—at the expense of other, more diverse, and less visible interests. Significantly, many of the funds and resources used in this public subsidy arrangement are provided not by the people of Indianapolis, who are most likely to benefit from the real estate development, but by diverse sources throughout the state of Indiana and across the United States.

One need only consider the various ways in which the federal government can subsidize local development for a selected city and project. The federal government, for example, can provide a city or project with grants through the Urban Development Action Grant (UDAG) program or with other direct subsidies through revenue sharing. Funds necessary to support these grants and revenue-sharing programs come from the general tax revenues or from printing additional money, which adds to the money supply and the national debt.[1] The tax-based funding method allows revenues raised from the entire national populace to be redirected to benefit the redevelopment efforts of any given locality, such as downtown Indianapolis. Similarly tax-based funding can be accomplished indirectly by providing federal tax incentives for specific types of redevelopment, such as in enterprise zones, or by providing a 25 percent tax credit for historic preservation as in the Indianapolis Union Station project. By using the indirect tax-based funding approach, the federal government forgoes collecting tax dollars from certain special interest projects. This creates a financial incentive for that type of project, but means the federal government must raise revenue from other taxpayers in order to make up for the incentives it provides the special interest group. The net result is that numerous taxpayers with diverse interests contribute to subsidy programs directed to identifiable and cohesive special interest groups. In the case of urban revitalization, this means subsidies to selected cities and projects.

Like these tax-based funding methods, general revenue-sharing schemes allow the federal government to shift the receipts from one state or locality to another state or locality for the latter's benefit.[2] Additionally, the federal government can provide grant money and subsidies out of deficit spending. Deficit spending, however, is merely another form of tax-based funding, in that all Americans pay for its negative impact on the value of the dollar and on the national economy, while the special interest recipient reaps all the benefits.

State programs to assist particular urban centers serve much the same function as federal programs. To the extent that revenues generated on a statewide basis are used to benefit a particular city or project, such a cross-subsidy benefits the special interest group able to employ political means. State tax incentives in the form of enterprise zones and tax abatement legislation also serve the special interest groups at the expense of other, less organized interests.[3]

Federal and state subsidies can be used in yet another even more indirect way to redirect revenues from one group of people to another. Consider, for example, the city that proclaims a willingness to fund its part of a co-financed real estate project. Rather than relying on state or federal subsidies, it will provide only a locally funded loan subsidy for the new project. Even though this scheme may require people from throughout the city to subsidize the chosen project, it can be argued that on this smaller scale, the local level, at least those asked to pay—city residents—also will be the most likely to benefit from the project. To the extent that the city does not require local taxpayers to offset fully the loan-financing subsidy for the project, however, the city may end up seeking nonproject-related subsidies from federal and state sources for budget shortfalls, such as welfare, health, and transportation programs. In other words, the city can gamble on the local subsidy program because it knows that, ultimately, another level of government will step in with additional revenues for essential services.

Given this situation, one must ask, who really gains from this complicated cross-subsidy and co-financing activity? Is there really a cohesive notion of a city as a special interest group? A city, of course, represents a political vehicle for the expression of the political interests of its key constituents. In the realm of urban development, these key constituents are the politicians and business people most likely to benefit from redevelopment efforts. For example, the case of Indianapolis outlined earlier revealed that a single developer is involved in at least four major co-financed projects. Such developers clearly benefit from the subsidies of co-financing activities. Similarly, real estate professionals—lawyers, brokers, and bankers—benefit from the increase in local business activity, as do local union workers, such as construction workers and those employed to clean and service the new buildings. Local politicians also gain favor and enhance their reputations by pointing to the new buildings, activities, and projects generated for their local constituents.[4]

These results seem wonderful until we realize that the buildings, activities, and profits generated for a city like Indianapolis come at the expense of equivalent or perhaps greater activity that could have occurred elsewhere but for the intervention of political means. Thus, it should be no great surprise that Indianapolis has become a comparatively richer or nicer place to live. This has been possible, after all, by making other parts of the state and country comparatively poorer.[5]

Clearly, several conclusions can be drawn from this analysis of the economic and political implications of emerging relationships in urban development activities. First, the involvement of all levels of government in co-financing activities allows numerous direct and indirect wealth transfers to occur between citizens and taxpayers. Second, the indirectness of the methods employed to achieve this income redistribution makes it difficult to obtain good information on the actual costs and benefits of government involvement in co-financing activities. Indeed, it is not only difficult to determine the true costs and benefits of these programs, it is nearly impossible to determine who bears these costs. It is relatively easy to point to the new office building or shopping center constructed in downtown Indianapolis. It is next to impossible, however, to determine which taxpayers actually paid for the project and, more important, which towns and people elsewhere in the state or country lost out on real estate projects or jobs because of the advantage Indianapolis gained from public funds. Third, the political means favor an allocation of resources to established cities. Therefore, they perpetuate a tyranny of the status quo because the established cities represent current, identifiable political and business interests that are better able to harness government power for their own interests. As a result, established cities are able to use grants and other co-financing subsidies to attract and retain businesses that would otherwise relocate to new or economically more desirable communities. Finally, the use of the political means results in resource allocations that do more than simply transfer wealth from 'A' to 'B.' To the extent that political means redirect the investment and resource allocations of the marketplace, there is a net social loss in economic activity because scarce resources are no longer used for their most valued and, therefore, most efficient purposes.[6] Thus, in addition to 'A' losing wealth to 'B,' society suffers a net total loss because fewer total benefits can be derived from resources used in an inefficient manner.

These conclusions, it seems, are essentially unaffected by the political rhetoric made popular in the days of the Reagan administration's push for a New Federalism.[7] New Federalism is a political phrase meant to distinguish the Reagan vision from that of earlier New Deal liberal administrations. The distinction in vision, as applied to the way urban revitalization programs are conceived and administered, however, is more one of form than of substance.[8] To understand this distinction, it is first necesssary to describe briefly both approaches.

The New Deal philosophy carries with it all the baggage of the welfare state that has grown since the rapid expansion of federal government programs under the Roosevelt administration.[9] New Dealers are generally perceived as people who support an active federal government and who envision a need for federal answers and responses to both state and local problems. New Federalism, on the other hand, envisions a reduction in the role of the federal government and a countervailing increase in the role of state and local governments to resolve their own problems.[10] New Federalism is supposed to allow for diversity and experimentation, while returning control of government planning and expenditures to the people.[11] The notion of returning government to the people is meant to conjure up images of small town meetings and participative government free of the excessive manipulation of the special interest groups that frequent the halls of the nation's capital.[12]

Despite the different emphasis in their visions, New Deal programs and those of New Federalism are actually not so dissimilar. Both approaches focus on the use of political means to attain politically desired outcomes. The only real difference between the two is the method by which benefits are bestowed upon favored special interest groups. Moving political decision making from the nation's capital to the fifty state capitals can affect the influence of specific special interest groups, but as long as political means are used to reallocate the resources in the marketplace, the process of government expropriation from the many to the few will continue. For example, enterprise zones and many of the urban redevelopment techniques used by cities, such as Indianapolis, are considered programs consistent with New Federalism. Yet such programs thrive on special interest groups' ability to capture the use of the political means for their own benefit. Although the special interest group dynamics of such an environment may be predictable, it is a process that is detrimental to the maintenance of the delicate balance required, in the classical liberal checks and balances system, between public and private power sources.

What then is the significance of New Federalism? Besides the rhetorical appeal of the appearance of local, popular decision making, New Federalism is an effective method of transferring the power associated with political means. New Deal programs concentrate political power at the national level by way of the federal government. By virtue of federal government sponsorship, programs and regulations have a uniform, national application. This means that liberal New Deal interests, with the support of a high concentration of legislative power and votes in the populous industrial states, can have national influence. Programs that capture the benefits of political means are assured of no competition from individual states that might wish to reject a program. States are not allowed to reject a program because the problem addressed by the legislation is deemed to be of national, rather than state or local, concern. Given the political makeup of the federal government, it was perfectly logical for the conservative special interest groups, which supported President Reagan, to favor a shift in power from the national to the state level. In this way conservative special interests could employ the political means at the state and local levels in those states and communities in which they were well represented, even if they would lack sufficient votes at the national level to overturn or replace New Deal programs. Thus, the key distinction between New Deal and New Federalism approaches was New Federalism's ability to shift political power to a forum more favorable to those special interest groups aligned with the Reagan administration.

The political shift between New Deal and New Federalism involved a reconstruction of legal economic discourse from liberal to conservative. As such, a new set of ideological guideposts structured official legal, political, and economic conversation. This change in structure favored a conversational form receptive to employment of state power in pursuit of a conservative social agenda. While the rhetoric of New Federalism seems significantly different from that of the New Deal, it is evident that there is less to this alleged difference than meets the eye. Fundamentally, both political approaches seek to allocate resources according to political rather than economic means. The result of New Federalism, therefore, is not to change the relationship of the state to the individual, but merely to change the identity of the special interests likely to benefit from the exercise of the state's power.

This view of the political process currently supporting urban development efforts raises questions of whether the political and economic dynamics of these programs can actually lead to an emergence of the prosperous urban environment necessary for fueling long-term economic growth, job creation, and capital formation. Jane Jacobs argues in her recent book, *Cities and the Wealth of Nations*, that government loan, grant, and subsidy programs can provide only short-term and short-lived benefits.[13] Furthermore, spending on development loans, grants, and subsidies is the entire benefit to be expected from these programs.[14] According to Jacobs, these programs can play little part in the economic life of the revitalizing city other than temporarily reducing unemployment and alleviating poverty.[15] In essence Jacobs asserts that urban development and revitalization is a creative process and not merely an accumulation of capital goods. She is in concurrence with the distinguished economist Israel Kirzner in recognizing that the true measure of wealth under capitalism and the primary source of economic development is found in the unleashing of a creative process of discovery and spontaneous social order.[16] Jacobs's critique of current trends in urban development operates at the level of process, and she argues, therefore, that development cannot be purchased. No matter how well-intentioned a government loan, grant, or subsidy program may be, the process of urban revitalization is likely to be more successful if achieved by the spontaneous interaction of individuals rather than attempts to plan and purchase specific capital goods and developmental outcomes.[17] Examining the reasons behind this assessment of redevelopment programs is necessary in order to appreciate its implications for formulating new approaches to urban life.

Jacobs says that the economic strength of an urban center and its extended regions depends on the vitality of their import-replacing capacity. Import replacement is an essential part of long-term growth potential and capital formation. Cities are dynamic and not static; they must respond to changes in economic circumstances. Granting government-sponsored incentives or transplanting industrial factories to new locations cannot turn an economically weak area into a prospering, import-replacing city region.[18]

In order to highlight the significance of import-replacing activities, Jacobs outlines the role imports play in the city economy.[19] First, cities use their imports.[20] Second, imports to a city region demonstrate the earning power of its export work. This is true to the extent that imports are purchased with funds earned by the city's export economy rather than with loans, grants, or subsidies made available from sources outside the region.[21] The source of the city's import funds is crucial, because only through developing its export productivity can a city nurture the dynamic interaction of suppliers and producers that is all-important to its economy.[22] Third, imports serve as candidates for replacement by local production.[23] But, as Jacobs points out, replacement cannot occur without the foundation of dynamic interaction that first must be laid by the process of earning the imports.[24] In short, "development cannot be given. It has to be *done*. It is a process, not a collection of capital goods."[25]

In order to explain this creative process better, Jacobs uses as an example northern Georgia and its ability in recent years to attract numerous transplant industries from other parts of the country. The transplant industries have added jobs and money to the regional economy, but Jacobs argues that they have not really transformed the Atlanta area into a truly prosperous import-replacing region.[26] Rather than encouraging import replacement, most of the transplant industries have only added to the servicing and distribution functions of the Atlanta region. Although such activities add jobs and payrolls to the local economy, Jacobs tells us that they can easily fail to nurture the creative and interactive process of discovery that is essential to long-term wealth creation and sustained urban development. Jacobs's story of Lockheed's Marietta works, one of the largest manufacturing complexes in the entire southeastern United States, illustrates the reason for this result.[27]

Lockhead was founded as a fledgling enterprise based in Los Angeles.[28] During its early years, the company relied heavily on local suppliers and businesses to furnish equipment and to help develop new ideas and sources of capital.[29] The local city economy also provided employees and consumers for Lockheed's products and services.[30] These local people learned to apply their many talents and attention to a wide variety of work necessary to support the growing industry of which Lockheed was an increasingly important part. Such work and interaction is the breeding ground for new work and ideas that lead to dynamic city life and to a prosperous import-replacing economy. By the time Lockheed was able to move to northern Georgia several years later, however, the company was in many ways self-sufficient.[31] It supplied many of its own items, services, and skills that formerly had been furnished by independent suppliers in the Los Angeles region.[32] The company's marketing, servicing, and communications lines were so well developed that Lockheed could have placed a major manufacturing facility in almost any location.[33] Marietta, Georgia, was chosen, but the facility transplanted there was tied to the major enterprise still headed in Los Angeles.[34] In short, Lockheed's Marietta facility provided jobs, but it did not interact with the local city region as a source of supplies and services in the way that Lockheed originally had in Los Angeles. Lockheed did not help support local producers and thus failed to reproduce in northern Georgia, even in microcosm, the sort of dynamic and creative environment it had inspired in Los Angeles.[35]

In another example Jacobs discusses the Tennessee Valley Authority (TVA) and its inability to stimulate the emergence of an import-replacing city despite the investment of tremendous amounts of government money and resources.[36] She generally applauds the TVA administrators' skills and success in executing their mission and does not fault TVA itself for the continued poverty in the region.[37] Instead, she finds fault in the use of government loan, grant, and subsidy programs.[38] The many projects the TVA undertook in the region produced project-related jobs, but did not create significant numbers or kinds of city jobs necessary for the accumulation of excess capital.[39] The region, rather than developing local producers for local needs, continued to depend on imports.[40] Furthermore, nearly all development continued to be financed with capital generated from outside rather than within the region.[41] Thus, the government-related subsidies generated by the TVA temporarily helped to reduce unemployment and alleviate poverty. But rather than fostering import-replacing activities, subsidies merely provided additional funds for local people to import goods, services, and capital from outside the region.[42] As long as the region remained without significant import-replacing activities, it required continued subsidies to maintain its current economic standard of living.

Jacobs's analysis and examples have important implications for the use of co-financing arrangements in the drive for urban revitalization. The use of public assistance or financing in redevelopment projects would seem to require, at the very least, a selection of projects consistent with the goals of achieving or enhancing a city's import-replacing ability. This means that the projects must do more than provide an influx of short-term jobs and outside capital infusion. They must stimulate a dynamic interaction between local suppliers and producers that will enhance the city's export economy. Jacobs is telling us that export and import-replacing activities are the essential part of spontaneous interactive learning and creative discovery. Only when a city earns its own import funds and develops a diversified and versatile economy can it hope to achieve long-term economic success.

The current range of urban development and revitalization projects that some cities have undertaken hardly seems worthy of the task at hand. The subsidized development of downtown office buildings and hotels, or the desire to preserve historic structures by turning them into fast food and retail centers, is hardly the type of activity likely to bring forth long-term gains for a local city economy. In the short run, such projects might provide project-oriented jobs, as did the TVA, and they will generate a series of minimum wage retail and service jobs. There will also be new or renovated buildings for local politicians to point to as signs of progress, and an appearance of urban vitality will result from the short-term construction activity. Without a strong import-replacing economy, however, the new buildings may be merely shifting uses between different parts of the city or region rather than fostering long-term economic growth and creative interaction. And, while it may be a matter of pride for local residents to enhance the downtown skyline at the expense of the suburbs or other potential business locations, it becomes questionable whether such projects merit the use of public funds and resources.

For cities facing a decline in their industrial and commercial manufacturing bases, it hardly seems possible that economic prosperity will result from replacing skilled jobs and export capacity with a nonexport economy based on restaurants, shops, hotels, and numerous downtown attractions similar to those springing up like clones all across America. Nonetheless, for political reasons it seems that urban development and revitalization activities have taken this direction. These activities, when well orchestrated, can produce real and necessary changes for a local economy. As was illustrated by the Lockheed and TVA examples, however, the successful transplanting of specific industrial facilities to a city region or the use of government loans, grants, and subsidies cannot, in themselves, create a successful, import-replacing region.

Without the import replacement prerequisite, a city region has no foundation for a lasting period of economic growth and prosperity. The absence of strong export and import-replacing trade indicates the lack of a creative environment of interaction and discovery. Such a deficiency cannot support real long-term economic prosperity because prosperity and wealth, like individual liberty, are inevitably linked to the creative discovery process and spontaneous social order. Once this inherent link between the classical liberal conceptions of individual liberty and wealth is understood, it becomes apparent that current trends in urban development and revitalization are harmful for both liberty and prosperity. Jacobs illustrated this point well when she wrote about the process of urban development as a process of creative capital, a view consistent with the process of protecting individual liberty in classical liberal discourse concerning the relationship between law and economics.

Chapter 15
The Philosophical Constraints on Urban Development

Up to this point, discussion of urban development and revitalization has focused on describing the nature of urban development activities and their political and economic dynamics. A philosophical evaluation, however, is also important because the analysis of development activities raises a fundamental philosophical question about the effect these programs have on traditional notions of individual liberty and the relationship between the state and private enterprise in a capitalist society.[1] This section will focus on philosophical constraints on development activities, which have two primary foundations useful for a philosophical evaluation. The first foundation reflects an understanding of the proper and limited role of government in a capitalist society. The second involves the normative role of law in facilitating social order.

A capitalist society, in which private individuals own the means of production, provides a framework for the protection of individual liberty.[2] Individual liberty in this context refers to a view of social relationships that provides for personal autonomy over one's thoughts and actions.[3] This personal autonomy is not limitless, however, and the concept of individual freedom in a market economy or *laissez faire* social organization requires governmental restrictions of antisocial behavior that, if left unchecked, would disintegrate social cooperation and civilization.[4] In the absence of a commitment to anarchy, the difficulty lies in determining the extent to which government can properly restrict an individual's behavior while still preserving a free society based on individual liberty. This issue, of course, has been debated extensively elsewhere,[5] and the entire theoretical underpinnings of limited government will not be restated here. My purpose is rather to set out a framework for legal economic discourse concerning the protection of individual liberty and the boundaries of legitimate state action in urban development and revitalization.

From this philosophical perspective many urban development activities, as currently conceived, do run afoul of traditional classical liberal notions of government's legitimate role in a society based on the preservation of free enterprise and individual liberty. This is not to say that classical liberals would consider all governmental attempts to foster urban development and revitalization impermissible. On the contrary, there are ways in which urban development could be made more acceptable to classical liberals, and these will be addressed in the recommendations chapter. Before considering recommendations for structuring future development programs, however, one must understand the philosophical problems with current activities.

The first philosophical problem is the substitution of political means for economic means.[6] This substitution is harmful because it removes the decision-making process of resource allocation from the marketplace, which reflects impersonal individual value determinations, and replaces it with the personal dynamics of special interest groups. In this way, the state becomes the means by which one group of people can legally exploit other members of society. The political means, thus, allows special interest groups to use government power to fulfill personal gains unavailable to individuals or groups in the impersonal marketplace. This consequence is aggravated by the various forms of legal and economic discourse that reject natural rights and allow the state unlimited activity.

In contrast to other, more statist views of law and economics, classical liberalism prefers individuals acting through the marketplace to make resource allocations and discourages attempts to circumvent the market process by government intervention, unless such intervention is required to assure individual liberty and human dignity. Although it may be possible for classical liberal theory to support government programs providing individuals with minimal levels of health care, shelter, and food, it is hard to see how such an approach can justify support for broadly based subsidies to one real estate developer, project, or city over another.

The first objection of classical liberals to many current urban development and revitalization activities is based on a simple principle. If Indianapolis or any other city is really worth investing in, then private developers will make that investment without having taxpayers subsidize their cost and risk. To the extent that private investors are not willing to invest in Indianapolis or any other city, they will invest in an alternative location or project, presumably more valuable because they are willing to invest without a subsidy. After all, hotels, shopping centers, office buildings, and restaurants are not like dams or airports. The former are types of investments in which private enterprise always has invested. Thus, the primary objective of many current urban development and revitalization arrangements is not to encourage activities that otherwise would not occur, but rather to encourage these activities in locations apparently deemed undesirable for investment by private parties. Because these subsidies result in public misallocations of resources—allocations blurring public/private distributions and contrary to those determined by individuals in the marketplace—they are objectionable.

The second objection of classical liberals to current urban development efforts is twofold. First, promoting a program that results in some form of governmental ownership of many of a city's most prominent office, hotel, and retail properties eliminates the impartial decision-making ability of local city officials. Second, it covertly reduces the ability of independent private capital to act as a check on government power.

Local city officials lose their ability to make impartial decisions regarding the direction of future growth when they have already staked millions of dollars of public funds and their own political futures on specific downtown projects. Having invested, for instance, in a particular shopping center or office building complex, the city has a vested interest in assuring some degree of financial success for the project, even if that means using its police powers to prevent future entry of more desirable, competitive private projects.[7] Assuring a project's success also may mean additional subsidies to support already "sunk funds" if the market response to the project is less than anticipated. An additional consequence of these subsidies, even when the city does not block market entry, is that the unsubsidized private developer may be unable to compete as a result of the comparative advantage his or her competitors gain by their use of public funds. In any of these situations the problem is clear. Expecting impartiality from a city government that owns profit-making enterprises is akin to putting Exxon Corporation in charge of the American oil industry and allowing it to oversee the activities of all its competitors, real or perceived.

The ability of private capital to act as a check on government power is a function of private capital's diversity and independence from the government. In a system of free enterprise, diverse individuals within the society are allowed to accumulate wealth and use it to support challenges to the exercise of government power.[8] In this way, private sources of wealth place resources that can serve as a check against the state beyond the state's reach.[9] To a certain extent, current urban development activities covertly reduce this private source of capital and its ability to check the power of the state. This occurs because co-financing and public/private partnerships reduce diversity of wealth by subsidizing select developers and preventing market entry by others. It also reduces the independence of private capital by linking the selected developer's interests to those of the city. Consequently, the blurring between public and private property rights contributes to the diminished ability of one power source to act as a counterbalancing check on the other. Ultimately, the destruction of this delicate balance between competing power sources results in the collapse of the creative and spontaneous environment necessary for long-term prosperity and wealth generation.

A third classical liberal objection to current urban development activities is that a fundamental prerequisite to efficient resource allocation, in a market-oriented economy, is the availability of information concerning the relative costs of alternative actions. Philosophically, this information is important because the expression of individual liberty through the marketplace is based in part on the premise that people are reasoning beings who will make rational economic choices based on the information available to them.[10] Thus, it is necessary to assess urban development programs from the perspective of their current ability to provide the public with adequate information.

Many current urban development activities benefit from the use of the political means which allows funds to be raised from a much wider population than that likely to receive the benefit of a particular project. The process of mixing sources of public funds and playing local, state, and federal income sources against each other makes it nearly impossible for the average urban resident to assess the value of a given project relative to its cost. This fund-mixing process is also undesirable because it obscures market information and hinders individual decision making. And the lack of definite information with which to judge a government official's performance makes him or her less accountable.

In addition to these objections that are based primarily on consideration of the proper and limited role of government in a free society, there are grounds for objection based on the normative role of law in facilitating social order. They rely on the notion that in a free society affirmative enforcement of all laws at all times is impractical, if not impossible, and that limited law enforcement resources require a legal system to depend substantially on voluntary compliance.[11] In order for this normative acceptance of laws to occur, a significant segment of the populace must view the enforcing state and its operative legal system as legitimate.[12]

Michael Hoeflich has considered this problem of normative acceptance of the law in conjunction with voluntary compliance under federal tax laws.[13] His analysis reveals that it is possible for a set of legal rules, such as the tax code, to lose its normative value over time. As this happens, people no longer feel obligated to pay their taxes, but rather treat the tax laws as a game in which they match wits with government bureaucrats.[14] In part, Hoeflich's observed decline in voluntary compliance can be attributed to a popular perception that the tax code, as structured, has long been merely a compilation of special interest benefits and burdens rather than a principled approach to sharing the costs of government.[15] As a result, the tax laws are less easily accepted, and this, of course, leads to a reduction in the tendency towards "law abidingness."[16] Ultimately, this process can lead to the disintegration of social order when the legal structure is no longer viewed as legitimate.

This analysis is equally applicable to considerations of many urban development activities. For instance, a typical response to objections against using project-specific zoning and financing to encourage development in downtown Indianapolis is: So what if Indianapolis gets a few dollars? Chicago, New York, Louisville, and other cities also get a few dollars, maybe even more than their fair share. In other words, the political and economic dynamics of outcome-specific planning and development appear to make such activities subject to the same problems as tax laws. To the extent that outcome-specific planning and financing arrangements are perceived as commitments to special political interest groups rather than as principled approaches to genuine social problems, they will lose their normative acceptance. The legitimacy of such urban development activities and, ultimately, the legitimacy of the political structure that supports such interest-oriented legislation will be called into question.

It becomes clear, at least to the classical liberal, that current outcome-specific planning and financing activities raise fundamental philosophical questions about urban development. The degree to which government should be involved in private market activities and the degree to which these activities affect principles necessary for social order are both called into question.

The transformation, therefore, of legal economic discourse into one that speaks freely of public/private partnerships, co-financing, and mutual cooperation in urban planning, validates norms that are antilibertarian (anti-individualist), rejects natural rights, and ultimately destroys the delicate societal balance necessary for the preservation of the creative discovery process. Consequently, individual liberty, in the classical liberal sense, is destroyed and replaced with a conception of liberty for the community or liberty for the state. Experts are summoned to plan and manage the seemingly anarchistic marketplace. In return, the individual is provided with a less creative, less expressive, and less dynamic environment in which personal political connections replace formerly impersonal market exchanges. The transformation is profound and it puts power into the hands of the state, which, by virtue of its monopoly on the coercive exercise of public power, presents a far more devastating risk to individual liberty than any perceived weakness in the operation of the free market.

The key to understanding this problem is simple. It is the same one that emerges in discussions of commercial monopoly. Although some legal economists argue that monopoly is bad because it is inefficient and it does not make good use of scarce resources, I have argued that monopoly is fundamentally harmful because it lacks a sufficient counterbalancing power source.[17] Monopoly, in a metaphorical sense, embodies the problems of the unlimited state, wherein individuals are subject to the whims or despotism of the sole exerciser of power. Monopoly is harmful because it destroys viable alternatives, it represses creativity, and thus undermines individual autonomy. In this sense, the collapse of the public/private sphere distinction in urban development leads to the destruction of the delicate balance necessary to preserve freedom.

Chapter 16
Recommendations for Proper Urban Development

Having described both the political and the economic dynamics of outcome-specific planning and financing activities, together with their philosophical constraints, I will now consider recommendations for future action in real estate law and urban development. Classical liberal philosophy provides a useful approach in formulating recommendations because it provides a method of analysis for legal economic discourse that encompasses notions of natural law, inalienable rights, and the commitment of limited government to supplying and protecting the moral and normative imperatives of human dignity. It is important to understand that classical liberalism does not take an amoral approach to economic analysis such as that used and advocated by conservative legal economists. Nor does it simply adhere to the false scientific principle of wealth maximization as the ultimate morality of the marketplace. Classical liberalism requires a constant and continuous dialogue on the subject of human dignity that may lead to the determination of government's proper role in the protection of individual liberty within the context of an organized social structure.[1]

Classical liberalism, therefore, does not proscribe planning and financing activities. On the contrary, it provides a framework for taking into account the factors discussed in this book and using them to formulate a perspective or approach consistent with the requirements of a free market economy. A free market economy, in the classical liberal sense, is concerned with both market efficiency and preservation of individual liberty through a moral and limited approach to government. Similarly, the free market metaphor and classical liberal theory provide a structure for legal economic discourse that promotes underlying norms and values considered essential to individual liberty. The recommendations for future planning and financing activity that follow are consistent with classical liberal views on the relationship between law, economics, and the state.

For classical liberals, government's proper and legitimate role is limited to those activities necessary to correct instances of market failure and protect human rights essential to the concept of individual liberty. Government arguably has a proper role to play in certain planning and financing activities. Permissible planning and financing activities, however, must proceed by general rules and comply with two essential requirements. First, the projects selected for development must be of a type not typically produced in the private marketplace. Market failure exists because natural market forces do not provide for adequate investment in the desired type of project. Second, the projects selected must serve a function essential to preserving the human dignity of individuals within the society. Both these requirements must be accomplished within a context that, nonetheless, supports the continued functioning of the private market while assuring the potential for the growth of more dynamic, import-replacing city regions.

These general criteria are put forth as norms that should be incorporated as central elements in any dialogue concerning urban development and revitalization. They are guidelines for both legal and economic discourse expressly recognized and embodying a concern for all of the specific value functions outlined in this book concerning classical liberal theory. Although seemingly simple, they are meant to direct the structure and content of legal economic discourse. The validation of a particular approach to urban development and revitalization must, consequently, involve a persuasive dialogue that conforms to the guidelines and value structures of classical liberal discourse and are meant to have a substantive impact on the future direction of urban revitalization and development.

On the basis of these general criteria, many current planning and financing activities seem impermissible. This conclusion is true even though government has a legitimate role to play in promoting urban redevelopment. Subsidizing shopping centers, hotels, office buildings, and restaurants, for instance, is hardly compatible with limiting government planning and financing activities to the types of projects involving inadequate investment in the private market. Private enterprise has always invested in shopping centers, hotels, office buildings, and restaurants, and these projects continue to be the focus of substantial private investment. It also seems difficult to contend seriously that subsidizing these particular types of projects is necessary to assure the protection of human dignity and individual liberty. People

living in the street without food, shelter, or minimal medical care
hardly need a room at a luxury hotel or additional high-priced cloth-
ing boutiques.[2]

Supporters of planning and financing for shopping centers, hotels,
office buildings, and restaurants typically respond to these challenges
with counterarguments. They argue that despite continued private
investment in these types of real estate projects, the private marketplace is unable to assure that these projects are located properly.
Outcome-specific planning and financing proponents assert that un-
derinvestment in the downtown urban center is an indication of market failure. This lack of investment, however, is not market failure.
The private marketplace is allocating resources to the production of
the very types of projects the city seeks to subsidize. The location
question is merely a disagreement as to where private capital should
be invested within a particular market or city region. Investors using
their own resources are bound to seek the best return for their investment. Their choice of location, therefore, should be at least as
good as, if not better than, the location choices of politicians seeking
to spend someone else's money.

A city confronting a decline in its downtown urban center should
examine the political and economic reasons for it. Excessive taxation
or zoning restrictions may be responsible, or a decline in police efforts to control crime and provide for safety on the streets. These
reasons, however, require political attention to correct their specific
causes. Outcome-specific planning and financing as a mechanism for
subsidizing particular special interests and selected real estate projects cannot lead to the creation of a sustained and vibrant urban
economy because they do little or nothing to enhance the city's creative import-replacing capacity.

A second challenge to criticism of current urban development
strategies is based on the asserted value of trickle-down job creation.
Planning for and investing in downtown shopping centers, hotels, office buildings, and restaurants is supposed to create job opportunities
for the unskilled and unemployed. The development of such projects
undoubtedly generates a number of unskilled and low-paying jobs,
but there are several problems with the asserted value of subsidizing
such efforts. First and foremost is that these subsidies suffer from all
the problems associated with Jane Jacobs's analysis of transplant industries and government subsidies.[3] Transplant industries and government subsidies may be able to provide temporary relief for the
unemployed or the impoverished, but they can neither develop nor
sustain an import-replacing city because they do not emerge from the
spontaneous and creative interaction of urban life. Although such

programs result in the ability to purchase jobs and capital, they fail because urban development is not merely a collection of capital goods; it is a process. Thus, they fail to create the dynamic urban economy that is necessary for true long-term economic growth and prosperity.[4] Without the ultimate development of an enhanced import-replacing city economy, trickle-down job creation is of nominal value. The subsidized urban economy lacks the true economic foundations of an integrated city region and, therefore, is unable to develop the necessary economic opportunities that will allow unskilled workers to advance within the market structure.[5] This is not to say that no benefit accrues to the unemployed from these projects, but it does suggest that policies that encourage import-replacing activities rather than those that merely subsidize current selected projects can better provide trickle-down job opportunities.

The second problem with the trickle-down assertion is that current projects result in urban gentrification, which can have negative effects equal to or greater than any asserted benefits to the unskilled and unemployed people living in or near the downtown center.[6] Gentrification occurs when middle-class and upper-income people are attracted to the downtown area because of the increase in upscale shopping, eating, and working opportunities.[7] In the process, low-income people are displaced either by the acquisition of their property for selected real estate projects or by rising rents and land costs.[8] Despite potential increases in the downtown urban tax base, the disruption of established neighborhoods and the dislocation of the urban poor represent a social cost that classical liberals must consider in evaluating current government-sponsored urban development programs. As a consequence, the alleged value of trickle-down job opportunities is offset, at least in part, by the problem of gentrification.

The third problem with the trickle-down assertion is that it ignores simple economic realities about job creation. As long as money is not stuffed in a mattress, it will be used, and jobs will be created with that money.[9] For instance, the use by a city of one million dollars in tax revenues to subsidize a business that employs a number of people means that the one million dollars that would have been available for individuals to invest in the marketplace has been invested for them by the city.[10] Individuals in possession of the money would have purchased more goods and services than they otherwise were able to and thereby would have increased job opportunities. All things being equal, the one million dollars is still only one million dollars and the jobs created by one project merely mean the loss of potential jobs elsewhere. This economic reality relates back to the first problem discussed in connection with the trickle-down assertion and supports the conclusion that trickle-down benefits, resulting from policies that favor creative import-replacing activities, would be greater than the benefits generated by current practices of planning and financing specific real estate projects.

Ultimately, the arguments in favor of subsidizing the construction of shopping centers, hotels, office buildings, and restaurants through outcome-specific planning and financing must be viewed as special interest arguments used to justify the use of political means. The unsupported assertion that the location problem for such real estate projects is, in itself, evidence of market failure merely covers the preference of special interests for a different location for resource employment. Similarly, the actual benefits from trickle-down job creation, at best, are much less valuable than those proclaimed by the special interests that will benefit from construction of the subsidized real estate projects. The supporters of many current outcome-specific planning and financing activities demonstrate the typical attitudes and practices analyzed here. Although their personal objectives may be completely rational and predictable as a matter of self-interested economics or public choice theory, their conduct is normatively undesirable. By recognizing the normative faults and consequences of these special interest programs, one can begin to appreciate the need to reformulate the criteria by which we judge these activities. A normative change in our views of these programs can lead to a recalculation of their economic desirability and can result in the promotion of different values and norms.

Given this classical liberal perspective on many current urban development activities, it is now possible to discuss specific recommendations. These will follow in three parts. First, the permissible types of projects for government-sponsored planning and finance will be outlined. Second, guidelines for government participation will be established. Third, recommendations will be made concerning alternative approaches to urban development that would improve the urban economic environment in ways consistent with creative import-replacing activities.

Permissible projects for government-sponsored planning and financing, within a general rules approach, must satisfy a two-part test by being the type of project the private market fails to provide and by serving a function essential to preserving individual human dignity. On these grounds, a classical liberal must reject government sponsorship of shopping centers, hotels, office buildings, and restaurants. In order to meet this two-part test, a completely different list of projects must be developed. An outline of acceptable projects would include the following: low-income housing to provide basic shelter for the poor, day care facilities for low-income people and the underemployed to allow them to engage more fully in the marketplace, and job training and retraining facilities to develop the working potential of the poor and to retrain workers displaced by the dynamics of the local employment market.

The projects outlined above are examples of projects the private market is unlikely to invest in because the poor, unemployed, and underemployed lack the purchasing power to make such investments profitable. These are not projects in which substantial investment is occurring elsewhere. Rather, they are projects that would receive no substantial private investment but for the assistance of government. Because the market truly fails to produce these projects, government-sponsored planning and financing activities could be justified as one method of assisting in these projects' development.

Under the second part of the two-part test of acceptability, each of the acceptable projects is designed to address the basic and fundamental rights of individuals. These projects raise the issue of government subsidies to a certain class of people when the private market fails to allocate resources for their use. This is fundamentally a moral question that cannot be resolved by simple utilitarian cost-benefit analysis. An appeal to economic analysis that fails to incorporate an understanding of moral philosophy and inalienable rights fails to serve a valuable purpose in resolving many of our nation's most pressing social problems. The focus on morality in economic analysis is consistent with the classical liberal philosophy. Access to both basic shelter and job training opportunities are within the confines of reasonable expectations for individual liberty and human dignity. They are, in modern American society, the fundamental equivalents of Adam Smith's concern for providing a basic education to every individual regardless of wealth. The obligation to provide such services falls on the government precisely because it is a fundamental reason *for* government, it is essential to individual liberty, and it is unlikely to be provided by the private marketplace. Thus, projects that aid the poor, such as those outlined above, are acceptable for government sponsorship.

Even if one disagreed with this proposition, however, it would be incumbent upon the dissenter, in a classical liberal discourse, to demonstrate that no moral basis supports providing such minimal services to the poor. And even if that demonstration were made, it would not justify the current outcome-specific planning and financing of shopping centers, hotels, office buildings, and restaurants that bear little or no relationship to the protection of basic fundamental rights.

The change in the direction of government planning and financing activities suggested by the outline of acceptable projects is essential to preserving the proper and limited role of government in a free society. By requiring that government, acting by general rules, limit its activities to those cases in which there is true market failure *and* in which there is a moral basis to protect an individual's liberty, the role of limited government is preserved. Government action in these situations is no different from government action in providing for public roads or other infrastructure and service needs. When private individuals cannot profitably provide infrastructure and services important to the concept of social order, economists generally have accepted a governmental role. The recommended reordering of urban development activities would be consistent with the traditionally accepted principles of limited government.

An acceptable project requires government planning and financing activities to be restricted by certain guidelines, which have three requirements. First, guidelines must delimit the liability attached to a city acting in a public/private partnership or co-financing capacity in order to complete an acceptable project with a private developer. Second, in order to preserve individual liberty in a capitalist society, meaningful constitutional limitations must be placed on government-sponsored activities. Third, adequate information must be available for assessing the costs and benefits of government-sponsored projects and making government more accountable for its conduct.

Local governments engaged in public/private partnerships or co-financing activities as part of their urban development strategy ought to be held to the same standards of liability and obligation as a private developer or lender. Governmental activities in this area are similar to their private market counterparts. Therefore, local governments should not enjoy lower standards of commercially reasonable conduct. Making local government stand on equal footing with private developers chosen for co-financing activities also encourages a more business-like approach to the construction and completion of projects. It should also make the full cost of engaging in co-financing activities more apparent to local government officials and their constituents and thereby provide a more fully informed decision-making process.

Constitutional limitations on government planning and financing activities must be of substance rather than merely form. A free society based on a limited governmental role must require sound justifications for employing the government's power in the pursuit of economic development. Current constitutional limitations on government activities that restrict competition in the private sector and employ both public funds and the power of eminent domain are easily circumvented. Current trends indicate a growing acceptance of broadly defined public welfare justifications that can permit government activity in the private real estate development sector of the economy. In order to prevent eventual full scale governmental intrusion into the traditional activities of the private marketplace, government assistance to private developers must be limited to those types of projects previously outlined as acceptable. Constitutional restrictions ought to prevent outcome-specific planning or financing of shopping centers, hotels, office buildings, and restaurants because these projects do not involve traditional grounds for government activity. Justifications for using governmental powers, such as condemnation, ought to be limited to those few cases in which a market failure exists and the project is essential to protect individual human dignity. This limitation, of course, would drastically restrict the type of activities government could support through use of its police and purse power, but in a free society based on a capitalist structure, the role of government should be limited.

Adequate information is essential for assessing the costs and benefits of a government-sponsored urban development project and for making government more accountable for its conduct. Providing information, however, means more than publishing expected budget and return items in the local newspaper. This, of course, is not to say that such publication is without merit, but only that it does not provide full information or demonstrate the significance of cost items. In order to insure better information for the decision-making process, two requirements must be met. First, to receive the primary benefits of the completed project the city should internalize as best as possible the entire cost of an urban development project. Second, to the extent that nonlocal funds are used in an acceptable urban development project, access to the outside funds should be linked to a local commitment to facilitate creative import-replacing activity.

Internalizing the cost of a co-financing project would require a city to finance its own activities, just as an unsubsidized private individual must do in buying goods or services in the private marketplace. Local politicians should engage in a convincing dialogue in order to get sufficient local support for their proposed projects. Without a source of nonlocal funds or cross-subsidies upon which to draw, local residents would carry the full cost of the city project. In this way, co-financing arrangements would be subject to close scrutiny because local taxpayers would see the exact result of the government's use of their money. Every individual would be able to see exactly what other projects or investments were given up in order to pursue the selected one. This would allow for a more informed decision-making process and would give substance to the notion that, as the potential recipients of an improved urban environment, the local residents should be willing to pay the full cost of the benefits they hope to enjoy.

In a less than ideal world, it may be impossible to avoid the politics that make nonlocal funds available to cities seeking to engage in specific government-sponsored urban development projects. It may even be appropriate to have outside funds made available to a city in certain limited circumstances. A city may be extremely poor or may be experiencing dramatic changes in its local economy that place many residents on unemployment and welfare. Such a city would be unable to afford certain limited but otherwise permissible projects. As long as planning and financing activities are limited to projects that benefit low-income people, the use of nonlocal funds can be justified provided those funds are linked to the encouragement of creative import-replacing activity. Linkage is important because, ultimately, subsidies for urban development projects remain just that, regardless of their origin, and in order to foster long-term economic growth and opportunity, a city must escape its need for subsidies and develop a strong and dynamic local economy. Thus, for instance, the receipt of federal funds may be predicated on the city's elimination or reduction of negative business restrictions, such as rent controls or excessive zoning requirements that discourage investment. In this way, nonlocal funds are made available at the expense of eliminating bad local economic policy, rather than as a way to use outside funds to offset the undesirable effects of local special interest legislation.[11]

Given these recommendations for acceptable projects, a city still has ways in which to encourage commercial economic development. The methods employed must be compatible with the need to facilitate creative import-replacing activities within the city region. Furthermore, the steps taken to encourage economic activity should be of a general rather than outcome-specific nature. In other words, government policy should be expressed by general rules applicable to all people, rather than by specific rules designed to create incentives for specific enterprises or special interest groups.[12]

Instead of local politicians trying to second-guess the marketplace or create specific incentives for select special interest groups, the process of general rules should be aimed at enhancing the economic environment of the entire city. Examples of this type of program include across-the-board reductions in local taxes, streamlining and reducing the discretionary nature of planning and zoning regulations, and expending city revenue on traditional infrastructure and services, such as roads, which enhance all types of economic activity. A city also might seek to enhance its economic environment by actively promoting competitive reductions in statewide income taxes, promoting right-to-work laws, or reducing unnecessary economic regulation of business. Finally, a city might engage in a study of its strengths and weaknesses and expend revenue to promote its economic advantages through furnishing information to the private marketplace. Such urban policies would promote an environment conducive to creative import-replacing activities necessary for achieving economic growth and, at the same time, protect the free flow of capital, technology, labor, and ideas.

Acceptable types of projects for urban development are limited and can be justified only when there is true market failure, and the government's involvement in correcting the market failure is within the traditional, limited confines of activity necessary to insure individual liberty. These requirements dramatically reduce the problems associated with the use of political means. When properly implemented, these requirements reduce governmental intrusion into the marketplace and allow individual preferences to enjoy the largest possible expression consistent with the needs of society and individual liberty. When properly restricted, government can protect individual liberty and human dignity while avoiding complete capture by special interest groups bent on employing the power of the state to exploit others in ways not possible in the competitive marketplace.

The recommendations above dramatically reduce the philosophical problems with promoting government ownership in a society that, in pursuit of individual liberty, should be committed to a capitalistic structure in which the means of production are owned by private individuals. As long as government-sponsored planning and financing arrangements are limited to the types of projects recommended here, the government will not intrude on significant private market activity and, therefore, should be able to maintain its ability to make impartial decisions concerning urban planning and development. At the same time, people engaged in private market activities will be forced to continue to compete in the marketplace without linking the financial success of their commercial projects to the city's ownership interest, and this should preserve a greater independence and diversity in the debate over urban policy. Likewise, to the extent that individuals appreciate more clearly the costs and benefits of their activity they will make better decisions, and all actors, including the government, will be made more accountable.

To the extent that these recommendations preserve the limited function of government and provide a moral and philosophical framework for engaging in a legal economic discourse concerning urban policy, they are less likely to lose their normative value. These recommendations represent a reasoned and principled approach to urban revitalization and are not merely an attempt to expand the grab bag of subsidies available for special interest groups. Additionally, they are based on traditional classical liberal values of individual liberty, free enterprise, and a government role limited to instances of market failure and protection of fundamental moral values concerning individual human dignity. Consequently, they are normatively more desirable in the long run than many current urban development practices.

These recommendations are consistent with classical liberal philosophy, as well as with Jane Jacobs's observations about the necessary path to long-term economic growth, prosperity, and opportunity. Only through enhanced import-replacing activity can true economic progress continue, for government loans, grants, and subsidies can provide only short-term relief for urban problems without correcting the structural and ideological difficulties underlying these problems.

Finally, these recommendations are significant because they focus on general rather than specific outcomes in the legal, political, and economic arrangements that govern urban life. A return to general principles in planning and zoning law would greatly reduce the current emphasis on discretionary action through the political process. Similarly, the limited nature of project financing recommended in this chapter will reduce the incentive for private individuals to look to governmental police and purse power in an effort to enhance unfairly their relative position in the competitive marketplace. Only by reducing the increasing scope of state power can our society overcome the dynamics of the current political process. Only by limiting the state to action within a framework of general rules and principles can we preserve the dynamic give and take of a properly functioning checks and balance system. And, only by a return to classical liberal values can we maintain the impersonal and spontaneous evolution of our society, an evolution that seems in every way preferable to personal influence in the political process and the return to serfdom in the age of state-sponsored capitalism.

Chapter17
Conclusion

The trend toward ever-increasing statism is not the product of any organized conspiracy. It is the product of a complex social dynamic that is fueled by a misplaced faith in scientific discourse and in planning. It leads to an overreliance on the exercise of state power for the achievement of personal goals and ambitions.

It is time to question the current direction of American social, political, and economic conduct; to reevaluate the merits and values by which American society functions; and to reconsider the norms promoted by the current transformation of American legal economic discourse.

Looking closely at almost any part of American social and cultural fabric will reveal deep insights into the nature and quality of our national character. I have focused on legal, economic, and political arrangements affecting urban development and revitalization. My observations disclose characteristics reflected in, and reflections of, the society around us. They are potentially devastating for those who retain aspirations of individual liberty and freedom within a free society concerned for the human dignity of each of its members. American society has become so driven by a myopic quest for the visible results of its materialistic designs that it fails to see how the end product of its labor may promote an ideological framework that changes the structure and content of legal economic discourse, thereby undercutting the values and norms of natural and inalienable rights, human dignity, and individual autonomy once held dearly.

In their quest for new office buildings, shopping centers, and restaurants, cities such as Indianapolis have engaged in new legal, economic, and political arrangements that will have dramatic long-term effects on the cultural character of the community and the nation. The world as it is cannot exist for long in contradiction to the way we perceive it, or want it to be, without ultimately leading us to reevaluate our values or reconfigure the reality around us. Thus, cities such as Indianapolis must face the consequences of individualist and free market rhetoric contradicted by substantial central planning and state ownership. The transformation in legal and economic thinking, which evidences itself in the legal arrangements emerging in Indianapolis and other cities, reveals an ideological shift that affects both the structure and the content of legal and economic discourse. This shift has real and substantive consequences for the protection and promotion of certain underlying values and norms. The legal and economic discourse that validates extensive public intervention into the private marketplace, promotes extensive governmentally sponsored planning and discretionary approval of real estate development, employs specific outcome-oriented legislation, and rejects the impersonality of individual empowerment in the free marketplace thereby undermining individual freedom, creativity, and spontaneous social order. It is fundamentally inconsistent with the values and norms of classical liberal theory no matter how many office buildings, restaurants, shopping centers, and hotels are constructed over the philosophical ashes of natural rights, human dignity, and individual liberty.

In the end, either the American people will have to give in to the statist ideology of their political, economic, and legal leadership or that leadership will have to be changed. For the sake of the continued prosperity of the human spirit and of the individual liberty required to make that spirit soar, I can only hope that this book will lead its readers to select the latter form of change.

Notes

Chapter 1

1. For one attempt to provide an account of the corresponding decline in liberalism, see A. Ekirch, THE DECLINE OF AMERICAN LIBERALISM (1967).

2. *See* J. Jacobs, CITIES AND THE WEALTH OF NATIONS—PRINCIPLES OF ECONOMIC LIFE (1984); J. Jacobs, THE ECONOMY OF CITIES (1969); J. Jacobs, THE DEATH AND LIFE OF GREAT AMERICAN CITIES (1961).

3. *See* R. Malloy, LAW AND ECONOMICS—A COMPARATIVE APPROACH TO THEORY AND PRACTICE (1990).

4. *See* Malloy, *A Sign of the Times—Law and Semiotics*, 65 TULANE L. REV. (1990) [hereinafter Malloy, SIGNS]; Malloy, *Is Law and Economics Moral? Humanistic Economics and a Classical Liberal Critique of Posner's Economic Analysis*, 24 VAL. U.L. REV. 147 (1990); Malloy, *The Limits of "Science" in Legal Discourse—A Reply to Posner*, 24 VAL. U.L. REV. 175 (1990).

5. *See* Malloy, SIGNS, *supra* note 4; R. Kevelson, THE LAW AS A SYSTEM OF SIGNS (1988); R. Kevelson, FOUNDATIONS OF SEMIOTICS (1987).

6. R. Duckworth, J. Simmons & R. McNulty, THE ENTREPRENEURIAL AMERICAN CITY 6–8 (1986). Reprinted and distributed by the Department of Housing and Urban Development, this book specifically praises Indianapolis.

7. L. Levathes, *Indianapolis: City on the Rebound*, 172, NATIONAL GEOGRAPHIC 230–59 (Aug. 1987).

8. D. Jackson, *Indianapolis: A Born-Again Hoosier Diamond in the Rust*, SMITHSONIAN 70–80 (June 1987).

9. R. Bamberger & D. Parham, *Leveraging Amenity Infrastructure—Indianapolis's Economic Development Strategy*, 43 URBAN LAND 12–18 (Nov. 1984).

10. F. Maier, *A Rust-Belt Relic's New Shine*, NEWSWEEK, Sept. 9, 1985, at 26.

Chapter 2

1. *See* Mandelker, *Public Entrepreneurship: A Legal Primer*, 15 REAL EST. L.J. 3 (1986). *See also* R. Duckworth, J. Simmons & R. McNulty, THE ENTREPRENEURIAL AMERCIAN CITY 6–8 (1986) [hereinafter Duckworth].

2. *See* Duckworth, *supra* note 1; L. Levathes, *Indianapolis: City on the Rebound*, 172 NATIONAL GEOGRAPHIC 230–59 (Aug. 1987); D. Jackson, *Indianapolis: A Born-Again Hoosier Diamond in the Rust*, SMITHSONIAN 70–80 (1987); R. Bamberger & D. Parham, *Leveraging Amenity Infrastructure—Indianapolis's*

Economic Development Strategy, 43 URBAN LAND 12–18 (Nov. 1984); F. Maier, *A Rust-Belt Relic's New Shine,* NEWSWEEK, Sept. 9, 1985, at 26.

3. I spent three and a half years in Indiana as an undergraduate at Purdue University and three years as a faculty member of the Indiana University Law School in Indianapolis. During those three years as a faculty member, I spent considerable time talking to people about the city and downtown development activities.

4. For example, I was interviewed by the INDIANAPOLIS STAR for a story concerning a major downtown mall that the city wanted to help finance. At the time the state legislature was hotly debating ways to subsidize the mall. I asked the reporter when the story would run, and he responded that the analysis of the mall with pro and con opinions would not appear until *after* the legislature voted on the issue. It seemed no coincidence that the paper had up until then written predominantly prodevelopment articles. The report that eventually came out after a favorable legislative vote was in the Business Section of the paper as an *Extra* Feature. *See* INDIANAPOLIS STAR, May 12, 1987, at 23–27.

5. *See* CITIES REBORN 28 (R. Levitt ed. 1987).

6. *Id.* at 35–37.

7. *Id.* at 60.

8. *Id.* at 69–92.

9. *Id.* at 106–20.

10. *Id.* at 120–27.

11. *Id.*

12. *Id.*

13. *Id.* at 127–30.

14. *Id.*

15. *Id.* at 154.

16. *Id.* at 193–98.

17. *Id.*

18. *Id.*

Chapter 3

1. *See* F. Hayek, THE CONSTITUTION OF LIBERTY 397–417 (1960) [hereinafter Hayek, LIBERTY].

2. *See id.* at 397–98; M. Friedman, CAPITALISM AND FREEDOM 5–6 (1962 reissued 1982) [hereinafter Friedman, CAPITALISM].

3. *See* Friedman, CAPITALISM, *supra* note 2, at 4–6.

4. Hayek, LIBERTY, *supra* note 1, at 400–401.

5. For a general historical account of Adam Smith, see J. Rae, LIFE OF ADAM SMITH (1895); E.G. West, ADAM SMITH–THE MAN AND HIS WORKS (1976) [hereinafter West, ADAM SMITH]. As these histories point out Smith was a scholar in multiple disciplines. He taught and wrote in the areas of English literature, logic, moral philosophy, natural theology, ethics, jurisprudence, and political expediency. Smith was more than a simple political economist. His best-known works are A. Smith, AN INQUIRY INTO THE NATURE AND CAUSES OF THE WEALTH OF NATIONS (E. Cannon ed. 1976; first published in 1776, now in two volumes) [hereinafter Smith, WEALTH OF NATIONS], and A. Smith, THE THEORY OF MORAL SENTIMENTS (E. West ed. 1976; first pub-

lished in 1759) [hereinafter Smith, MORAL SENTIMENTS]. In addition to these well-known works, Smith was also responsible for A. Smith, ESSAYS ON PHILOSOPHICAL SUBJECTS (J. Bryce & W.P.D. Wightman eds. 1980) [hereinafter Smith, ESSAYS]; A. Smith, LECTURES ON JURISPRUDENCE (R. Meek, D. Raphael & L. Stein eds. 1978) [hereinafter Smith, LECTURES]; A. Smith, LECTURES ON RHETORIC AND BELLES LETTERS (J. Bryce ed. 1983) [hereinafter Smith, RHETORIC].

Smith, ESSAYS is an interesting collection of works. It includes essays on such topics as astronomy, ancient physics, ancient logic and metaphysics, the external senses, the imitative arts, music, dance, poetry, and English and Italian verse. Included among the essays is Smith's notable work "The History of Astronomy," pages 32–105. This was one of Smith's first major works elaborating his view of philosophy, and gives some early indications of how he would derive a theory of spontaneous social order:

> Philosophy is the science of the connecting principles of nature. Nature, after the largest experience that common observation can acquire, seems to abound with events which appear solitary and incoherent with all that go before them, which therefore disturb the easy movement of the imagination; which make its ideas succeed each other, if one may say so, by irregular starts and sallies; and which thus tend, in some measure, to introduce those confusions and distractions we formerly mentioned. Philosophy, by representing the invisible chains which bind together all these disjointed objects, endeavours to introduce order into this chaos of jarring and discordant appearances, to allay this tumult of the imagination, and to restore it, when it surveys the great revolutions of the universe, to that tone of tranquillity and composure, which is both most agreeable in itself, and most suitable to its nature. (*Id.* at 45–46 [footnote omitted])

Smith, LECTURES is based on authenticated lecture note materials of two separate students of Adam Smith, one covering Smith's lectures during 1762–1763 and the other dated 1766. These student notes have been carefully reviewed with respect to other known works of Smith and they are believed to reflect accurately Smith's lectures on the subject. It should be noted that student notes of the time were basically a verbatim transcript of lectures because there were no books for the course.

The notes for the lectures in Smith, RHETORIC come from the time when Smith was lecturing on this subject during 1762–1763. The lectures demonstrate Smith's knowledge of writing and style. He taught students how to structure arguments, advocate views, and write in an appealing manner. He included discussions of legal reasoning (*id.* at 171–79) and legal oration (*id.* at 179–84). In one section, Smith explained the origin of language. In describing its historical and social evolution, he tracks similar discussion of the development of law and social order found in his LECTURES ON JURISPRUDENCE (*id.* at 203–26). Basically, economic progress and the increasing complexity of social interaction require an ever-increasing complexity and formalism in the development of language (*id*). Elsewhere in this book, Smith made some interesting comments. He discussed, for instance, the fact that language and style are class-based and therefore can be used to bolster elitism and discriminate against members of other "less desirable classes" (*id.* at 4–5). On another page, Smith lectured on the rules of style and expression and wrote:

This you'll say is no more than common sense, and indeed it is no more. But if you'll attend to it all the Rules of Criticism and morality when traced to their foundation, turn out to be some Principles of Common Sence which every one assents to; all the business of those arts is to apply these Rules to the different subjects and shew what their conclusion is when they are so applied. (*Id.* at 55 [footnotes omitted])

6. *See generally* M. Friedman, BRIGHT PROMISES, DISMAL PERFORMANCE (W. Allen ed. 1983); Friedman, CAPITALISM, *supra* note 2; M. Friedman & R. Friedman, FREE TO CHOOSE (1980) [hereinafter Friedman, FREE TO CHOOSE]; M. Friedman & R. Friedman, TYRANNY OF THE STATUS QUO (1984) [hereinafter Friedman, TYRANNY]; Hayek, LIBERTY, *supra* note 1; F. Hayek, THE COUNTER-REVOLUTION OF SCIENCE-STUDIES ON THE ABUSE OF REASON (1952) [hereinafter Hayek, ABUSE OF REASON]; F. Hayek, LAW, LEGISLATION AND LIBERTY; vol. 1 RULES AND ORDER (1973) [hereinafter Hayek, RULES AND ORDER]; vol. 2 THE MIRAGE OF SOCIAL JUSTICE (1976) [hereinafter Hayek, SOCIAL JUSTICE]; vol. 3 THE POLITICAL ORDER OF A FREE PEOPLE (1979) [hereinafter Hayek, A FREE PEOPLE]; F. Hayek, THE ROAD TO SERFDOM (1944) [hereinafter Hayek, ROAD TO SERFDOM].

7. *See* E.G. West, ADAM SMITH, *supra* note 5, at 42.

8. *See* West, *Adam Smith's Two Views on the Division of Labour*, 1964 ECONOMICA 26. West comments:

> The Wealth of Nations was an essay in "conjectural history." This meant the systematic study of the effect of legal, institutional, and general environmental conditions upon human progress, a branch of study that had started with Montesquieu, and was taken up not only by Smith, but also by his Scottish friends and colleagues, Lord Kames, Hume, Ferguson, and Millar. This field of study today would be called sociological evolutionism, and there can be no doubt of Adam Smith's preoccupation with it throughout his book. (*Id.*)

9. *See* Buchanan, *The Justice of Natural Liberty*, 5 J. LEGAL STUD. 1, 2–5 (1976) [hereinafter Buchanan, *Liberty*]; Skinner, *Economics and History—The Scottish Enlightenment*, 1965 SCOTTISH J. POL. ECON. 1 [hereinafter Skinner, *Economic History*].

10. *See* Skinner, *Economic History, supra* note 9, at 1–2.

11. *See id.* at 3–4. Skinner compares the historical approach of Smith and other members of the Scottish Enlightenment to the philosophic and scientific approaches of Hegel and Vico (*id.* at 4). This approach, he says, also has been referred to as "theoretical history" (*id.* at 4).

12. *See id.* at 5.

13. *Id.*

14. *See* Smith, LECTURES, *supra* note 5, at 13, 401. (The original and greatest part of a person's natural rights result from a person merely being a person.) "The origin of natural rights is quite evident. That a person has a right to have his body free from injury, and his liberty free from infringement unless there be a proper cause, nobody doubts" (*id.* at 401). Smith's position is similar to the notions of Thomas Aquinas, who did not see human rights as the same as property rights because human rights are based on the very essence of man—his humanity. *See* AN AQUINAS READER 39–104 (M. Clark ed. 1972); *see also* Devine, *Adam Smith and the Problem of Justice in Capitalist Society*, 6 J. LEGAL STUD. 399, 404 (1977) (comparing Smith to Aquinas); *see*

generally J. Finnis, NATURAL LAW AND NATURAL RIGHTS (1980) (an excellent book on the place and value of natural law theory in legal analysis).

15. *See* I Smith, WEALTH OF NATIONS, *supra* note 5, at 20, 111–58, 276–78. Here, Smith argued that the educated philosopher is equal to the street porter (*id.* at 20). It is only class distinction and social privilege that has allowed the one to pursue a division of labor dramatically different from the other (*id.*). As to perfect liberty, Smith saw its manifestation in the marketplace as the free mobility and equality of labor (*id.* at 111–58). He argued that most inequality of labor is a result of government policy and regulation that restricts labor's mobility and bargaining power (*id.*). Smith did not believe government was the only problem in the abridgement of perfect liberty. He argued that monopolies and conspiracies of powerful merchants and capitalists were also to blame (*id.*). Smith wrote, for instance, "People of the same trade seldom meet together, even for merriment and diversion, but the conversation ends in a conspiracy against the public, or in some contrivance to raise prices" (*id.* at 144). He went on to argue that government regulations should not encourage such conspiracies against the public by granting treatment or licensing cartels that solidify the interests of the members (*id.*). Elsewhere, Smith warned that the interests of the capitalists are not necessarily the interests of the public. He warned against being taken in by the capitalists when they sought laws and regulations (*id.* at 276–79). He said that such requests come "from an order of men, whose interest is never exactly the same with that of the public, who have generally an interest to deceive and even oppress the public, and who accordingly have, upon many occasions, both deceived and even oppressed it" (*id.* at 278); *see also* Smith, MORAL SENTIMENTS, *supra* note 5, at 112–38. (Smith discussed the reasons why people strive for wealth. It is clear that he did not adhere to inequality as the manifestation of the true capacity of those who were poor rather than rich. Instead, he assured the reader that poor people are not poor because of divine will or inherent inferiority.)

16. *See* I Smith, WEALTH OF NATIONS, *supra* note 5, at 132–59; II Smith, WEALTH OF NATIONS, *supra* note 5, at 95. Smith wrote, "To prohibit a great people, however, from making all that they can of every part of their own produce, or from employing their stock and industry in the way that they judge most advantageous to themselves, is a manifest violation of the most sacred rights of mankind" (*id.*).

17. *See* I Smith, WEALTH OF NATIONS, *supra* note 5, at 344–45. Smith noted that "those exertions of the natural liberty of a few individuals, which might endanger the security of the whole society, are, and ought to be, restrained by the laws of all governments; of the most free, as well as of the most despotical" (*id.*).

18. II Smith, WEALTH OF NATIONS, *supra* note 5, at 312–486.

19. *See* Buchanan, *Liberty, supra* note 9, at 6–9. Smith was more concerned with a just society than with utilitarian calculations. According to Buchanan, "There was, to Smith, no trade-off between 'efficiency' and 'equity,' in the more familiar modern sense. As a general principle of social order, the freedom of individual choice would produce efficiency; but it would also be a central attribute of any social order that was just" (*id.* at 7); *see also* Coase, *Adam Smith's View of Man*, 19 J. L. & ECON. 529, 543–46 (1976) (arguing that Smith viewed man neither as a mere profit maximizer nor as a utility maximizer).

20. *See* Smith, LECTURES, *supra* note 5, at 314–15 (the rise of law and of independent judges protects liberty by restraining others and the state from wholesale infringement of liberty); Smith, MORAL SENTIMENTS, *supra* note 5, at 264–71, 274–82 (discussing the role of general rules and norms in social order); II Smith, WEALTH OF NATIONS, *supra* note 5, at 49–50, 125 (discussing how securing liberty for individuals under law allows not only for a more just society but also for more industry and prosperity); *see generally* Hayek, LIB-ERTY, *supra* note 1, at 220–28 (Smith believed in economic and social activity under the general rule of law. Economic freedom, therefore, meant freedom under law and not the absence of government intervention).

21. *See* II Smith, WEALTH OF NATIONS, *supra* note 5, at 171. Smith commented: "To hurt in any degree the interest of any one order of citizens, for no other purpose but to promote that of some other, is evidently contrary to that justice and equality of treatment which the sovereign owes to all the different orders of his subjects" (*id.*).

22. *See id.* at 339–400. Smith wrote:

> By necessaries I understand, not only the commodities which are indispensably necessary for the support of life, but whatever the custom of the country renders it indecent for creditable people, even of the lowest order, to be without. A linen shirt, for example, is strictly speaking, not a necessary of life. The Greeks and Romans lived, I suppose, very comfortably, though they had no linen. But in the present times, through the greater part of Europe, a creditable day-labourer would be ashamed to appear in public without a linen shirt, the want of which would be supposed to denote that disgraceful degree of poverty, which it is presumed, no body can well fall into without extreme bad conduct. Custom, in the same manner, has rendered leather shoes a necessary of life in England. . . . under necessaries therefore, I comprehend, not only those things which nature, but those things which the established rule of decency have rendered necessary to the lowest rank of people. (*Id.* [footnote omitted])

23. *See* I Smith, WEALTH OF NATIONS, *supra* note 5, at 111–58 (Smith discussed how bad government policy and conspiracy of private groups infringes on natural liberty).

24. *See* Smith, LECTURES, *supra* note 5, at 270–79, 314–15. Smith also said:

> The system of government now supposes a system of liberty as a foundation. . . . One security for liberty is that all judges hold their offices for life and are entirely independent of the king. Everyone therefore is tried by a free and independent judge, who are also accountable for their conduct. Nothing therefore will influence them to act unfairly to the subject, and endanger the loss of a profitable office and their reputation also; nothing the king could bestow would be an equivalent. The judge and jury have no dependence on the crown. (*Id.* at 271)

See also Smith, MORAL SENTIMENTS, *supra* note 5, at 264–71, 274–82; II Smith, WEALTH OF NATIONS, *supra* note 5, at 237–44. The judicial power must be separated from the executive power to preserve liberty and to create the norm that impartial justice, free from politics and the influence of the rich, protects each individual.

25. Individual liberty is freedom from coercion by the arbitrary will of another or others. Hayek, LIBERTY, *supra* note 1, at 11–21. It is not a right to

do anything one desires, for the exercise of individual liberty embodies within it a respect for the liberty of others. *See id.*; Friedman, CAPITALISM, *supra* note 2, at 14–21; *see generally* J.S. Mill, ON LIBERTY 53–86 (D. Spitz ed. 1975). Fundamentally, individual liberty is a view of social relationships that provides for personal autonomy over one's own thoughts and actions free from the outside coercive interference of others. *See* Hayek, LIBERTY, *supra* note 1, at 13; M. Rothbard, THE ETHICS OF LIBERTY 35–43 (1982) (discussing the natural right to seek interpersonal relations and voluntary exchanges). Coercive interference occurs when an individual's circumstances or environment is controlled by another to the extent that, in order to avoid a greater evil, the individual is forced to act not according to his or her own designs, but to serve the ends of another. Hayek, LIBERTY, *supra* note 1, at 21. This coercion of the individual is "evil precisely because it thus eliminates an individual as a thinking and valuing person and makes him a bare tool in the achievement of the ends of another" (*id.*). Personal autonomy is not, however, limitless. The concept of individual freedom in a market economy or *laissez faire* social organization requires governmental restriction on certain behavior that, if left unchecked, would disintegrate social cooperation and civilization. *See* L. von Mises, HUMAN ACTION 279–87 (rev. ed. 1963). Thus, within the confines of a free society, modern-day Smithians agree that the state can be a legitimate vehicle for protecting individual liberty from the coercive interference of others, even though the state may impose some limitation on the rights of individuals to engage in certain behavior.

26. *See* Skinner, *Economic History, supra* note 9, at 14–18.

27. *See* Smith, LECTURES, *supra* note 5, at 14–37, 200–290, 401–38. Although these citations are to areas containing significant discussion of the stages of development, Smith's analysis of jurisprudence throughout LECTURES is made with constant reference to these different stages. I Smith, WEALTH OF NATIONS, *supra* note 5, at 420–45; II Smith, WEALTH OF NATIONS, *supra* note 5, at 231–44; *see generally* Smith, RHETORIC, *supra* note 5, at 201–26. This chapter of RHETORIC is entitled "Consideration Concerning the First Formation of Languages and the Different Genius of Original and Compounded Languages."

28. *See supra* note 27.

29. *Id.*

30. *Id. See also* I Smith, WEALTH OF NATIONS, *supra* note 5, at 7–26 (discussing the division of labor that is not a result of planning, but one that emerges slowly and spontaneously as a result of human nature. The division of labor increases productivity and brings forth a better standard of living. In a commercial society with a division of labor, everyone becomes a merchant—a buyer of much and a seller of special skills); Smith, LECTURES, *supra* note 5, at 340–55 (discussing the division of labor's ability to help even the poorest member of society even when it seems that the rich get the greatest part of any social benefit).

31. *See supra* note 27; *see also* J. Galbraith, THE ANATOMY OF POWER (1983) [hereinafter Galbraith, POWER]. In POWER, Galbraith focuses on the sources and the nature of power in discussing social evolution. Much of Galbraith's analysis provides a modern and expanded consideration of the concepts explored by Adam Smith.

32. *See supra* note 5. Smith wrote: "The more improved any society is and the greater length the several [sic] means of supporting the inhabitants are

carried, the greater will be the number of their laws and regulations necessary to maintain justice, and prevent infringements of the right of property."
Smith, Lectures, *supra* note 5, at 16.

33. *See supra* note 27.

34. *Id.*

35. *See* II Smith, Wealth of Nations, *supra* note 5, at 432–45; Smith, Lectures, *supra* note 5, at 194–99, 225–28, 261–64.

36. *See supra* note 35; *see generally* T. Veblen, The Theory of The Leisure
Class (New American Library ed. 1953) (interesting comparisons of the theory of social evolution and the status of the leisure class).

37. *See supra* note 35; *see also* II Smith, Wealth of Nations, *supra* note 5,
at 325–38. Smith, in the course of discussing religious institutions, addressed
the power of the Roman Catholic Church. Smith compared the Roman Catholic clergy to the various lay lords throughout Europe, but observed that the
latter were more powerful because of the shared interest of their unity and
because a spiritual claim supported their secular exercise of power. Thus, for
Smith, the Roman Catholic Church was the greatest threat to civil government and to liberty. But, like the great lay lords, the advent of commerce and
the increasing division of labor destroyed much of the Church's power base.
See generally Galbraith, Power, *supra* note 31. This book contains similar insights into the basis and evolution of power from a historical perspective.

38. Capitalism puts power, in the form of resources and wealth, in the
hands of private citizens, thereby assuring a power base outside the reach of
the state that can be used to protect individuals from the state. Similarly, the
state has powers and resources that enable it to protect weaker individuals
from the more powerful. *See generally* Friedman, Capitalism, *supra* note 2;
Hayek, Liberty, *supra* note 1; Hayek, Road to Serfdom, *supra* note 6; *see also*
Malloy, *The Political Economy of Co-Financing America's Urban Renaissance*, 40
Vand. L. Rev. 67, 95–119 (1987) [hereinafter Malloy, *Political Economy*];
Malloy, *Equating Human Rights and Property Rights—The Need for Moral Judgment in an Economic Analysis of Law and Social Policy*, 47 Ohio St. L.J. 163,
166–71 (1986) [hereinafter Malloy, *Human Rights*].

39. *See* I Smith, Wealth of Nations, *supra* note 5, at 111–44, 157–58,
276–78, II Smith, Wealth of Nations, *supra* note 5, at 161–65 (numerous
examples of regulations, restrictions, trade practices, and government policies, that demonstrate the efforts of special interests to dominate or exploit
other individuals or the general public); Smith, Lectures, *supra* note 5, at
208. Smith commented:

> But here when . . . some have great wealth and others nothing, it is nec-
> essary that the arm of authority should be continually stretched forth, and
> permanent laws or regulations made which may ascertain the property of
> the rich from the inroads of the poor, who would otherwise continually
> make incroachments upon it. . . . Laws and government may be considered
> in this and indeed in every case as a combination of the rich to oppress the
> poor, and preserve to themselves the inequality of the goods which would
> otherwise be soon destroyed by the attacks of the poor. (*Id.*)

See also Malloy, *Political Economy, supra* note 38, at 67–134 (explaining the way
in which special interest politics shape improper decisions about urban revitalization programs).

40. *See supra* note 38; *see also* Smith, Lectures, *supra* note 5, at 247–64

(explaining how the balance between lords and the British king had a similar effect in helping to secure liberty because each had sufficient power and resources to need the other); A. Hogue, ORIGINS OF THE COMMON LAW (1966). This brief history of the common law makes the same point about the balance of power in Great Britain as does Smith in LECTURES.

41. *See supra* note 32 (including the quoted material from Smith).

42. *See* I Smith, WEALTH OF NATIONS, *supra* note 5, at 18, 477–78; Smith, MORAL SENTIMENTS, *supra* note 5, at 275, 297–307, 379–82. Smith argues in favor of the invisible hand concept and against central planning.

43. *See* I Smith, WEALTH OF NATIONS, *supra* note 5, at 477–78. Smith observed:

> He generally, indeed, neither intends to promote the public interest, nor knows how much he is promoting it . . . by directing that industry in such a manner as its produce may be of the greatest value, he intends only his own gain, and he is in this, as in many other cases, led by an invisible hand to promote an end which was no part of his intention. Nor is it always the worse for society that it was no part of it. By pursuing his own interest he frequently promotes that of the society more effectually than when he really intends to promote it. I have never known much good done by those who affected to trade for the public good. It is an affection, indeed, not very common among merchants, and very few words need be employed in dissuading them from it. (*Id.*)

44. *See* Smith, MORAL SENTIMENTS, *supra* note 5, at 297–307. Smith also commented:

> It is to no purpose that the proud and unfeeling landlord views his extensive fields, and without a thought for the wants of his brethren, in imagination consumes himself the whole harvest that grows upon them. The homely and vulgar proverb, that the eye is larger than the belly, never was more fully verified than with regard to him. The capacity of his stomach bears on proportion to the immensity of his desires, and will receive no more than that of the meanest peasant. The rest he is obliged to distribute among those who prepare, in the nicest manner, that little which he himself makes use of. . . . The rich only select from the heap what is most precious and agreeable . . . in spite of their natural selfishness and rapacity, though they mean only their own conveniency, though the sole end which they propose from the labours of all the thousands whom they employ be the gratification of their own vain and insatiable desires, they divide with the poor the produce of all their improvements. They are led by an invisible hand to make nearly the same distribution of the necessaries of life which would have been made had the earth been divided into equal portions among all its inhabitants; and thus, without intending it, without knowing it, advance the interest of the society. (*Id.* at 304)

45. I Smith, WEALTH OF NATIONS, *supra* note 5, at 18.

46. *See* Smith, MORAL SENTIMENTS, *supra* note 5, at 71–72 (selfishness is not the proper motivation); *id.* at 499–508 (denouncing Hobbes and his theory of self-interest and self-love); *id.* at 161–65 (self-interest is different from selfishness). Smith explained:

> And hence it is, that to feel much for others, and little for ourselves, that to restrain our selfish, and to indulge our benevolent, affections,

constitutes the perfection of human nature; and can alone produce among mankind that harmony of sentiments and passions in which consists their whole grace and propriety. (*Id.* at 71–72)

Smith also noted: "Sympathy, however, cannot, in any sense, be regarded as a selfish principle" (*id.* at 501). Smith further stated:

Every man is, no doubt, by nature first and principally recommended to his own care; and as he is fitter to take care of himself, than of any other person, it is fit and right that it should be so. Every man, therefore, is much more deeply interested in whatever immediately concerns himself, than in what concerns any other man . . . though every man may according to the proverb, be the whole world to himself, to the rest of mankind he is a most insignificant part of it. Though his own happiness may be of more importance to him than that of all the world besides, to every other person it is of no more consequence than that of any other man. . . . When he views himself in the light of which he is conscious that others will view him, he sees that to them he is but one of the multitude, in no respect better than any other in it. . . . [H]e must upon this, as upon all other occasions, humble the arrogance of his self-love, and bring it down to something which other men can go along with. (*Id.* at 161–62)

47. *Id.* at 297–307.
48. *Id.* at 299–301.
49. *Id.* at 297–307.
50. *Id.*
51. *Id.*
52. *Id.* at 300–301.
53. *Id.* at 297–307. In discussing the hardship of the poor relative to the life of the rich Smith concluded:

In what constitutes the real happiness of human life, they are in no respect inferior to those who would seem so much above them. In case of body and peace of mind, all the different ranks of life are nearly upon a level, and the beggar, who suns himself by the side of the highway, possesses the security which Kings are fighting for. (*Id.* at 305)

54. *Id.* at 251–52.
55. *Id.* at 69, 166–69. Smith commented, "It is thus that man, who can subsist only in society, was fitted by nature to that situation for which he was made. All the members of human society stand in need of each other's assistance, and are likewise exposed to mutual injuries" (*id.* at 166). He also noted, "Man, it has been said, has a natural love for society, and desires that the union of mankind should be preserved for its own sake, and though he himself was to derive no benefit from it" (*id.* at 169). *See also* I Smith, WEALTH OF NATIONS, *supra* note 5, at 17–18 (people depending on interaction in society).
56. *See supra* note 46.
57. *See* Smith, MORAL SENTIMENTS, *supra* note 5, at 47–74. In MORAL SENTIMENTS, Smith argued that "[a]s we have no immediate experience of what other men feel, we can form no idea of manner in which they are affected, but by conceiving what we ourselves should feel in the like situation" (*id.* at 47). Smith also stated:

[U]pon all occasions, his own sentiments are the standards and measures by which he judges of mine . . . to approve or disapprove, therefore, of the opinions of others is acknowledged, by everybody, to mean no more than to observe their agreement or disagreement with our own. But this is equally the case with regard to our approbation or disapprobations of the sentiments or passions of others. (*Id.* at 59)

58. *Id.*
59. *Id.* at 200–232. Smith contended:

And, in the same manner, we either approve or disapprove of our own conduct, according as we feel that, when we place ourselves in the situation of another man, and view it, as it were, with his eyes and from his station, we either can or cannot entirely enter into and sympathize with the sentiments and motives which influenced it. (*id.* at 203)

Later, Smith noted: "Our first ideas of personal beauty and deformity are drawn from the shape and appearance of others, not from our own. We soon become sensible, however, that others exercise the same criticism upon us" (*id.* at 205).
60. *Id.* at 71, 200–260, 352, 422 (discussions of the concept of the "impartial spectator"). Smith stated: "We endeavour to examine our own conduct as we imagine any other fair and impartial spectator would examine it (*id.* at 204).
61. *Id.* at 204–7. Smith stated:

Were it possible that a human creature could grow up to manhood in some solitary place, without any communication with his own species, he could no more think of his own character, of the propriety or demerit of his own sentiments and conduct, of the beauty or deformity of his own mind, than of the beauty or deformity of his own face. (*Id.* at 204)

62. *Id.* at 208–321.
63. *Id.* at 212, 264–97.
64. *See supra* note 46 (pursuit of self-interest in the marketplace not the same as selfishness).
65. *See* Smith, MORAL SENTIMENTS, *supra* note 5, at 161–63, 236. Smith also observed:

In the race for wealth, and honours, and preferments, he may run as hard as he can, and strain every nerve and every muscle, in order to outstrip all his competitors. But if he should justle, or throw down any of them, the indulgence of the spectators is entirely at an end. It is a violation of fair play, which they cannot admit of. (*Id.* at 162)

"One individual must never prefer himself so much even to any other individual as to hurt or injure that other in order to benefit himself, though the benefit to the one should be much greater than the hurt or injury to the other" (*id.* at 236).
66. *Id.* at 212, 264–97.
67. *Id.* at 264.
68. *Id.* at 232–60, 314.
69. *See* Smith, LECTURES, *supra* note 5, at 14–37, 200–290, 401–38 (concerning the advancing stages of society); Smith, MORAL SENTIMENTS, *supra*

note 5, at 265–82, 290 (reference to general rules in moral matters as well as in matters of justice); I Smith, WEALTH OF NATIONS, *supra* note 5, at 420–45; II Smith, WEALTH OF NATIONS, *supra* note 5, at 231–44 (also concerning the advancing stages of society); *see also* Smith, MORAL SENTIMENTS, *supra* note 5, at 167. Smith noted that society itself could not exist without justice.

70. *See* Hayek, LIBERTY, *supra* note 1, at 220–28. Hayek writes:

> The classical argument for freedom in economic affairs rests on the tacit postulate that the rule of law should govern policy in this as in all other spheres. We cannot understand the nature of the opposition of men like Adam Smith or John Stuart Mill to government "intervention" unless we see it against this background. Their position was therefore often misunderstood by those who were not familiar with that basic conception; and confusion arose in England and America as soon as the conception of the rule of law ceased to be assumed by every reader. Freedom of economic activity had meant freedom under the law, not the absence of all government action. The "interference" or "intervention" of government which those writers opposed as a matter of principle therefore meant only the infringement of that private sphere which the general rules of law were intended to protect. They did not mean that government should never concern itself with any economic matters. . . .
>
> To Adam Smith and his immediate successors, the enforcement of the ordinary rules of common law would certainly not have appeared as government interference; nor would they ordinarily have applied this term to an alteration of these rules or the passing of a new rule by the legislature so long as it was intended to apply equally to all people for an indefinite period of time. . . . There is perhaps no aim which they would not have regarded as legitimate if it was clear that the people wanted it; but they excluded as generally inadmissible in a free society the method of specific orders and prohibitions. (*Id.* at 220–21)

71. One way of evaluating Smith's concern for general rules is through his various discussions in THE THEORY OF MORAL SENTIMENTS. Smith asserted that the need for justice is essential to the fabric of human society. Smith, MORAL SENTIMENTS, *supra* note 5, at 167. Providing for a system of justice is the role of civil government and it is an important role for assuring social cooperation (*id.* at 157–59, 166–72). Part of knowing how to achieve justice is knowing what behavior is proper in society. For Smith, right and proper behavior involves harmonizing personal conduct with the general principles and rules of morality and moral sentiments then prevailing in the community (*id.* at 261–82). Finally, after emphasizing the need for general rules of morality, Smith turned to the relationship between positive law and moral sentiments (*id.* at 535–37). He concluded that positive law is an effort to implement a system of natural jurisprudence, but that it is inevitably imperfect in its attempt (*id.*). Nonetheless, systems of positive law deserve recognition for their authority, since they embody the best attempts to articulate the moral sentiments of human beings in different ages and nations (*id.*). Thus, there is a clear recognition that an understanding of the rules of moral sentiments is linked to an understanding of justice and the systems of positive law. Furthermore, it would seem that the concern for general rules of morality would carry over into concern for general rules of positive law.

72. *See supra* notes 70, 71. Smith was concerned about special interest

groups that sought special as opposed to general rules of law in order to advance their own interests over that of the public. *See* I Smith, WEALTH OF NATIONS, *supra* note 5, at 111–44, 157–58, 276–78; II Smith, WEALTH OF NATIONS, *supra* note 5, at 161–65 (numerous examples of regulations, restrictions, trade practices, and government policies that demonstrate the efforts of special interests to dominate or exploit other individuals or the general public). *See generally* Malloy, *Political Economy, supra* note 38, at 67–134 (explaining how special interest politics shape improper decisions about urban revitalization programs).

73. *See supra* notes 42–53 and accompanying text; *see generally* Hayek, RULES AND ORDER, *supra* note 6, at 35–54. Hayek discusses spontaneous social order as it relates to law and social cooperation.

74. *See* Hayek, A FREE PEOPLE, *supra* note 6, at 1–19.

75. *Id.*

76. *Id.*

77. *Id.*

78. *See* Smith, LECTURES, *supra* note 5, at 7.

79. *See supra* note 38.

80. *See* Smith, MORAL SENTIMENTS, *supra* note 5, at 157–60, 166–71 (a proper balance must be struck for government activity to occur without destroying liberty).

81. *See* II Smith, WEALTH OF NATIONS, *supra* note 5, at 231–44. Smith commented:

> The rich, in particular, are necessarily interested to support that order of things, which can alone secure them in the possession of their own advantages. Men of inferior wealth combine to defend those of superior wealth in the possession of their property, in order that men of superior wealth may combine to defend them in the possession of theirs . . . Civil government, so far as it is instituted for the security of property, is in reality instituted for the defense of the rich against the poor, or of those who have some property against those who have none at all. (*Id.* at 256 [footnote omitted]

Smith makes a similar point elsewhere in his writing. Smith, MORAL SENTIMENTS, *supra* note 5, at 126–32. Smith writes:

> Men in the inferior and middling stations of life, besides, can never be great enough to be above the law, which must generally overawe them into some sort of respect for, at least, the more important rules of justice. . . . [F]ortunately for the good morals of society, these are the situations of by far the greater part of mankind. (*Id.* at 128)

Thus, Smith recognized that civil government treats the poor differently from the rich. Although the rich may be "above" the law, the poor are not. *See* Smith, LECTURES, *supra* note 5, at 208 ("Laws and government may be considered in this and indeed in every case as a combination of the rich to oppress the poor").

82. *See* II Smith, WEALTH OF NATIONS, *supra* note 5, at 231–44 (only with the accumulation of wealth does society need civil government and laws to protect the rich and their property); *see also* Smith, LECTURES, *supra* note 5, at 14–37, 200–290, 401–38 (discussed in various ways in connection with the stages of social development).

83. I Smith, WEALTH OF NATIONS, *supra* note 5, at 426; II Smith, WEALTH OF NATIONS, *supra* note 5, at 231–44; Smith, MORAL SENTIMENTS, *supra* note 5, at 208–10.

84. *See supra* notes 14–53 and accompanying text.

85. *See supra* note 38. Modern-day Smithians, classical liberals, and libertarians are in agreement on this concept.

86. *See* Malloy, *Political Economy, supra* note 38, at 119–32.

87. *See* Smith, MORAL SENTIMENTS, *supra* note 5, at 157–60, 166–72.

88. *See* II Smith, WEALTH OF NATIONS, *supra* note 5, at 208–446. The government is to provide for (1) the national defense, (2) the administration of justice, and (3) the maintenance of certain public works. Government is to protect natural liberty without favoring manufacturing or mercantilism over agriculture or vice versa.

89. *Id.*

90. *Id.* at 282–309.

91. *Id.* at 302–9; *see also* Rosenberg, *Adam Smith on the Division of Labour: Two Views or One?*, 1965 ECONOMICA 127 [hereinafter Rosenberg, *Labour*]; West, *Division of Labour, supra* note 8, at 23–32; West, *The Political Economy of Alienation: Karl Marx and Adam Smith*, 21 OXFORD ECON. PAPERS 1 (1969).

92. *See* sources cited *supra* note 91.

93. *Id.* Smith wrote:

> In the process of the division of labour, the employment of the far greater part of those who live by labour, that is, of the great body of the people, comes to be confined to a few very simple operations; frequently to one or two. But the understandings of the greater part of men are necessarily formed by their ordinary employments. The man whose whole life is spent in performing a few simple operations, of which the effects too are, perhaps, always the same, or very nearly the same, has no occasion to exert his understanding, or to exercise his invention in finding out expedients for removing difficulties which never occur. He naturally loses, therefore, the habit of such exertion, and generally becomes as stupid and ignorant as it is possible for a human creature to become. The torpor of his mind renders him, not only incapable of relishing or bearing a part in any rational conversation, but of conceiving any generous, noble, or tender sentiment, and consequently of forming any just judgment concerning many even of the ordinary duties of private life. ... [I]n every improved and civilized society this is the state into which the labouring poor, that is, the great body of the people, must necessarily fall, unless government takes some pains to prevent it. (II Smith, WEALTH OF NATIONS, *supra* note 5, at 302–3)

94. *See* sources cited *supra* note 91.

95. *Id.*

96. *See* II Smith, WEALTH OF NATIONS, *supra* note 5, at 302–9.

97. *Id.* Not only are the rich more able than the poor to afford the cost of education, but rich children are given jobs and training that better exercise their intelligence.

98. *Id.* Smith observed: "Though the state was to derive no advantage from the instruction of the inferior ranks of people, it would still deserve its attention that they should not be altogether uninstructed" (*id.* at 308–9).

99. *Id.* at 302–9.

100. This, it seems, is relatively clear from Smith's discussion of the marketplace in his book WEALTH OF NATIONS. But Smith also made a comment of interest in his LECTURES ON JURISPRUDENCE when he acknowledged that the rich will always be able to outbid the poor for goods or services that they both desire. *See* Smith, LECTURES, *supra* note 5, at 358. Thus, the poor are at once limited in their ability to demand the production of goods and services for their benefit and also subject to being outbid for limited goods and services which are of interest to those with more wealth.

101. *See* II Smith, WEALTH OF NATIONS, *supra* note 5, at 302–9.

102. *See supra* notes 14–26 and accompanying text.

103. *See* Smith, LECTURES, *supra* note 5, at 207, 311–30, 401–7.

104. *Id.*

105. *Id.* at 311–30, 401–7.

106. *Id.* at 207, 311–30, 401–7. Smith asserts that the relationship between the citizen and the state evolves as a part of his historical depiction of the stages of social evolution rather than as a result of a social contract. Within this evolutionary process two principles emerge that induce people to enter into civil society. Smith calls these the principles of authority and utility.

107. *Id.*

108. *Id.*

109. *See, e.g,* Smith, MORAL SENTIMENTS, *supra* note 5, at 212–97 (concerning social norms and the process of morals and general rules).

110. Smith allowed for a continuing reevaluation of government. First, since the relationship between the individual and the government is based on historical evolution not contract, it follows that as society continues to evolve it cannot be limited to its earlier legal framework. We do not engage in a search for the meaning of an earlier social contract but rather escape the contract metaphor and evaluate government in light of a changing context. *See* Smith, LECTURES, *supra* note 5, at 207, 311–30, 401–7. Second, Smith was concerned with the relationship between natural justice and positive law. He viewed systems of positive law not as the perfection of natural justice but as the imperfect embodiment of historical understandings of societal norms in pursuit of natural justice. *See* Smith, MORAL SENTIMENTS, *supra* note 5, at 535–37. Therefore, for Smith, it seems that positive law and government must be continually evaluated in light of the changing norms and moral sentiments that evolve in pursuit of natural justice.

Chapter 4

1. *See* F. Hayek, LAW, LEGISLATION, AND LIBERTY: vol. 1 RULES AND ORDER (1973); vol. 2 THE MIRAGE OF SOCIAL JUSICE (1976); vol. 3 THE POLITICAL ORDER OF A FREE PEOPLE (1979).

2. *See* A. Nock, OUR ENEMY, THE STATE 29 (1976) [hereinafter Nock, THE STATE]. According to Nock:

[The] idea rests upon certain assumptions that experience has shown to be unsound; the first one being that the power of the ballot is what republican political theory makes it out to be, and that therefore the electorate has an effective choice in the matter. It is a matter of open and notorious fact that nothing like this is true. Our nominally republican system is actually built on an imperial model, with our professional politicians standing in the place of the praetorian guards; they meet from time to time, decide what can be "got away with," and how, and who is to do it; and the electorate votes according to their prescriptions. (*Id.*)

Nock's position could be supported by John Kenneth Galbraith. Galbraith argues that the state possesses access to the means of power and that the state, through conditional power, gets people to respond to or believe in concepts that serve those in power, without accurately portraying the real world. *See* J. Galbraith, THE ANATOMY OF POWER (1983).

3. *See, e.g.*, M. Kaus, H. Fineman, J. McCormick, E. Clift, M. Starr & D. Pedersen, *Adventures in Campaignland*, NEWSWEEK, Feb. 1, 1988, at 18–23.

4. *See, e.g.*, L. Tribe, AMERICAN CONSTITUTIONAL LAW 18–545 (1988).

5. *See* M. Friedman, CAPITALISM AND FREEDOM 7–21 (1962 reissued 1982) [hereinafter Friedman, CAPITALISM].

> The fundamental threat to freedom is the power to coerce, be it in the hands of a monarch, a dictator, an oligarchy, or a momentary majority. The preservation of freedom requires the elimination of such concentration of power to the fullest possible extent and the dispersal and distribution of whatever power cannot be eliminated—a system of checks and balances. (*Id.* at 15)

6. *See generally* Nock, THE STATE, *supra* note 2, 23–35 (1983) (concentrating power in the state and progressively removing decision making from the individual and from local government leads to the destruction of liberty).

7. *See* Malloy, *Market Philosophy in the Legal Tension between Children's Autonomy and Parental Authority*, 21 IND. L. REV. 889 (1988).

8. *See* Friedman, CAPITALISM, *supra* note 5, at 1–36 (1982) (asserting that capitalism is a necessary but not sufficient basis for freedom). Friedman comments:

> Viewed as a means to the end of political freedom, economic arrangements are important because of their effect on the concentration or dispersion of power. The kind of economic organization that provides economic freedom directly, namely, competitive capitalism, also promotes political freedom because it separates economic power from political power and in this way evokes the one to offset the other. . . .
>
> History suggests only that capitalism is a necessary condition for political freedom. Clearly it is not a sufficient condition. Fascist Italy and Fascist Spain, Germany at various times in the last seventy years, Japan before World Wars I and II, tzarist Russia in the decades before World War I— are all societies that cannot conceivably be described as politically free. Yet, in each, private enterprise was the dominant form of economic organization. (*Id.* at 9–10)

9. The most recent example is the power of the British government to control the BBC and deny broadcasting coverage of certain elected political representatives. *See* G. Mott & E. Jones, *A Loss of Liberties*, NEWSWEEK, Oct. 31, 1988, at 47 (reporting on the BBC denial of access to elected Sinn Fein leader Gerry Adams).

10. *See generally* D. Funk, GROUP DYNAMIC LAW: INTEGRATING CONSTITUTIVE CONTRACT INSTITUTIONS (1982); D. Funk, GROUP DYNAMIC LAW: EXPOSITION AND PRACTICE (1988); Michelman, *Norms and Normativity in the Economic Theory of Law*, 62 MINN. L. REV. 1015–48 (1978).

11. *See* S. Gould, Ever Since Darwin (1977); S. Gould, The Mismeasure of Man (1981). Gould is famous for his theories on creative evolution.

Chapter 5

1. *See* A. Nock, Our Enemy, The State (2d ed. 1983). This book first appeared in 1935. It represents a classic challenge to the role of the state. For Nock the state is a vehicle for class exploitation rather than a means for organizing society within certain limits that protect individual liberty. Nock refers to the limited entity that protects individual liberty as government. He argues:

> [T]here are two methods, or means, and only two, whereby man's needs and desires can be satisfied. One is the production and exchange of wealth; this is the *economic means*. The other is the uncompensated appropriation of wealth produced by others; this is the *political means*. The State, then, whether primitive, feudal or merchant, is the *organization of the political means*. Now since man tends always to satisfy his needs and desires with the least possible exertion, he will employ the political means whenever he can—exclusively, if possible; otherwise, in association with the economic means. He will, at the present time, that is, have recourse to the state's modern apparatus of exploitation; the apparatus of tariffs, concessions, rent-monopoly, and the like. (*Id.* at 46–47)

2. *See, e.g.,* M. Olson, The Logic of Collective Action: Public Goods and the Theory of Groups (1971); J. Buchanan & G. Tullock, The Calculus of Consent: Logical Foundations of Constitutional Democracy (1962); J. Buchanan, Public Finance in Democratic Process (1967); Tullock, *Problems of Majority Voting*, 67 J. Pol. Econ. 571 (1959); Macey, *Promoting Public—Regarding Legislation Through Statutory Interpretation: An Interest Group Model*, 86 Colum. L. Rev. 223 (1986); Farbar & Frickey, *The Jurisprudence of Public Choice*, 65 Tex. L. Rev. 873 (1987); Lee, *Politics, Ideology, and the Power of Public Choice*, 74 Va. L. Rev. 191 (1988); Sunstein, *Interest Groups in American Public Law*, 38 Stan. L. Rev. 29 (1985); Tollison, *Public Choice and Legislation*, 74 Va. L. Rev. 339 (1988); Macey, *Transaction Costs and the Normative Elements of the Public Choice Model: An Application to Constitutional Theory*, 74 Va. L. Rev. 471 (1988); Macey, *Public Choice: The Theory of the Firm and the Theory of Market Exchange*, 74 Cornell L. Rev. 43 (1988).

3. *See infra* Chapter 9.

4. It is a basic assumption of economics that market allocations, by definition, are efficient and result in resources being put to the most valued use. Two excellent texts on basic economics are A. Alchian & W. Allen, Exchange & Production—Competition, Coordination & Control (1983), and R. Lipsey & P. Steiner, Economics (4th ed. 1975). For a text on economic analysis applied to law and the notion of the marketplace and efficiency, see R. Posner, Economic Analysis of Law (3d ed. 1986) [hereinafter Posner, Economic Analysis]. Chapters 1 and 2 of Posner's work provide background on economic assumptions, while the remainder of the book applies an amoral and simplistic economic method to a variety of legal issues.

5. *See* Nock, *supra* note 1, at 46–48.

6. *See* F. Hayek, The Constitution of Liberty 20–21 (1960). Hayek

discusses the evil of coercion and the conflict between coercion and individual liberty.

> Coercion, however, cannot be altogether avoided because the only way to prevent it is by the threat of coercion. Free society has met this problem by conferring the monopoly of coercion on the state and by attempting to limit this power of the state to instances where it is required to prevent coercion by private persons. The coercion which a government must still use for this end is reduced to a minimum and made as innocuous as possible by restraining it through known general rules, so that in most instances the individual need never be coerced unless he has placed himself in a position where he knows he will be coerced. (*Id.* at 21)

See also L. von Mises, HUMAN ACTION 280–81 (1966) (arguing that liberty is best preserved within society by putting coercive power in the hands of government and then restricting government by rule of law); F. Hayek, THE ROAD TO SERFDOM 72–87 (1944) (discussing the nature of general rules and the protection of individual liberty); F. Hayek, LAW, LEGISLATION, AND LIBERTY: vol. 1 RULES AND ORDER (1973).

> The thesis of this book is that a condition of liberty in which all are allowed to use their knowledge for their purposes, restrained only by rules of just conduct of universal application, is likely to produce for them the best conditions for achieving their aims; and that such a system is likely to be achieved and maintained only if all authority, including that of the majority of people, is limited in the exercise of coercive power by general principles to which the community has committed itself. (*Id.* at 55)

7. *See supra* note 2 (references to various materials on Public Choice Theory).

8. *Id.*

9. *See, e.g.,* Friedman, *Free Markets and Free Speech,* 10 HARV. J.L. & PUB. POL'Y. 1, 7 (1987) (rejecting a slave society even if proven to be more efficient than a free society); Malloy, *Is Law and Economics Moral? Humanistic Economics and a Classical Liberal Critique of Posner's Economic Analysis,* 24 VAL. U.L. REV. 147 (1990); Malloy, *The Limits of "Science" in Legal Discourse—A Reply to Posner,* 24 VAL. U.L. REV. 175 (1990); Malloy, *Invisible Hand or Sleight of Hand? Adam Smith, Richard Posner, and the Philosophy of Law and Economics,* 36 KAN. L. REV. 209 (1988). *See contra,* R. Posner, THE ECONOMICS OF JUSTICE 86 (1983) (approving slavery in some circumstances as efficient); Posner, *Wealth Maximization Revisited,* 2 NOTRE DAME J.L. ETHICS & PUB. POL'Y. 85–105 (1985) (approving slavery on efficiency grounds).

10. *See* Nock, *supra* note 1, at 36–48; F. Hayek, LAW, LEGISLATION AND LIBERTY: vol. 1 RULES AND ORDER (1973); vol. 2 THE MIRAGE OF SOCIAL JUSTICE (1976); vol. 3 THE POLITICAL ORDER OF A FREE PEOPLE (1979) [hereinafter collectively Hayek, LAW, LEGISLATION AND LIBERTY]. In this three-volume work, Hayek not only argues that the democratic process is a way of coordinating the desires and objectives of special interest groups, but he goes on to argue that democracy inevitably leads to socialism, statism, and the loss of individual liberty. *See also* M. Friedman & R. Friedman, TYRANNY OF THE STATUS QUO (1984) [hereinafter Friedman, TYRANNY]. This book condemns the Reagan administration for continuing to use government as a political means to aid special interests despite Reagan's rhetoric to the contrary.

11. *See* Hayek, Law, Legislation and Liberty, *supra* note 10; see also Posner, Economic Analysis, *supra* note 4, at 491–507.

12. *See* Hoeflich & Malloy, *The Shattered Dream of American Housing Policy—The Need for Reform*, 26 B.C.L. Rev. 655, 663–70, 681–83 (1985) (discussing rent regulations and their implications); H. Hazlitt, Economics in One Lesson 127–33 (1979) (discussing rent controls).

13. *See* Hoeflich & Malloy, *supra* note 12, at 655, 663–70, 681–83.

14. *See generally* M. Friedman, Bright Promises, Dismal Performance 359–72 (W. Allen ed. 1983) (discussing trade, protectionism, and embargoes); H. Hazlitt, *supra* note 12, at 74–84 (discussing how tariffs work and their short-term and long-term effects).

15. *See* Coase, *The Problem of Social Cost*, 3 J.L. & Econ. 1 (1960).

16. *See* Friedman & Friedman, Tyranny, *supra* note 10.

Chapter 6

1. G. Hardin, *Tragedy of the Commons*, 162, Science 1243 (1968).

2. *See* R. Malloy, Law and Economics: A Comparative Approach to Theory and Practice 14–47 (1990); A. Polinsky, An Introduction to Law and Economics 11–24 (1983); R. McKenzie & G. Tullock, The New World of Economics—Explorations into the Human Experience (1975); L. Phillips & H. Votey, Economic Analysis of Pressing Social Problems (1974). *See also* Dolan, *Environmental Policy and Property* in Property in a Humane Environment 209–24 (S. Blumenfeld ed. 1974).

3. *See e.g.*, D. Pegrum, Transportation—Economics and Public Policy (3d ed. 1973); J. Kneafsey, Transportation Economic Analysis (1975); D. Locklin, Economics of Transportation (1972).

4. *See, e.g.*, Phillips & Votey, Economic Analysis, *supra* note 2.

5. *See, e.g.*, Hoeflich, *Of Reason, Gamesmanship, and Taxes: A Jurisprudential and Theoretical Approach to the Problem of Voluntary Compliance*, 2 Am. J. Tax Pol'y 9 (1983) (looking at the rise in coercion and gamesmanship in the tax compliance area).

Chapter 7

1. *See, e.g.*, S. Macedo, The New Right v. the Constitution (1986).

2. *See* M. Friedman, Capitalism and Freedom 14–21 (1962 reissued 1982).

3. *See* Malloy, *Equating Human Rights and Property Rights—The Need for Moral Judgment in an Economic Analysis of Law and Social Policy*, 47 Ohio St. L.J. 163–177 (1986); National Conference of Catholic Bishops, Economic Justice For All—Pastoral Letter on Catholic Social Teaching and the U.S. Economy (1986). *See also* Novak, *The Liberal Society as Liberation Theology*, 2 Notre Dame J.L. Ethics & Pub. Pol'y 27 (1985); *Symposium on The Economy*, 2 Notre Dame J.L. Ethics & Pub. Pol'y 1–358 (1985); *Symposium on the Catholic Bishops' Pastoral Letter on the U.S. Economy*, 5 St. Louis Univ. Pub. L. Rev. 277–515 (1986); *The Catholic Church Speaks Out on Poverty: Ethics and Economics: Hearings Before The Joint Economic Committee* 99th Cong., 2d Sess. 1 (1986). *See generally* J. Finnis, Natural Law and Natural Rights (1980).

4. In addition to simple humanistic notions that people are not doormats, there are three distinct bases for recognizing this, which are outlined by H.L. Mencken. *See* H.L. Mencken, TREATISE ON RIGHT AND WRONG 14 (1977). *Theological* systems of morality are based in religious doctrine. *Logical* systems of morality stem from philosophical inquiries and seek to justify human conduct on purely logical grounds. *Biological* theories of morality originate in Darwin's work "The Descent of Man," wherein the moral passions of man are linked to instinct and are alleged to be observable in many lower animals (*id.* at 1–62).

5. *See* L. von Mises, HUMAN ACTION 279–87 (1963).

6. *See, e.g.,* L. Tribe, AMERICAN CONSTITUTIONAL LAW 1302–1435 (1988).

7. No country for instance has ever enjoyed the benefits of *laissez faire* or the freedom and individual liberty possible under Adam Smith's conception of capitalism. *See* J. Gray, LIBERALISM 26–36 (1986) (there has never been a true period of *laissez faire*); L. Friedman, A HISTORY OF AMERICAN LAW 177–79, 440, 454, 465 (1985) (supporting the notion that *laissez faire* in America has been long on rhetoric and short on reality); A. Nock, OUR ENEMY, THE STATE (1983).

Chapter 8

1. L. von Mises, HUMAN ACTION 279–87 (1963).

2. *See* F. Hayek, THE CONSTITUTION OF LIBERTY 200–228 (1960).

3. *Id.*

4. *See generally* F. Hayek, LAW, LEGISLATION AND LIBERTY: vol. 1 RULES AND ORDER 35–54 (1973) (discussing spontaneous social order as it relates to law and social cooperation).

5. *See* F. Hayek, LAW, LEGISLATION AND LIBERTY: vol. 3 THE POLITICAL ORDER OF A FREE PEOPLE 1–19 (1979).

6. *Id.*

7. *See* Malloy, *The Political Economy of Co-Financing America's Urban Renaissance,* 40 VAND. L. REV. 67–134 (1987).

8. *See* Hoeflich & Malloy, *The Shattered Dream of American Housing Policy—The Need for Reform,* 26 B.C.L. REV. 655–90 (1985); Malloy, *The Economics of Rent Control—A Texas Perspective,* 17 TEXAS TECH L. REV. 797–809 (1986).

9. *See* THE REPORT OF THE PRESIDENT'S COMMISSION ON HOUSING (1982).

10. *See* Hoeflich & Malloy, *Housing Policy, supra* note 8.

11. *See* 21 LAND USE DIGEST 1 (Aug. 1988) (a study by the Manhattan Institute for Policy Research found a strong link between rent control and the degree of homelessness in different U.S. cities).

12. *See* M. Friedman & R. Friedman, FREE TO CHOOSE 109–12 (1980) (arguing that effects of most subsidy programs have been negative and, rather than helping people needing homes, programs really only benefitted landowners, builders, and sellers); Olsen, *Housing Programs and the Forgotten Taxpayer,* 66 THE PUBLIC INTEREST 97, 102–8 (1982); *see also* THE REPORT OF THE PRESIDENT'S COMMISSION ON HOUSING 27–48 (1982).

13. *See* Friedman, FREE TO CHOOSE, *supra* note 12, at 253–70. In addition to raising taxes or printing money, the government can also enter the financial markets to borrow from the public.

14. *See* ULI—The Urban Land Institute, *Tax Expenditures for Real Estate* 18

LAND USE DIG. 3 (Jan. 15, 1985) (for fiscal years 1984–1989 total cost of lost revenue to federal government as a result of tax benefits for real estate estimated at $320 billion).

15. *See, e.g.,* Malloy, *Is Law and Economics Moral? Humanistic Economics and a Classical Liberal Critique of Posner's Economic Analysis,* 24 VAL. U.L. REV. 147 (1990); Malloy, *The Limits of "Science" in Legal Discourse—A Reply to Posner,* 24 VAL. U.L. REV. 175 (1990). Both articles argue for the importance of keeping morality and natural rights expressly in our discourse.

Chapter 9

1. *See* R. Malloy, LAW AND ECONOMICS—A COMPARATIVE APPROACH TO THEORY AND PRACTICE (1990) [hereinafter Malloy, LAW AND ECONOMICS].

2. *See* L. von Mises, HUMAN ACTION (1966).

3. *See* A. Smith, THE THEORY OF MORAL SENTIMENTS 69, 166–69 (E. West ed. 1976). Smith commented: "It is thus that man, who can subsist only in society, was fitted by nature to that situation for which he was made. All the members of human society stand in need of each other's assistance, and are likewise exposed to mutual injuries" (*id.* at 166). He also noted: "Man, it has been said, has a natural love for society, and desires that the union of mankind should be preserved for its own sake, and though he himself was to derive no benefit from it" (*id.* at 169). *See also* A. Smith, THE WEALTH OF NATIONS (vol. 1 at 17–18) (E. Cannon ed. 1976) (people depend on interaction in society).

4. *See, e.g., infra* notes 27, 29, 32.

5. *See* FASCISM—A READER'S GUIDE (W. Laquer ed. 1976) [hereinafter FASCISM]. *See also* J. Stone, *Theories of Law and Justice of Fascist Italy,* 1 MOD. L. REV. 177–97 (1937).

6. *See supra* note 5.

7. *See* F. Hayek, THE CONSTITUTION OF LIBERTY 400–401 (1960).

8. *See* A. Nock, OUR ENEMY, THE STATE 45 (1983). Nock states:

> Republicanism permits the individual to persuade himself that the state is his creation, that state action is his action, that when it expresses itself it expresses him, and when it is glorified he is glorified. . . . Lincoln's phrase, "of the people, by the people, for the people" was probably the most effective strike of propaganda ever made in behalf of republican state prestige. (*Id.* at 45)

9. G. Stuteville & Scott L. Miley, *High Time to Herald Hoosiers' Heyday,* INDIANAPOLIS STAR, April 2, 1987, at 1, col. 1.

> If ever there was a time when it was o.k. to be from Indiana, when people from this great state could stand and shout, without shame, to the world "WE ARE THE HOOSIER!"—then now must certainly be that time. We have the NCAA basketball trophy. (*Id.*)

> We have coach Bobby Knight. (*Id.*)

> The bottom line is that each of the little occurrences, triumphs and victories add up to a heck of a lot. That forms the basis of our personality and characteristic as a state.
> Everything like an I.U. championship stands by itself, but it's all part of

a greater whole that is the common personality we have as a state. (*Id.* at 10, col. 1)

See also P. Richards, *Reagan Honors I.U. Champs in Storybook Day*, INDIANAPOLIS STAR, April 4, 1987, at 1, col. 1; P. Richards, *Indiana Captures NCAA Title*, INDIANAPOLIS STAR, March 31, 1987, at 1, col. 1.

10. *See* Malloy, *Invisible Hand or Sleight of Hand? Adam Smith, Richard Posner and the Philosophy of Law and Economics*, 36 KAN. L. REV. 209–59 (1988); Posner, *The Ethics of Wealth Maximization: Reply to Malloy*, 36 KAN. L. REV. 260–66 (1988); Malloy, *The Merits of the Smithian Critique: A Final Word on Smith and Posner*, 36 KAN. L. REV. 267–74 (1988). Posner has written many articles which are discussed and evaluated in Malloy, *Invisible Hand, supra*. For a sample of key works by Posner, see R. Posner, ECONOMIC ANALYSIS OF LAW (1986); R. Posner, THE ECONOMICS OF JUSTICE (1983) [hereinafter Posner, ECONOMICS OF JUSTICE]; Posner, *An Economic Theory of the Criminal Law*, 85 COLUM. L. REV. 1193–1231 (1985).

11. *See* Posner, *Law and Economics Is Moral*, 24 VAL. U.L. REV. 163 (1990) (arguing against natural rights). *See also* Malloy, *Invisible Hand, supra* note 10, at 209 (arguing that Posner rejects natural rights and the role of morality and is, therefore, outside the classical liberal tradition of Adam Smith).

12. *See* Posner, ECONOMICS OF JUSTICE, *supra* note 10, at 76–77. Posner states:

> Another implication of the wealth-maximization approach, however, is that people who lack sufficient earning power to support even a minimum standard of living are entitled to no say in the allocation of resources unless they are part of the utility function of someone who has wealth. This conclusion may seem to weight too heavily the individual's particular endowment of capacities. If he happens to be born feebleminded and his net social product is negative, he would have no right to the means of support even though there was nothing blameworthy in his inability to support himself. (*Id.* at 76)

See also Posner, *Wealth Maximization Revisited*, 2 NOTRE DAME J.L. ETHICS & PUB. POL'Y. 85, 101 (1985). "There is for good or ill nothing in the ethic of wealth maximization which says that society has a duty to help the needy" (*id.*).

13. *See* Malloy, *Invisible Hand, supra* note 10, at 242–54.

14. *Id.* at 248–51. *See also* Reuter, *A Just Use of Economics or Just Use Economics* (Book Review), 70 CALIF. L. REV. 850 (1982); Schmalbeck, *The Justice of Economics: An Analysis of Wealth Maximization as a Normative Goal* (Book Review), 83 COLUM. L. REV. 488 (1983); Kennedy, *Cost-Benefit Analysis of Entitlement Problems: A Critique*, 33 STAN. L. REV. 387 (1981).

15. *See* Malloy, *Invisible Hand, supra* note 10; Malloy, *A Final Word on Smith and Posner, supra* note 10.

16. *See, e.g.*, T. Sowell, CIVIL RIGHTS: RHETORIC OR REALITY? (1984); W. Williams, THE STATE AGAINST BLACKS (1982). (Both of these books use conservative theory.)

17. Under Posner's system, certain variables may be included or excluded from the calculation. For instance, the impact on family harmony may not be included. Thus, if the value to each of the parties of their transactions in sex was +2, their total utility would be +4. If we estimate the impact on street crime to be +1 then the transaction should be permitted (+4 versus +1). If

we assume an impact against family harmony of +1 then we have +4 versus +2 and the transaction should still be allowed, even though we have taken a new variable into consideration. But, if we suppose that the impact on street crime is a +3 and the impact against family harmony is a +2, then we have a +4 increase in utility to the parties at the expense of a +5 negative impact on the rest of society. Thus, the transaction is no longer a socially desirable exchange. Obviously, the difficulty in such social planning is determining the variables to use and their respective values. *See generally* E.F. Schumacher, SMALL IS BEAUTIFUL—ECONOMICS AS IF PEOPLE MATTERED (1973). In criticizing the extensive efforts to reduce all human behavior and rights to market formulations, Schumacher has harsh words for economists and for efforts such as Posner's. Schumacher says that in the market:

> Everything is equated with everything else. To equate things means to give them a price and thus to make them exchangeable. To the extent that economic thinking is based on the market, it takes the sacredness out of life, because there can be nothing sacred in something that has a price. Not surprisingly, therefore, if economic thinking pervades the whole of society, even simple non-economic values like beauty, health or cleanliness can survive only if they prove to be 'economic.'
>
> To press non-economic values into the framework of the economic calculus, economists use the method of cost/benefit analysis ... [I]t is a procedure by which the higher is reduced to the level of the lower and the priceless is given a price. It can therefore never serve to clarify the situation and lead to an enlightened decision. All it can do is lead to self-deception or the deception of others; for to undertake to measure the immeasurable is absurd and constitutes but an elaborate method of moving from preconceived notions to foregone conclusions; all one has to do to obtain the desired results is to impute suitable values to the immeasurable costs and benefits. The logical absurdity, however, is not the greatest fault of the undertaking: what is worse, and destructive of civilisation, is the pretense that everything has a price or, in other words, that money is the highest of all values. (*Id.* at 45–46)

Schumacher's comments are consistent with the moral dimensions of the approach of Adam Smith and the classical liberals. His comments also seem to be similar to the Catholic Bishops' recent comments on the U.S. economy. The Bishops remind us that one important criterion in evaluating an economy is the way in which people are treated and the degree to which it incorporates moral principles. NATIONAL CONFERENCE OF CATHOLIC BISHOPS, PASTORAL LETTER, ECONOMIC JUSTICE FOR ALL: CATHOLIC SOCIAL TEACHING AND THE U.S. ECONOMY (Nov. 13 1986), reprinted in Nat'l Cath. Rep., Jan. 9, 1987, at 1.

18. *See generally* A. Shand, THE CAPITALIST ALTERNATIVE—AN INTRODUCTION TO NEO–AUSTRIAN ECONOMICS 15–31 (1984) (efforts at perfecting mathematical economic models are misguided); F. Hayek, THE COUNTER-REVOLUTION OF SCIENCE—STUDIES ON THE ABUSE OF REASON (1952) [hereinafter Hayek, ABUSE OF REASON] (there is an inherent unpredictability and indeterminacy in human knowledge—the future is not only difficult to predict, but is inherently unpredictable); B. Ackerman, SOCIAL JUSTICE IN THE LIBERAL STATE (1980) [hereinafter Ackerman, SOCIAL JUSTICE] (just as Ackerman argues that the liberal dialogue cannot be ended by divine appeal to

the word of God, a dialogue on law and economics cannot be ended merely by invoking the wealth maximization principle).

19. *See* Malloy, *Invisible Hand, supra* note 10; Malloy, *Is Law and Economics Moral? Humanistic Economics and a Classical Liberal Critique of Posner's Economic Analysis,* 24 VAL. U.L. REV. 147 (1990); Malloy, *The Limits of "Science" in Legal Discourse—A Reply to Posner,* 24 VAL. U.L. REV. 175 (1990) [hereinafter Malloy, *Legal Discourse*]; III LAW AND SEMIOTICS (R. Kevelson ed. 1990; *see* chapter by Malloy, *Of Icons, Metaphors, and Private Property—The Recognition of "Welfare" Claims in the Philosophy of Adam Smith*).

20. *Supra* note 19.

21. *Id.*

22. *Id. See also* Posner, ECONOMICS OF JUSTICE, *supra* note 10, at 86 (approving slavery in some circumstances as efficient); Posner, *Wealth Maximization Revisited, supra* note 12 (approving slavery on efficiency grounds).

23. *See, e.g.,* Malloy, *Invisible Hand, supra* note 10, at 242–50; Malloy, *Legal Discourse, supra* note 19, at 175–81.

24. *See* Malloy, *Legal Discourse, supra* note 19, at 175–81.

25. *Id.*

26. *Id.*

27. *See, e.g.,* Ackerman, SOCIAL JUSTICE, *supra* note 18.

28. *See* Malloy, LAW AND ECONOMICS, *supra* note 1.

29. This I believe is the ultimate conclusion to be reached from reading Dworkin and Ackerman. *See* Ackerman, SOCIAL JUSTICE, *supra* note 18; B. Ackerman, RECONSTRUCTING AMERICAN LAW (1983); R. Dworkin, LAW's EMPIRE (1986); R. Dworkin, TAKING RIGHTS SERIOUSLY (1978). *See also* Hyde, *Is Liberalism Possible?* 57 N.Y.U. L. REV. 1031–58 (1982).

30. *See* Malloy, LAW AND ECONOMICS, *supra* note 1, at Chapter 5.

31. *See* Ackerman, SOCIAL JUSTICE, *supra* note 18.

32. *See, e.g.,* Kennedy, *Form and Substance in Private Law Adjudication,* 89 HARV. L. REV. 1685–1778 (1976); Tushnet, *An Essay on Rights,* 62 TEX. L. REV. 1363–1403 (1984); M. Kelman, A GUIDE TO CRITICAL LEGAL STUDIES (1987); Unger, *The Critical Legal Studies Movement,* 96 HARV. L. REV. 561–675 (1983). A general bibliography of Critical Legal Studies can be found in Kennedy & Klare, *Bibliography of Critical Legal Studies,* 94 YALE L.J. 461 (1984). For a general introduction to the feminist theory related to Critical Legal Studies, see *Women In Legal Education—Pedagogy, Law, Theory and Practice,* 38 J. LEGAL EDUC. 3 (1981).

33. *See* Malloy, LAW AND ECONOMICS, *supra* note 1, at Chapter 6.

34. *Id. See also* Kennedy, *Form and Substance, supra* note 32 (looking at the theoretical implication of rules versus standards).

35. *See* Malloy, LAW AND ECONOMICS, *supra* note 1, at Chapter 6.

36. *See* Kelman, CRITICAL LEGAL STUDIES, *supra* note 32, at 63.

37. *See, e.g.,* FREEDOM, FEMINISM, AND THE STATE (W. McElroy ed. 1982); R. Nozick, ANARCHY, STATE, AND UTOPIA (1968) [hereinafter Nozick, ANARCHY]; A. Nock, OUR ENEMY, THE STATE (1983); R. Epstein, TAKINGS—PRIVATE PROPERTY AND THE POWER OF EMINENT DOMAIN (1985) [hereinafter Epstein, TAKINGS]; M. Rothbard, FOR A NEW LIBERTY—THE LIBERTARIAN MANIFESTO (1978); M. Rothbard, THE ETHICS OF LIBERTY (1983).

38. *See, e.g.,* A. Rand, PHILOSOPHY: WHO NEEDS IT? (1982).

39. *See* Nozick, ANARCHY, *supra* note 37.

40. *See* Epstein, TAKINGS, *supra* note 37.

41. *See* Malloy, LAW AND ECONOMICS, *supra* note 1, at Chapter 7.

42. Epstein, TAKINGS, *supra* note 37, at 5–6.

43. *See* Malloy, LAW AND ECONOMICS, *supra* note 1, at Chapter 7.

44. *See supra* Chapter 3 discussing Smith and classical liberal theory.

45. For excellent examples of classical liberal scholarship, see M. Friedman, BRIGHT PROMISES, DISMAL PERFORMANCE (W. Allen ed. 1983); M. Friedman, CAPITALISM AND FREEDOM (1962 reissued 1982) [hereinafter Friedman, CAPITALISM]; M. Friedman & R. Friedman, FREE TO CHOOSE (1980) [hereinafter Friedman, FREE TO CHOOSE]; M. Friedman & R. Friedman, TYRANNY OF THE STATUS QUO (1984) [hereinafter Friedman, TYRANNY]; F. Hayek, THE CONSTITUTION OF LIBERTY (1960) [hereinafter Hayek, LIBERTY]; F. Hayek, ABUSE OF REASON, *supra* note 18; F. Hayek, LAW, LEGISLATION AND LIBERTY: vol. 1 RULES AND ORDER (1973) [hereinafter Hayek, RULES AND ORDER]; F. Hayek, LAW, LEGISLATION AND LIBERTY: vol. 2 THE MIRAGE OF SOCIAL JUSTICE (1976) [hereinafter Hayek, SOCIAL JUSTICE]; F. Hayek, LAW, LEGISLATION AND LIBERTY: vol. 3 THE POLITICAL ORDER OF A FREE PEOPLE (1979) [hereinafter Hayek, A FREE PEOPLE]; F. Hayek, THE ROAD TO SERFDOM (1944) [hereinafter Hayek, ROAD TO SERFDOM]. *See also* Malloy, *Invisible Hand, supra* note 10; Malloy, *A Final Word on Smith and Posner, supra* note 10; Malloy, *The Political Economy of Co-Financing America's Urban Renaissance*, 40 VAND. L. REV. 67–134 (1987); Malloy, *Equating Human Rights and Property Rights—The Need for Moral Judgment in an Economic Analysis of Law and Social Policy*, 47 OHIO ST. L.J. 163–77 (1986) [hereinafter Malloy, *Human Rights*].

46. *See* Malloy, *Human Rights, supra* note 45. *See generally* J. Schumpeter, CAPITALISM, SOCIALISM AND DEMOCRACY 190–91 (1950) (morality and one's sense of justice are important in evaluating the merits of any particular social, political, or economic structure).

47. *See* Friedman, CAPITALISM, *supra* note 45, at 1–36. For Friedman's comments on this issue, see *supra* note 8, Chapter 4.

48. Friedman, *Free Markets and Free Speech*, 10 HARV. J.L. & PUB. POL'Y. 1, 7 (1987).

49. *See* Hayek, LIBERTY, *supra* note 45, at 11–21.

50. *See generally* Hayek, RULES AND ORDER, *supra* note 45; Hayek, SOCIAL JUSTICE, *supra* note 45; Hayek, A FREE PEOPLE, *supra* note 45. For a discussion on spontaneous social order, law, and government, see Hayek, RULES AND ORDER, *supra* note 45, at 35–54.

51. *See supra* note 50.

52. *See* Smith, MORAL SENTIMENTS, *supra* note 3, at 264.

53. *See* Friedman, CAPITALISM, *supra* note 45, at 161–202 (the alleviation of poverty through a negative income tax as a guaranteed income); Friedman, FREE TO CHOOSE, *supra* note 45, at 150–88 (public education and the use of a voucher system); Malloy, *Human Rights, supra* note 45, at 163; Malloy, *America's Urban Renaissance, supra* note 45, at 67, 112–33.

54. *See* sources cited *supra* note 53.

55. *See* Hoeflich & Malloy, *The Shattered Dream of American Housing Policy—The Need for Reform*, 26 B.C.L. REV. 655 (1985).

56. *Id.*

57. *Id.*

Chapter 10

1. *See generally* J. Campbell, THE POWER OF MYTH (1988); J. Campbell, MYTHS TO LIVE BY (1988); J. Campbell, THE INNER REACHES OF OUTER SPACE—METAPHOR AS MYTH AND AS RELIGION (1986); J. Campbell, THE HERO WITH A THOUSAND FACES (1949).

2. *See* Malloy, *Is Law and Economics Moral? Humanistic Economics and a Classical Liberal Critique of Posner's Economic Analysis*, 24 VAL. U.L. REV. 147 (1990); Malloy, *The Limits of "Science" in Legal Discourse—A Reply to Posner*, 24 VAL. U.L. REV. 175 (1990). Both articles refer to Adam Smith's work and assert as Smith did that we learn morality, first principles, etc. from experience.

Chapter 11

1. *See generally* J. Reps, THE MAKING OF URBAN AMERICA—THE HISTORY OF CITY PLANNING IN THE UNITED STATES (1965); D. Hagman & J. Juergensmeyer, URBAN PLANNING AND LAND DEVELOPMENT CONTROL LAW (2d ed. 1986) [hereinafter Hagman, PLANNING].

2. *See* B. Siegan, LAND USE WITHOUT ZONING (1972) [hereinafter Siegan, ZONING]; *see also* Sigman, *Non-Zoning in Houston*, 13 J. L. & ECON. 71 (1971).

3. *See* Siegan, ZONING, *supra* note 2.

4. *See* J. Feagin, FREE ENTERPRISE CITY: HOUSTON IN POLITICAL–ECONOMIC PERSPECTIVE (1988).

5. Village of Euclid v. Amber Realty Co., 272 U.S. 365 (1926).

6. *See* Hagman, PLANNING, *supra* note 1.

7. *Id.*

8. *Id.*

9. *See* B. Siegan, OTHER PEOPLE'S PROPERTY (1976); R. Babcock, THE ZONING GAME (1966); R. Babcock & C. Sieman, THE ZONING GAME REVISITED (1985).

10. *See, e.g.,* Taub, *Exactions, Linkages, and Regulatory Takings: The Developer's Perspective* 20 URB. LAW. 515 (1988); Toombs, *The Linkage of Infrastructure Costs to Private Development*, 3 REAL EST. FIN. J. 40 (Fall 1987); Comment, *Opening the Door for Boston's Poor: Will "Linkage" Survive Judicial Review?* 14 B.C. ENVTL. AFF. L. REV. 447 (1987).

11. *See* M.B. Johnson, RESOLVING THE HOUSING CRISIS (1982) (in particular Chapter 6 by Robert Ellickson).

12. *See id. See also* Southern Burlington County v. Township of Mount Laurel, 67 N.J. 151, 336 A.2d 713 (1975); Oakwood At Madison, Inc. v. Township of Madison, 72 N.J. 481, 371 A.2d 1192 (1977); Southern Burlington County v. Township of Mount Laurel, 92 N.J. 158, 456 A.2d 390 (N.J. 1983).

13. For a recent analysis of the takings power, see an interesting book with a libertarian perspective, R. Epstein, TAKINGS—PRIVATE PROPERTY AND THE POWER OF EMINENT DOMAIN (1985) [hereinafter Epstein, TAKINGS].

14. *See generally* Mandelker, *Public Entrepreneurship: A Legal Primer*, 15 REAL EST. L.J. 3 (1986).

15. *See generally* Epstein, TAKINGS, *supra* note 13; Callies, *Property Rights: Are There Any Left?* 20 URB. LAW. 597 (1988); Epstein, *Takings: Descent and Resurrection*, 1987 SUP. CT. REV. 1.

16. *See* Lawrence, *Constitutional Limitations on Governmental Participation in*

Downtown Development Projects, 35 VAND. L. REV. 277 (1982) (revealing that there is very little limitation on government participation); Malloy, *The Political Economy of Co-Financing America's Urban Renaissance*, 40 VAND. L. REV. 67–134 (1987). *See also* Sax, *Takings and the Police Power*, 74 YALE L.J. 36 (1964).

17. *See supra* note 16.

Chapter 12

1. *See* Malloy, *The Political Economy of Co-Financing America's Urban Renaissance*, 40 VAND. L. REV. 67–134 (1987) (discussing these programs in detail).

2. *Id.*

3. For additional information on these types of activities, see CITIES REBORN (R. Levitt ed. 1987); G. Stout & J. Vitt, PUBLIC INCENTIVES AND FINANCING TECHNIQUES FOR CODEVELOPMENT (1982); W.A. Barnes, DOWNTOWN DEVELOPMENT: PLAN AND IMPLEMENTATION (1982); R. Witherspoon, CODEVELOPMENT: CITY REBUILDING BY BUSINESS AND GOVERNMENT (1982).

Chapter 13

1. *See* Forstall & Starsinic, *The Largest U.S. Metropolitan Areas*, URB. LAND. Sept. 1984, at 32–33 (relying on 1982 figures derived from the Population Division, U.S. Bureau of the Census).

2. *See* R. Bamberger & D. Parham, *Leveraging Amenity Infrastructure—Indianapolis's Economic Development Strategy*, 43 URB. LAND. 12–18 (Nov. 1984) [hereinafter Bamberger & Parham], at 12, 14.

3. *Id.* at 13–14.

4. *Id.*

5. *Id.* at 13.

6. *Id.* In addition, 4,000 more jobs were lost in 1983 by the closing of a Western Electric facility (*id.* at 17).

7. *Id.* at 12–18.

8. *Id.* at 13.

9. *Id.* at 16.

10. *Id.* at 12–18. *See generally* Goodman & Nutting, *A Tale of Four Cities: Investment Activity in "Dying Downtowns,"* URB. LAND, March 1985, at 32, 33. Support for real estate development projects is illustrated by the way Indianapolis spends its allocations of Community Development Block Grant Funds (CBDG). In 1985 Indianapolis spent about 50 percent of its CBDG funds on real estate development while the national average for other cities was only 11 percent, the remaining money being used for direct assistance to low and moderate income residents in accordance with the CBDG program's original objective. Johnston, *Housing Funds Go Elsewhere*, INDIANAPOLIS NEWS, Nov. 17, 1986, at 25, col. 1.

11. *See* Swiatek, *Tax Dollars Are Working Hard in City Real Estate Developments*, INDIANAPOLIS STAR, Sept. 1, 1985, at 11–12, col. 2; Bamberger & Parham, *supra* note 2, at 12–18.

12. *See supra* note 11.

13. *See, e.g., id.* For example, the One North Capitol project was unprofitable in its first full year of operation, so the city received no income. Two

West Washington was unprofitable for two years and is not expected to show a profit until at least 1988 (*id.*). *See also Pan Am Plaza Project Has Yet to Earn Keep,* INDIANAPOLIS NEWS, Nov. 16, 1989, A–9, col. 1. This article reveals that the city provided $5 million in land to a private developer to build an office building. The city acquired the land in a takings action in order to transfer it from one private party to another. After two years the property is not contributing to property taxes and is having financial difficulty.

14. Schramm, *Public-Private Projects Seeing Red,* INDIANAPOLIS STAR, June 12, 1900, at C1, col. 4.

15. *See* Swiatek, *supra* note 11.

16. Three of these projects are identified in Table 1 in the text and correspond with note 15, and they include One North Capital, Two West Washington, and Embassy Suites. *See supra* note 15.

17. *See* Wildey & Schneider, *Will Downtown Shopping Mall Help Indianapolis?* INDIANAPOLIS STAR, Oct. 21, 1985, at C1, col. 1; *see also* Schneider & Wildey, *Circle Centre–Mall Plan Unveiling Slated for Tuesday,* INDIANAPOLIS STAR, Oct. 20, 1985, at F1, col. 1; J. Swiatek, *On the Market—City Steadily Acquiring Property for Mall,* INDIANAPOLIS STAR, Sept. 13, 1988, at C1, col. 2; R. Schneider, *Circle Centre Mall to Cost $970 Million,* INDIANAPOLIS STAR, May 19, 1988, at A1, col. 4 (with new projects putting the total cost of the mall project at $970 million and the city's share at $250 million); R. Cady, *State Tied to Success of Downtown Project,* INDIANAPOLIS STAR, July 31, 1988, at A1, col. 1.

18. *See* Schneider & Wildey, *Mall Project Seen as Magnet to New Business,* INDIANAPOLIS STAR, Oct. 22, 1985, at C1, col. 1.

19. *Id.*

20. *Id.* at C8. Indianapolis hopes to get $15 million to $20 million in federal money for the project. The city also will arrange a package of tax abatement and TIF to assist in the development of the mall (*id.*). *See also* Schneider, *Delays May Benefit Proposed Circle Centre Mall,* INDIANAPOLIS STAR, July 20, 1986, at B5, col. 1. In addition to seeking federal grant money, the city hopes to subsidize the project by making mortgage financing available at substantially discounted interest rates (*id.*). *See also* Schneider, *Federal Loan Sought to Buy Ten Buildings for Downtown Mall,* INDIANAPOLIS STAR, Dec. 8, 1985, at A1, col. 4 (discussing city efforts to raise $9.5 million to buy property needed to assemble the land for the mall).

21. *See* Schneider, *City Builds Its Development Plans on Tax Financing,* INDIANAPOLIS STAR, June 1, 1986, at C3, col. 1; Schneider, *Moldthan Warns About Tax Increment Bonds,* INDIANAPOLIS STAR, June 19, 1986, at C5, col. 3; Newland & Petrosky, *Hudnut Proposes New Plan for Downtown Construction,* INDIANAPOLIS STAR, Oct. 10, 1985, at C7, col. 1. The city plans to borrow $23 million to finance projects related to hosting the 1987 Pan Am Games. The bulk of the money will come from TIF (*id.*). *See also* Indiana Continuing Legal Education Forum, REAL ESTATE DEVELOPMENT AND HOUSING LAW IV-6 (1986). Indiana also has adopted enterprise zones. Two significant features are the Indiana tax credit of up to $1,500 for each resident of an enterprise zone for whom a job is created and a credit, equal to 5 percent of the interest paid, against Indiana tax available to lenders making loans within an enterprise zone.

22. *See* Miley & Schneider, *Is Tax Abatement Worth the Gamble?* INDIANAPOLIS STAR, Feb. 2, 1986, at B8, col. 1 (identifying major projects that have benefited from substantial tax abatements ranging into many millions of dollars)..

23. *See* Swiatek, *supra* note 11; Bamberger & Parham, *supra* note 2. Co-financing arrangements have been used to develop and promote such projects as Market Square Arena (basketball), the Hoosierdome (football), and a world-class olympic natatorium. Progress is also underway in building a downtown park and zoo at White River State Park (*id.*). *See also* Swiatek, *"Plot" Will "Thicken" When Work Begins on Lower Canal Project,* INDIANAPOLIS STAR, Feb. 2, 1986, at 11, col. 2 (noting $7 million in federal funds to begin work on a riverwalk similar to that in San Antonio, Texas).

24. Among the projects illustrated in Table 2, *supra,* all but Merchant's Plaza involved the use of $12.5 million in Federal Urban Development Action Grant money. *See* Swiatek, *supra* note 11, at 12.

25. *See* Stall, *State of the Union,* INDIANAPOLIS MONTHLY, April 1986, at 60–76. The station's grand opening was April 26, 1986 (*id.* at 60).

26. *Id.* In its prime the train station had served two hundred trains a day (*id.*).

27. *Id.*

28. *See id.* at 60–76; Schneider, *Station Reopening To Be Major Gala,* INDIANAPOLIS STAR, Feb. 16, 1986, at A1, col. 1; *Union Station,* INDIANAPOLIS STAR, April 20, 1986, at K1–K16 (special section). The STAR devoted a sixteen-page special section of the Sunday paper to promoting the grand opening of Union Station on the following Saturday. The *Today Show* broadcast on NBC was one day before the grand opening. The local praise for the developer included a rags-to-riches story of a son of immigrant parents whose first entrepreneurial venture was a lawn-watering business. *See* Stall, *supra* note 25, at 74–75. The local hero, of course, stands to make a considerable profit from a venture that is substantially subsidized and promoted at the public expense.

29. *See* Table 1, *supra.*

30. *See* Stall, *supra* note 25, at 74. Congressman Andy Jacobs was a vocal opponent of the Union Station renovation and he was upset with the use of Federal Mass Transit Funds. He stated, "that money was meant for buses, not boutiques. . . . [A]t a time when student loans are cut and we are running up the God-awful deficits, I don't see the logic" (*id.*). Of course, Jacobs eventually did see the political logic and was responsible for assuring the continuation of a federal tax credit for the developers scheduled to be eliminated when the project still had $5 million in work left and the remaining tax credit was worth $1.25 million (*id.* at 74–75).

31. *Id.*

32. Even when the city did not directly condemn property, its method resulted in de facto takings. *See* K. Johnston, *Owners of Rost Building Sue City Over Mall Project,* INDIANAPOLIS NEWS, March 12, 1987, at 10, col. 1.

33. While I was living in Indianapolis, the city passed a moratorium on building on the Northside. This raised new interest in downtown.

34. *See* L. Levathes, *Indianapolis: City on the Rebound,* 172 NATIONAL GEOGRAPHIC 230–59 (Aug. 1987). Members of the very Republican Columbia Club boast "anything of importance in this town starts right here, . . . it's almost a law" (*id.* at 248). A local columnist complains "things get done quickly and smoothly around here because there's no dissent, . . . the rest of us kind of feel like spectators" (*id.* at 248).

35. *See, e.g.,* Forstall & Starsinic, *supra* note 1, at Chapter 2.

36. *See* Downtown Development Research Committee and Indiana Christian

Leadership Conference, Indianapolis, DOWNTOWN DEVELOPMENT FOR WHOM? (1980).

37. *See, e.g., Taxpayer Costs Continue When Construction Stops*, INDIANAPOLIS NEWS, Nov. 15, 1989, A12, col. 4. Not only have millions been spent to acquire such facilities, but they cost a significant amount to maintain. The Indiana University Natatorium, for instance, costs taxpayers about $450,000 a year in utility expenses (*id.*). The facility, although on the IUPUI campus, is considered to be a centerpiece of the city's redevelopment efforts with a focus on sports (*id.*).

38. *See* D. Penticuff, *State Won't Spring for Conference Center—IUPUI Students Forced to Pay Bond Retirement*, INDIANAPOLIS BUS. J., Nov. 16–22, 1987, at 8A, col. 2; M. McGrath, *IUPUI May Lose Hot Profit*, SAGAMORE, March 21, 1988, at 1, col. 1.

39. *See* J. Halliman, *Blacks Enjoying Little of Midtown Project Wealth*, INDIANAPOLIS STAR, May 29, 1988, at 1, col. 1 (this special report covered several pages of the paper and explained how minorities and the poor were not sharing in many of the projects undertaken by the city. *See also Social Ills Had to Wait a Turn*, INDIANAPOLIS NEWS, Nov. 18, 1989, A1, col. 2. The article outlines the tremendous expenditure of public funds and resources from the Lilly Endowment. Although over $4 billion have been spent on revitalization over the past two decades, only a small fraction of money has been directed toward the needs of the city's poor.

40. *See Shaping a City—The Lilly Legacy: Endowment is 5th Largest*, INDIANAPOLIS NEWS, Nov. 13, 1989, A1, col. 2. Conservative estimates are that, since 1937, the Lilly Endowment has given $425 million to Indianapolis projects (*id.*). This represents about 44 percent of all funds the private foundation has given away (*id.*). The Lilly Endowment is the fifth largest endowment in the United States, with current assets in excess of $2 billion (*id.* at A1 & A8).

41. *See, e.g., Shaping a City—The Lilly Legacy*, INDIANAPOLIS NEWS, Nov. 13–18. Written as a special story series, these reports focused on the Lilly Endowment activity in Indianapolis and its role as a key player in directing the political and public agenda. Many potential conflicts of interest are exposed, and it is shown that a handful of private businessmen managed to secure very profitable contracts, properties, and benefits as a result of their personal relationship with the political power structure of the city. The stories included in this report were very revealing, but like other reports in the local papers, they came well after the decision-making process was over. The stories also reveal the "good ole boy" attitudes in Indianapolis where the appearance of numerous conflicts of interest are brushed aside by personal assertions that all parties felt they acted fairly. It is almost as if their having said so makes it so.

42. *See Elite Panel Avoids Spotlight*, INDIANAPOLIS NEWS, Nov. 14, 1989, A1, A3–5, col. 1. This elite panel was the decision-making force behind public policy in Indianapolis (*id.*). The group was not subject to pubic scrutiny and its membership list includes the names of local businessmen, lawyers, bankers, and others who benefited financially from most of the projects they planned (*id.*). Furthermore, these are the "political fat-cats" who continually get press in Indianapolis for their civic commitment. Why doesn't the city spend more time praising the small business people who set up shop without subsidies and create real jobs and opportunities?

43. *Id.*

44. *Id.* This was basically an all-male, White, middle-class club that unofficially established the political and public agenda for the nation's twelfth largest city (*id.*). It was not representative of the community and the White male membership benefited from the activities undertaken (*id.*).

45. *Id.*

46. *Id.*

47. *See, e.g., Public Board Decisions Affect Members' Firms,* INDIANAPOLIS NEWS, Nov. 17, 1989, A1, A10–11, col. 1; *Business Opportunity Opened for Insiders,* INDIANAPOLIS NEWS, Nov. 16, 1989, A1, A8–9, col. 1. These reports reveal that members of the private City Committee had financial interests in many of the public/private ventures they promoted for the city's political agenda. The members also found their political and business power enhanced, as well as their finances, and in a number of instances their public roles put them in a position of making "public" decisions concerning their private business investments. In some cases open bidding for publicly supported projects was suspended and contracts were awarded to insiders.

48. *Id.*

49. A. Smith, THE WEALTH OF NATIONS, vol. 1, 144 (E. Cannon ed. 1976).

50. *Id.* at 278.

51. *See* E.M. Swift, *Now You See Him, Now You Don't,* SPORTS ILLUSTRATED, Dec. 15, 1986, at 84–100. Indianapolis not only built its Hoosierdome before it had a team to play in it, but "guaranteed the Colts $7 million in ticket and preseason radio and TV revenues for each of the first 12 years, plus the first $500,000 of revenue from the luxury boxes. On top of that, the city has built the Colts a new $4.4 million practice facility, which it has sold to Irsay (the Colts' owner) for one dollar" (*id.* at 100). *See also* H. Lancaster, *Tale of Two Cities: Why Football Mesmerizes Baltimore, Indianapolis,* WALL ST. J., Jan. 24, 1986, at 23, col. 4 (confirming the facts of the *Sports Illustrated* article and adding that Indianapolis subsidized interest costs on a $12.5 million loan to the Colts as part of the deal to get the team to relocate).

52. *Id.*

53. *See generally* Frieden & Sogalyn, DOWNTOWN, INC.: HOW AMERICA REBUILDS CITIES (1989); P. Eisinger, THE RISE OF THE ENTREPRENEURIAL STATE: STATE AND LOCAL ECONOMIC DEVELOPMENT POLICY IN THE UNITED STATES (1988). Both of these recent books present a positive interpretation of emerging trends in urban development and revitalization. They fail, however, to account for the dramatic normative changes that underlie emerging trends.

Chapter 14

1. *See* M. Friedman & R. Friedman, FREE TO CHOOSE 253–70 (1980).

2. *See* Hoeflich & Malloy, *The Shattered Dream of American Housing Policy—The Need for Reform,* 26 B.C.L. REV. 655, 681–83 (1985).

3. *See* Huddleston, *Taxpayers in Some Communities May Pay More in Tax Increments,* 19 LAND USE DIG. 2 (1986). Professor Jack Huddleston of the University of Wisconsin at Madison has examined the distribution of development costs among taxpayers in nineteen municipalities—nine of which used TIF—in Milwaukee County, Wisconsin. He found that residents of cities that did not use TIF for real estate projects effectively subsidized taxpayers in cities that did use TIF (*id.*). *See, e.g., Enterprise Zones,* 18 LAND USE DIG. 1

(1985) (noting that 26 states and more than 450 cities have adopted their own enterprise zone programs); Callies & Tamashiro, *Enterprise Zone: The Redevelopment Sweepstakes Begins*, 15 Urb. Law. 231, 268–71 (discussing state enterprise zone initiatives).

4. *See* Helyar & Johnson, *Tale of Two Cities—Chicago's Busy Center Masks a Loss of Jobs in Its Outlying Areas*, Wall St. J., April 16, 1986, at 1, col. 1. Chicago politicians have poured $1 billion into downtown incentives for construction, and the resulting activity has been favorable to the politicians, despite the fact the suburban areas are suffering (*id.*). *See also Review & Outlook—A Hunger for Money*, Wall St., J., Jan. 28, 1986, at 30, col. 1 (discussing how mayors use and rely on federal subsidies to satisfy the special interests of local friends and developers while claiming to be concerned with the poor and needy); *see generally Welfare for Developers*, Wall St., J., April 3, 1986, at 26, col. 1. This editorial discusses the tremendous amount of "welfare" being given to developers and related real estate professionals by way of local access to federal UDAG subsidies. The article asserts that states and districts with influential congressmen benefit greatly from the subsidies through extensive use of the political means. The editorial goes on to say:

> Of course, the UDAG boodle is defended on the ground that it helps the "poor." But 60% of UDAG funds have gone to commercial projects; developers promise new jobs but only two-thirds of those promised actually materialize, HUD estimates, and when you consider that UDAG money comes out of taxpayers' pockets, there is little reason to believe there is any net job "creation." Moreover, construction workers seldom are "poor." (*Id.*)

5. *Id. See* H. Hazlitt, Economics in One Lesson 36 (1979) [hereinafter Hazlitt] (discussing the predictable results of this process of wealth transfer).

6. *See* Hazlitt, *supra* note 5, at 40–48.

7. *See generally* Freilich, Frye & Carpenter, *The New Federalism—American Urban Policy in the 1980's: Trends and Directions in Urban, State and Local Government Law*, 15 Urb. Law. 159 (1983) (taking a complete look at Reagan's New Federalism, including urban development issues, tax issues, school issues, civil rights issues, and housing issues); Bollinger, *The Historic and Proper Place of Central Governments in Urban Redevelopment: The U.S. View*, 6 Urb. L. & Pol'y 53 (1983). Bollinger was Assistant Secretary for Community Planning and Development, United States Department of Housing and Urban Development, when he wrote this article. It reflects a New Federalism philosophy by stressing a strong national economy and the return of many state and local issues to state and local government. He sees the federal urban role as one of "urban facilitator," rather than provider, helping cities to be entrepreneurial and innovative in addressing their economic and community development needs (*id.* at 54). *See also* Wingo & Wolch, *Urban Land Policy Under the New Conservatism*, 5 Urb. L. & Pol'y 315 (1982) (arguing that the New Federalism is a conservative movement that favors commercial and industrial uses and rejects social welfare programs, all of which will lead to the "ghettoization" of the poor, the elderly, and the handicapped).

8. *See generally* M. Friedman & R. Friedman, Tyranny of the Status Quo (1984). In this book the Friedmans argue that much of the Reagan administration's rhetoric is unfulfilled. In actuality, Reagan had become trapped by special interest groups just as surely as the welfare Democrats, from whom Reagan tried to disassociate himself. Although the special interests may have

changed, the use of the political means and the tyranny of the status quo remain.

9. *See* Friedman, FREE TO CHOOSE, *supra* note 1, at 91–127, 228–29 (discussing the growth of the welfare state and the expansion of the federal government).

10. *See* Bollinger, *supra* note 7; Wingo & Wolch, *supra* note 7 (discussing the emphasis on local involvement and participation).

11. The theory is that putting power in state and local government creates a check on the federal government's power. At the same time, to the extent that government is responsive to the electorate, it is likely to be most responsive at the local level. See M. Friedman, CAPITALISM AND FREEDOM 7–21 (1962, reissued 1982). *But see* A. Nock, OUR ENEMY, THE STATE 29 (2d ed. 1983) (for a quote from Nock on this issue, see *supra* note 2, Chapter 4); J. Galbraith, THE ANATOMY OF POWER (1983).

12. Nock makes a further comment on the political process and its response to the rhetoric of returning government to the people. For his comments on this, see *supra* note 8, Chapter 9.

13. *See* J. Jacobs, CITIES AND THE WEALTH OF NATIONS 93–124 (1984) [hereinafter Jacobs, CITIES].

14. *Id.*

15. *Id.*

16. *See* I. Kirzner, DISCOVERY AND THE CAPITALIST PROCESS (1985).

These essays see market capitalism not simply as a set of institutions governing exchanges, not as a set of activities or prices (or both) continuously reflecting with attained accuracy the changing patterns of relative supply and demand, but as an ongoing *process of creative discovery*. What one witnesses in a market economy, at any point in time, are nothing but attempts by market participants to take advantage of newly discovered or created possibilities. In the course of seeking *these* plans, market participants notice, again, *further* market possibilities that had hitherto escaped attention. And so on. The process is kept continuously boiling by the incessant injection of unexpected changes and surprises. The process of creative discovery is never completed, nor is it ever arrested. (*Id.* at ix–x)

17. *See also* L. Harrison, UNDERDEVELOPMENT IS A STATE OF MIND (1985) (Harrison argues that the lack of development in Latin America is because of its mind-set or attitudes. A world vision of creative discovery is vital to economic development, while a static and elitist social structure coupled with discretionary state power is not helpful to economic development).

18. *See* Jacobs, CITIES, *supra* note 13.

19. *Id.* at 119–22.

20. *Id.* at 119.

21. *Id.*

22. *Id.* at 119. Jacobs clarifies this point by offering the following comparison:

Once we understand why unearned imports, whatever other usefulness they may have, are beside the point for catalyzing real economic development, we can understand, also, why the remittances that migrant workers send back to their poor home regions do so little to transform economic life there. Not having been earned right there, by city work, these benefits can play no part in economic life other than temporarily alleviating poverty. It is the same with all transfer payments from rich to poor regions. They alleviate poverty but inherently can do nothing to overcome the causes of poverty. (*Id.* at 122)

23. *Id.* at 119.
24. *Id.*
25. *Id.* (emphasis original).
26. *Id.* at 94–96.
27. *Id.* at 94.
28. *Id.* at 95.
29. *Id.*
30. *Id.*
31. *Id.*
32. *Id.* at 95–96.
33. *Id.*
34. *Id.*
35. *Id.* at 96.
36. *Id.* at 110–23. Jacobs describes the TVA efforts as attempts to create an artificial city region. She also points out that Knoxville, Tennessee, a city in the middle of the TVA area and home of the University of Tennessee, never was able to capitalize on the influx of TVA money. Knoxville never emerged as a successful or prosperous import-replacing city. She also notes that the region itself contained abundant natural resources and that the native people had a history of self-reliance and hard work. Furthermore, because the area had not developed as part of the earlier plantation economy of the South, many farmers in the region owned their own land. Despite all these strengths and the influx of enormous amounts of federal money for the TVA, no import-replacing city emerged.
37. *Id.* at 110–23.
38. *Id.*
39. *Id.* at 114.
40. *Id.*
41. *Id.* Jacobs also uses the example of massive subsidy programs in southern Italy as a comparison to the TVA experience (*id.* at 120–23). Historically, there has been a large gap between the wealth, prosperity, and job opportunities of the industrial regions of northern Italy and the impoverished, agricultural regions of southern Italy. Since the 1950s, the Italian government has provided loans, grants, and subsidies to build roads, power plants, schools, and housing to attract industries and to subsidize agriculture, in order to aid the southern part of the country (*id.* at 120–21). Industrial transplants were located at Bari and close to Naples. Although this massive Italian effort produced certain benefits, as did the TVA program, the long-term results have done little to decrease the poverty in the region, and the gap between northern and southern Italy is said to have increased over the period in question (*id.* at 121).
42. *Id.* at 110–23.

Chapter 15

1. *See* Kennedy, *Form and Substance in Private Law Adjudication*, 89 Harv. L. Rev. 1685 (1976). Although Kennedy focuses on the difference between

an individualist and an altruist view of law, his overriding theme stresses that all law is philosophy. Kennedy's discussion of individualism, however, is not a discussion of the classical liberal model of individual liberty. The classical liberal concern for individual liberty includes moral and natural law principles not fully shared by the Benthamite utilitarians that Kennedy discusses. *See also* Lanversin, *Land Policy: Is There a Middle Way?* 3 URB. L. & POL'Y 229 (1980). Lanversin argues that land policy varies with each country and is a function of political ideology because land rights or the lack thereof are defined by law and because government takes part in this process. Since land policy is universally political or ideological, one must consider these factors in evaluating given programs. *See also* Darin-Drabkin & Darin, *Let the State Control!* 3 URB. L. & POL'Y 217 (1980) (presenting an example of marxist philosophy applied to land policy).

2. *See* M. Friedman, CAPITALISM AND FREEDOM 1–36 (1962 reissued 1982) [hereinafter Friedman, CAPITALISM]. "The kind of economic organization that provides economic freedom directly, namely, competitive capitalism, also promotes political freedom directly because it separates economic power from political power and in this way enables the one to offset the other" (*id.* at 9).

3. *See* F. Hayek, THE CONSTITUTION OF LIBERTY 13 (1960) [hereinafter Hayek, LIBERTY]; *see also* M. Rothbard, THE ETHICS OF LIBERTY 35–43 (1983) (discussing the natural right to seek interpersonal relations and voluntary exchanges); Friedman, *supra* note 2, at 14–21. According to Friedman:

> The fundamental threat to freedom is power to coerce, be it in the hands of a monarch, a dictator, an oligarchy, or a momentary majority. The preservation of freedom requires the elimination of such concentration of power to the fullest possible extent and the dispersal and distribution of whatever power cannot be eliminated—a system of checks and balances. (*Id.* at 15)

4. *See* L. von Mises, HUMAN ACTION, 179–87 (2d ed. 1963); Hayek, LIBERTY, *supra* note 3, at 11–21 (1960). Within the confines of a free society, the state can be a legitimate collective vehicle for protecting the individual's liberty from the coercive interference of others (*id.*). *See also* Hayek, THE ROAD TO SERFDOM 82–83 (1944). The idea of government as a protector of individual freedom, however, does not mean that whatever the government does in the name of this protection is to be considered proper. Hitler may have gained power and acted in a strictly constitutional manner, but this would not make his rule "right" (*id.*).

5. *See, e.g.,* R. Epstein, TAKINGS: PRIVATE PROPERTY AND THE POWER OF EMINENT DOMAIN (1985) (arguing for limited government and addressing the theory behind it); Friedman, CAPITALISM, *supra* note 2; M. Friedman & R. Friedman, FREE TO CHOOSE (1980); Hayek, LIBERTY, *supra* note 3; D. Hume, ESSAYS—MORAL, POLITICAL, AND LITERARY 87–97 (2d ed. 1985); J. Mill, ON LIBERTY 53–106 (1975); R. Nozick, ANARCHY, STATE, AND UTOPIA (1974) (defending individual liberty and seeking to define the proper role of the state in a society that values the individual as the basis of freedom); von Mises, HUMAN ACTION, *supra* note 4; L. von Mises, PLANNING FOR FREEDOM (1952). *See also* A. Smith, LECTURES ON JURISPRUDENCE 200–458 (R. Meek, D. Raphael & L. Stein eds. 1978). This part of Smith's book deals with justice and the forms of legal relationships between the individual and the state and considers

different forms of government. Based on notes from Smith's lectures on jurisprudence at the University of Glasgow, it also presents an interesting look at Adam Smith as legal philosopher.

6. *See* A. Nock, OUR ENEMY, THE STATE (1983).

7. *See* Gruen, *Public/Private Projects—A Better Way for Downtowns*, URB. LAND, Aug. 1986, at 4. This very action has been taken in St. Paul, Minnesota, where city officials used their influence with the regional planning agency to block approval of a suburban shopping mall that would compete with a downtown shopping facility in which the city had an economic interest.

8. *See* Friedman, CAPITALISM, *supra* note 2, at 7–21; Malloy, *Equating Human Rights and Property Rights—The Need for Moral Judgment in an Economic Analysis of Law and Social Policy*, 47 OHIO ST. L.J. 163, 168–71 (1986).

9. *See supra* note 8.

10. *See* von Mises, HUMAN ACTION, *supra* note 4. Von Mises describes economics as the science of all human action and states that human action is necessarily always rational (*id.* at 19). *See also* Kuttner, *The Poverty of Economics*, ATLANTIC MONTHLY, Feb. 1985, at 74. Although this article is critical of the trends that favor model building in economics, it provides a good analysis of basic economic approaches. It also argues that economics, of whatever branch, is basically an ideologically charged undertaking (*id.* at 83). Relevant to the issue, the article refers to a position taken by Milton Friedman in his ESSAYS IN POSITIVE ECONOMICS. There Friedman argues that the information and rationality assumptions underlying economics do not have to be empirically true as long as they lead to an internally consistent model not refuted by data (*id.* at 79, citing M. Friedman, ESSAYS IN POSITIVE ECONOMICS [1953]).

11. *See* Malloy, *supra* note 8, at 166–68; *see also* Kornhauser, *The Great Image of Authority*, 36 STAN. L. REV. 349, 353–57 (1984) (arguing that law helps shape human conduct and thus serves a normative function); Michelman, *Norms and Normativity in the Economic Theory of Law*, 62 MINN. L. REV. 1015 (1978) (describing law as multidimensional with moral, social, political, and economic aspects); *see generally* L. Fuller, THE MORALITY OF LAW 33–94 (rev. ed. 1969) (arguing that governments' failure to observe certain guidelines in expecting people to obey the law would lead to reduced normative acceptance of the legal structure); H. Hart, THE CONCEPT OF LAW 83–114, 133–37 (1961) (discussing the internal point of view and how law becomes an internalized standard for assessing conduct); J. Schumpeter, CAPITALISM, SOCIALISM AND DEMOCRACY 190–91 (1950) (describing morality and one's sense of justice as important factors in the evaluation of the merits of a particular social or economic structure and, therefore, in the legitimization of that structure).

12. Malloy, *supra* note 8, at 166.

13. *See* Hoeflich, *Of Reason, Gamesmanship, and Taxes: A Jurisprudential and Theoretical Approach to the Problem of Voluntary Compliance*, 2 AM. J. TAX POL'Y 9 (1983) (viewing problems of tax compliance creatively and innovatively in relation to theories of gamesmanship and jurisprudence).

14. *Id.* at 37–65 (giving examples of "playing the game").

15. *Id.* at 9–88. "A recent English commentator on this problem of multipurpose tax systems has remarked that such a hodgepodge of conflicting interest and purposes cannot possibly succeed in convincing those who must bear the tax burden of the tax system's inherent worth and fairness" (*id.* at

12, *citing* H. Monroe, INTOLERABLE INQUISITION? REFLECTIONS ON THE LAW OF TAX [1981]).

16. Hoeflich, *supra* note 13.

17. *See* Malloy, *The Limits of "Science" in Legal Discourse—A Reply to Posner*, 24 VAL. U.L. REV. 175 (1990); Malloy, *Market Philosophy in the Legal Tension Between Children's Autonomy and Parental Authority*, 21 IND. L. REV. 889 (1988).

Chapter 16

1. It is important to understand that moral principles do not have to be based on any given religion or source. Moral principles for classical liberal thought can be found in notions of natural law and involve concepts of right and wrong sanctioned by theological, logical, and biological theories. *See* H. Mencken, TREATISE ON RIGHT AND WRONG 14 (1977). Mencken asserts that morality has existed among all peoples in one form or another (*id.* at 5). Additionally, people fundamentally agree that murder, theft, trespass, adultery, and false witness are examples of antisocial and immoral behavior (*id.* at 6–8). Despite general agreement on certain basic moral norms, the authority for individuals' moral beliefs can differ considerably over time and place (*id.* at 8–62). Mencken described the three theories of morality as follows: (1) theological, based in religious doctrine; (2) logical, stemming from philosophical inquiries and seeking to justify human conduct on purely logical grounds, rather than on the will of the gods; and (3) biological, originating in Darwin's work on THE DESCENT OF MAN, wherein man's moral passions are linked to instinct and are alleged to be observable in many lower animals (id. at 1–62).

2. Depending on the source of data used, 250,000 to 4,000,000 homeless people live in America. *See Homelessness: Demographics, Causes, and Cures in a Nutshell*, URB. LAND, May 1986, at 32.

3. *See* J. Jacobs, CITIES AND THE WEALTH OF NATIONS (1984).

4. *Id.*

5. *Id.*

6. *See* Bryant & McGee, *Gentrification and the Law: Combatting Urban Displacement*, 24 W.U.J. URB. & C. L. 43 (1983); McDougall, *Gentrification: The Class Conflict Over Urban Space Moves into the Courts*, 10 FORDHAM URB. L.J. 177 (1982); LeGates & Hartman, *Gentrification—Caused Displacement*, 14 URB. LAW. 31 (1982); Note, *Gentrification, Tipping, and the National Housing Policy*, 11 N.Y.U. REV. L. & SOC. CHANGE 255 (1982).

7. *See supra* note 6.

8. *See id.; see also, e.g.*, Downtown Development Research Committee & Indiana Christian Leadership Conference, INDIANAPOLIS: DOWNTOWN DEVELOPMENT FOR WHOM? 12–18 (1980) (noting the dislocation of residents and destruction of many low-income neighborhoods in order to make way for cofinanced redevelopment projects).

9. The money will be spent on goods and services or donated to charity, which will use it for goods and services. If the money is invested or saved, then the recipients of the investment or deposit will use it on loans to others. *See generally* H. Hazlitt, ECONOMICS IN ONE LESSON 177–90 (1979).

10. *Id.* at 31–36.

11. *See* Hoeflich & Malloy, *The Shattered Dream of American Housing Policy—*

The Need for Reform, 26 B.C.L. Rev. 665 (1985). This article discusses the many bad effects of local special-interest legislation in the housing area. In addition, it recommends limiting or eliminating federal funds for states that employ undesirable local housing regulations, such as rent controls (*id.* at 683–89).

12. See F. Hayek, The Constitution of Liberty 220–28 (1960) (*see supra* note 70 Chapter 3 for the text of Hayek's position on this point).

———

Index

Ackerman, Bruce, 6, 72, 73, 165–66
Alienation (alienates, alienated), 26, 63, 156
Altruistic (ism), 62, 74–75, 177
Atlanta, 119

Baltimore, 108, 110, 173
Boston, 13, 14, 93, 168

Capitalist (ism), 3, 12, 20–21, 26, 29–30, 32–33, 43, 49, 50, 52, 61, 73–74, 79–81, 85–86, 109, 118, 123, 136, 138–39, 144, 146–47, 149–50, 158, 161–62, 165, 167, 175, 177–78
Checks and balances, 3–4, 26, 30–37, 39, 49, 71, 72, 74, 76, 78, 86, 91, 111, 117, 139, 158, 177
Chicago, 4, 5, 46, 73, 127, 174
Classical liberal, ix, 3, 5, 14, 16–30, 37–40, 44, 49–56, 60–65, 68–69, 73–74, 76–83, 86, 91, 111–12, 117, 122, 124–27, 129–30, 132–34, 139, 141, 156, 160, 163–66, 168, 177, 179
Coase, Ronald, 147, 161
Coase Theorem, 41
Co-Financing, ix, x, 55, 98–112, 114–16, 120, 126–27, 135–36, 150, 162, 167, 169, 171, 179
Commons, tragedy of, 45–48, 161
Communitarian, 9, 38, 62–63, 70–76, 83
Community, liberty of, 62–64, 128
Condemnation, 95–96, 100, 107. See also Eminent domain; Taking
Conservative(s) (ism), 16–17, 29, 44, 61, 64–71, 73–74, 76, 79, 80, 83, 117–18, 129, 164, 174
Cost/benefit, 16, 18, 23, 26, 44, 59, 70, 115, 134, 136, 164–65

Critical Legal Studies (CLS), 70–76, 166

Deconstruction, 63, 76
Discourse (including dialogue), 2–3, 11, 15, 39–40, 50–52, 55–56, 60–85, 102, 111, 122, 129–30, 136, 140, 143, 160, 163, 165–66, 168, 179; legal economic, 2–3, 4, 5, 11–14, 36, 39, 50–51, 61–83, 111, 117, 123–24, 127, 129–30, 138, 140–41

Economic means, 1, 37–44, 89, 124, 159
Efficient (efficiency/inefficient), 3–5, 16, 18, 22, 40, 46, 54, 66, 68–71, 79, 90–91, 116, 126, 128–29, 147, 159–60, 166
Eminent domain, 13–14, 95–96, 106, 166, 168, 177. See also Condemnation; Taking
Enterprise zone(s), 100–102, 114, 117, 170, 173–74
Entrepreneur (ism), 10, 54, 85, 143, 168, 171, 173–74
Epstein, Richard, 77, 78, 166–68, 177
Externality (ies), 4, 21, 34, 73

Faith, 84–86
Fascist (ism), 33, 64, 163
Federalism, New, 116–18, 174
First principles, 62, 83–86
Free good, 35, 44–47
Friedman, Milton, ix, 16–17, 50, 80–81, 144, 146, 149–50, 158, 160–62, 167, 173–75, 177–78

Galbraith, John Kenneth, 149–50, 158, 175
Gentrification, 132, 179

Great Britain, 33, 101, 151, 158

Hayek, Friedrich, ix, 16–17, 65, 81, 144, 146, 148–50, 155, 157, 159–63, 165, 167, 177, 180
Hoeflich, Michael, x, 127, 161–62, 167, 173, 178–79
Houston, 90, 168
Human dignity, 1–3, 15–16, 18–19, 25–27, 29, 31, 40, 48–50, 52, 62, 68–69, 78–84, 86, 124, 129–30, 133–34, 136, 138–41
Hume, David, 16, 146, 177

Ideology (ideological), 1–5, 11, 15, 36, 48–50, 52, 60–86, 91–92, 102, 109, 111, 118, 139–41, 159, 177–78
Impartial spectator, 23, 153
Import-replacing, 118–21, 130–33, 136–39, 176
Inalienable rights. *See* Natural rights
Indiana, x, 4, 10, 65, 103–13, 144, 163, 170–71
Indianapolis, 4–5, 10–15, 40, 103–15, 117, 124, 127, 140–41, 143–44, 163–64, 169–73, 179
Indiana University, 65, 107, 144, 163–64, 172
Individual liberty, 1–3, 15–16, 18–22, 25–29, 31–33, 37, 40, 44, 48–54, 62, 66, 68, 77–83, 86, 97, 111–12, 122–24, 126–30, 134–35, 138–41, 148–49, 159–60, 162, 177
Industrial Development Bonds (IDBs), 100–102
Invisible hand, ix–x, 21–22, 151, 160, 164, 166–67

Jacobs, Jane, 118–22, 139, 143, 175–76, 179

Kaldor–Hicks criterion, 68
Kellman, Mark, 75, 166
Kirzner, Israel, 118
Knoxville, 176

Labor, division of, 19–20, 26–27, 29, 146–47, 149–50, 156
Laissez Faire, 16, 18, 53, 55, 86, 123, 149, 162
Land use, 85, 89, 90–91, 94, 98, 168

Law and economics, ix–x, 1–2, 4–5, 17, 24, 29, 50, 52, 54–56, 60–83, 122, 124, 143, 160–61, 163–64, 166–68
Law and semiotics, x, 3, 143, 166. *See also* Semiotics; Sign
Left communitarian. *See* Communitarian
Liberal(s) (ism), 16–17, 29, 37, 44, 61–62, 65, 70–76, 116–17, 143, 161–62, 165–66
Libertarian(s) (ism), 17, 29, 37, 44, 49, 51, 61, 65, 76–79, 82, 127, 156, 166, 168
Lilly Endowment, 107–108, 172
Linkage (linking), 13, 43, 93, 137, 168
London, 4
Los Angeles, 119, 120–21
Louisville (Kentucky), 13–14, 127

Malloy, Robin Paul, ix–x, 143, 150, 155–56, 158, 160–64, 166–69, 173, 180
Marx (Marxist/Neomarxist), 61–62, 65, 70–76, 83, 156
Metaphor(ical), x, 3–5, 30, 55, 60, 78, 82, 84–86, 128–29, 157, 166, 168
Mill, John Stuart, 149, 154, 177
Minimal, state, 76–79
Mises, Ludwig von, 61, 149, 160, 162–63, 177–78
Monopoly, 32, 39, 56, 82, 128, 159–60
Moral sentiments, 21–25, 27, 29, 68, 144–48, 151–57, 163

Natural rights (inalienable rights), 3, 17–19, 50, 52, 70–73, 76–84, 124, 127, 129, 134, 140–41, 146–47, 149, 161, 163, 177
Neoclassical (economic theory), 5, 39, 63, 66–70, 73, 76, 78–80
New Deal, 73, 77–78, 116–18
New Federalism. *See* Federalism, New
New York, 4–5, 57–59, 127
Norms (normative), 2–4, 9–12, 14–15, 23, 29, 33–36, 39–40, 48–49, 52, 60–62, 66, 82, 85–86, 111, 123, 126–27, 129, 133, 138–41, 148, 157–59, 164, 173, 178–79
Nozick, Robert, 77

Palo Alto (California), 94
Pareto efficiency, 68
Paris, 4

Pittsburgh, 13–14
Planned Unit Developments (PUDs), 92
Planning, 1, 2, 5, 13, 15–16, 21, 32, 36–37, 53, 72, 85, 89, 90, 92–98, 107, 127, 129–31, 133–41, 149, 151, 165, 168, 174
Police power, 32, 34, 39, 64, 89–97, 103, 107, 113, 136, 139, 169
Political means, 1, 11, 35, 37–44, 47, 89, 92–94, 96, 107, 113–17, 124, 126, 133, 138, 159–60, 175
Posner, Richard, ix–x, 66–71, 73–74, 79, 82, 159–61, 163–68, 179
Public choice, 5, 38–40, 111, 133, 159–60
Public entrepreneurism. See Entrepreneur
Public/private partnerships (ventures), 13–15, 34, 98–112, 125–27, 135, 173, 178
Purse power, 32, 39, 89, 98–103, 107, 113, 136, 139

Renaissance, ix–x, 9, 98, 103–12, 150, 162, 167, 169; counter-renaissance, 9–10, 103–12
Rent control, ix, 41, 43, 56–59, 82, 94, 137, 162, 180
Revenue Sharing, 58, 113–14
Rules, 75; general, 3, 18, 23–26, 53–60, 80–81, 86, 89–92, 130, 133, 135, 137, 139, 148, 154–55, 157, 160; special (outcome-specific), 3, 53–60, 89, 92, 107, 137

San Francisco, 93
Self-interest, 3, 21–22, 24, 66–67, 74, 110, 133, 151, 153
Semiotics, x, 3, 82, 143. See also Law and semiotics; Signs
Serfdom, 1–2, 37, 40, 43–45, 89, 98, 139, 146, 150, 167, 177
Sign(s), 37, 62–64, 78, 82, 121, 143. See also Law and Semiotics; Semiotics
Smith, Adam, ix–x, 3–4, 16–29, 32, 51–52, 69, 79, 80–81, 109, 134, 144–57, 160–67, 173, 177–78
Social contract, 28–29, 157
Special interest(s) (groups), 11, 18, 30, 35, 40–44, 47, 52, 54–55, 57, 59, 71, 112–18, 124, 127, 131, 133, 137, 139, 154–55, 160, 174, 180

Spontaneous social order, 21–22, 24–25, 30, 32, 37, 49, 54–55, 81–82, 111–12, 118, 122, 141, 155, 162
State capitalism (ist), 12, 107
Statist (ism), 1–2, 9, 30, 35–37, 44–45, 48–49, 65–66, 74, 76, 78–79, 85, 94, 109–10, 140–41, 160
State, liberty of, 62, 64–65, 69, 86, 128
St. Louis, 13–14
Symbolic. See Metaphor

Taking(s), x, 4, 14, 77, 95–96, 100, 166–69, 177. See also Condemnation; Eminent domain
Tax(es) (ation), 11, 13–14, 32, 34, 39, 55, 57–59, 73, 93–94, 99–102, 104, 106, 110, 113–14, 127, 131, 133, 137–38, 163, 169, 170–71, 178–79
Tax abatement, 100–102, 106, 114, 170
Tax Increment Financing (TIF), 100–102, 106, 170, 173
Tennesee Valley Authority (TVA), 120–21, 176
Tokyo, 4
Transaction costs, 4, 41, 73, 159
Trickle-down, 131–33

Urban development (urban revitalization), 1–2, 4–5, 9–10, 12–16, 40, 48, 52, 54–55, 61–62, 83, 85–86, 89, 95, 97–98, 101–102, 108, 111, 113–30, 132–33, 135–40, 155, 173–74
Urban Development Action Grant (UDAG), 113, 171, 174
Urban Socialism, 12, 85
Utility (Utilitarian), 16, 18–19, 22, 28–29, 134, 147, 157, 164–65, 177

Variance (zoning), 92

Wealth maximization, 3, 16, 22–23, 28, 66–70, 74, 79–82, 129, 160, 164, 166
Wealth of Nations, The (Adam Smith), 21, 22, 25–26, 144, 146–52, 154–57, 163, 173
Welfare, 69, 71, 79, 114, 116, 136–37, 166, 174–75

Zoning, 4, 54–55, 89–95, 106–107, 127, 131, 137, 139, 168

This book was set in Baskerville and Eras typefaces. Baskerville was designed by John Baskerville at his private press in Birmingham, England, in the eighteenth century. The first typeface to depart from oldstyle typeface design, Baskerville has more variation between thick and thin strokes. In an effort to insure that the thick and thin strokes of his typeface reproduced well on paper, John Baskerville developed the first wove paper, the surface of which was much smoother than the laid paper of the time. The development of wove paper was partly responsible for the introduction of typefaces classified as modern, which have even more contrast between thick and thin strokes.

Eras was designed in 1969 by Studio Hollenstein in Paris for the Wagner Typefoundry. A contemporary script-like version of a sans-serif typeface, the letters of Eras have a monotone stroke and are slightly inclined.

Printed on acid-free paper.